What Was I Thinking?

Getting your thoughts working for you, not against you

Updated and Revised Version 2015

Caspar McCloud and Linda Lange

WHAT WAS I THINKING?

Updated and Revised
May 2015

Originally Published by Destiny Image 2010

Life Application Ministries Publishing (LAMP)

Cover Design: LAMP

Printer: Createspace.com

Disclosure:

The Bible has tremendous insights as to why people have disease. We are ministers who seeks what the Bible says about these issues. We are not psychiatrists or medical doctor, nor do we seek to be in conflict with church beliefs or medical practices or theological differences. This book is for your information only and does not replace any medical advice.

We are simply administering the Scriptures according to I Corinthians 12, Psalm 103:3, 2 Corinthians 5:18-20, and Ephesians 4 as we hope to help shed some light on the mysteries of life we have addressed in this book to hopefully equip you with what you need to find your healing, freedom, restoration, and peace.

Acknowledgments

We want to first thank our Lord for every breath we take and for all and any gifts He has given us to help teach and minister in His all-powerful name of Jesus Christ of Nazareth.

We want to thank our families for supporting us as we dedicated time in writing this book. Caspar thanks his wife, Joan, and children, Derek and Hayley.

Linda gives special thanks to her husband, Tom, who has been instrumental in supporting her, helping her stay focused, encouraging her to write, and loving her unconditionally. These attributes not only helped her in writing this book, but has also helped her in her ministry in reaching others find their freedom.

We have been blessed with wonderful dedicated trust worthy friends whom we consider extended family members, and very thankful to God for each one of them. They are the ones, along with our family, whom the Lord used to shape our perceptions according to His most Holy Word and who were there to encourage us when we felt discouraged. They are the saintly ones who help lift up our arms, just as Aaron and Hur held up Moses' arms, so they could win another battle.

We want to give special acknowledgment to Henry Wright, pastor of Pleasant Valley Church, and his staff who mentored both Caspar and Linda over the last decade. Pastor Henry was most influential in teaching biblical and medical insights, which not only brought about healing and miracles but also enabled us to share those basic understandings to minister to and restore others worldwide.

Caspar must also thank Dr. Terri Allen, who came alongside him and gave tirelessly of herself to help him and so many others receive and assimilate many of these concepts so they may recover themselves out of the snare of the devil (see 2 Tim. 2:24-26).

Caspar thanks his longtime friend and mentor Phil Keaggy, who introduced him to Jesus Christ of Nazareth as a teenager and who has always been there for him.

We want to thank Sherri Stewart for transcribing and editing the material for the book. She worked many hours helping in this effort.

We want to acknowledge and thank Mike and Brenda Waldner, who tirelessly give of themselves to help run Caspar McCloud Ministries, Inc., and the entire board of directors and those in leadership roles. Without them, Caspar would not have been able to dedicate his time to writing this book, teaching, leading church services, and providing ministry. Thank you!

We want to thank Bishop Joe Mattera for helping and encouraging us to publish this book.

ENDORSEMENTS

What Was I Thinking? draws upon a wealth of personal experience to vividly demonstrate why the Bible says, "As a man thinks in his heart, so is he." Drawing on modern research, which certainly confirms much that I experienced with my patients when I worked as a family physician, this book teaches that right thinking does much more than just lead to good mental health; it lays the foundation for our overall physical well-being as well. Read, enjoy, prosper, and be in health!

Tony and Felicity Dale
Authors of The Rabbit and the Elephant
(with George Barna), and Renewing the Mind

What Was I Thinking? is full of wisdom and practical guidance about how to heal diseases by learning to think healthy thoughts. It is clear that our thoughts produce physical changes in our bodies. Thoughts that are based on faith, love, joy, peace, and forgiveness will produce health, and thoughts which are based on fear, worry, anger, and resentment will produce disease. This book will teach you how to be healed and stay healthy. I highly recommend that you give a copy to your doctor and ask your doctor to work with you to use these teachings in your healing process.

Peter Wyman, MD
Primary Care Internal Medicine

What was I Thinking? Instructive, compelling, packed with insight and practical wisdom. A book that dissects the mind-body connections, shattering common misconceptions and offering priceless wisdom that can save your life! Theologically, I may differ on a few points, but none that alter the foundational message in this book. As a physician for almost two decades, I have seen the dynamics explained in this book play out in countless patients. This is a must-read for everyone. Thank you, Caspar, for putting together such an important resource, written in an engaging, fun, easy-to-read, informative format with practical, ready-to-apply, life-changing principles. You can begin immediately to change your life with this road map on how to fulfill your unique destiny, walk in your God-given gifts, and experience the "abundant life" we were all meant to have.

Dr. Teresa Allen
Internist for Adult Health
and Preventative Medicine

Caspar's life is constructed on the rock of his faith, and this book shows you clearly how to find your own rock and to build on it.

Robert Lacey
Best-selling author and royal biographer to
HRM the Queen of England

In our ministry here in Thailand we serve many people with health and mental problems. What Was I Thinking?, written by Caspar, is an excellent, biblical, and readable resource helping people overcome their fears through greater trust and faith in God by the power of the Holy Spirit in their lives. I've known Caspar for some time; through applying the teachings of this book, he long since has overcome allergies and other health issues. My wife is also living victoriously over long-term back pain. Both came to grips with thoughts that produced fears and stresses in their lives, making me a believer in the spirit-mind-body connections that Caspar so clearly reveals in this book. Great teaching!

Rev. Alan Lawton
Missionary to Thailand with Pioneers

It's great to see Caspar use all the tools that God has blessed him with. When I first met him back in 1983, I knew he was a talented musician, but only recently have I learned what an amazing writer and person he is. I'm glad to know him and thankful that we have kept in touch after all these years. This is a great book!

Matt Bassionett
Musician
Joe Satriani and Ringo Starr All Starr Band

I once heard it said that if you sow a thought, you'll reap an action; sow an action, you'll reap a habit; sow a habit, you'll reap a lifestyle. Thank you for this book and for reminding us of the importance of our thought life! Well done!

Peter Furler
Newsboys

Caspar McCloud has been a personal friend of mine for twenty-odd years. My background was radically different from his. I was raised as a liberal, Jewish New Yorker with a drive to get involved in the entertainment industry. Caspar, a Christian from across the pond, was a musician and performer who was gifted enough to have the industry come searching for him. We were introduced in the early 1980s, by Michael Shrieve (Hall of Fame recipient and member of Santana), with whom I was working at the time. Caspar immediately became a faithful "mate" of mine, and unlike the hundreds of other industry stars and players with whom I have associated, has remained so ever since. We had lost contact with each other for several years, and when we finally connected again, it was as if no time had passed. Only now Caspar had a "secret" that he was ready to share with the world, and that was his faith in a higher being. I have always admired Caspar for being able to have true spiritual faith... something that he has tried to pass on to me for some time. I suggest that you read Caspar's first publication, Nothing Is Impossible, to get a grip on what makes this man tick. What Was I Thinking? will allow you to peak into Caspar McCloud's faith and will show you how this man is a true spiritual Bodhisattva.

Eliot Goldstein
Tour Assistance and Coordination
for Stadium Tours, which included
U-2 / Rolling Stones / Metallica / Ozzfests /
Bruce Springstein/ Fleetwood Mac
Independent Record Producer
Artist Management

Caspar McCloud's life proves the reality of the mind-body-spirit connection. Just as his heart stopped beating in 2001, a friend prayed and called his spirit to return and took authority over his dying body. His life since then has been a testimony to the power God gives us to take control of our thought life and the way that it impacts our spirit and body. McCloud's healing and subsequent life of victory shows us the timeless principles of freedom through truth. In What Was I Thinking?, he shows how you can live a life where your spirit plays its proper role with the result that you live a free and abundant life. Read it, put it into practice, and your life can't help but change!

Seth Barmes
CEO of Adventures in Missions

I am privileged to be able to call Caspar McCloud a friend and mentor. Since our very first conversation, I found myself challenged and encouraged by his words of faith and wisdom. What Was I Thinking? is an outstanding way to learn what it means to take your thoughts captive and what your thoughts really are capable of doing.

Ashley Dasher
Guitarist, Unhindered

It is with great pleasure that I recommend Pastor Caspar and Linda Lange's book, What Was I Thinking? It is scripturally rich and doctrinally sound. It pulls the reality of spiritual forces from without, as well as within, influencing our thought life, and, in turn, our world around us. We are indeed what we think, and this book not only reveals the negative sources of influence, but more importantly, shows us how to deal with it for the renewing of our minds for more productive service in the Kingdom of God.

Eddie T. Rogers
Founder, Revival in Power Ministries
and Revival Alliance International Network
Author, Supernatural: Living Under an Open Heaven
and The Power of Impartation

Never has a book of the Spirit opened with as warm or reassuring a tone as Caspar's address to "Papa God." Too often those who author books that offer to teach us how to improve our lives and spiritual/physical health bring with them the accusatory tone of a judgmental parent. *What Was I Thinking?* offers all the guidance of a considerate physician or parent, but with tenderness and good humor. In a clear, conversational tone and succinct, readable chapters, these authors open their arms to guide the lost, assure the frightened, assuage the ill, and nurture those battling with internal emptiness and strife. If the Holy Bible is our Owner's Manual to spiritual and physical health, What Was I Thinking? is surely, and thankfully, our Dummy's Guide to get us back on track toward all that Papa God wants us to be.

L.A. Pomeroy
Northampton, MA, Journalist

TABLE OF CONTENTS

PREFACE

Pastors Caspar McCloud (Caspar McCloud Ministries, Roswell, GA) and Linda Lange (Life Application Ministries, Mt. Aukum, CA) have put this book together from a couple of original teachings taught by Caspar McCloud at the Upper Room in Roswell, GA.

Caspar and Linda have been friends for several years and are board members on each of their ministries. While talking through the idea of putting these teachings in book form, Linda offered to assist in the task. They both have a heart to help people grasp these life changing principles and what better way but to get them in written form.

While Linda was working on the transcripts she started noticing things that the Lord was speaking to her about that would fit perfectly in the book. She told Caspar some of those thoughts and after prayerful consideration on both parts, decided to co-author. Interestingly enough, as they began writing, adding, and modifying the transcripts, both couldn't tell who was writing what and realized that this was truly the work of the Holy Spirit.

This book is presented as though they are talking to you personally. As ministers, it's their desire and joy to share what they have learned hoping that you find what you need for reconciliation, healing, and receiving all the blessings that God has promised to those who are His.

Beloved, I wish above all things
that thou mayest prosper and be in health,
even as thy soul prospereth

(3 John 1:2).

INTRODUCTION

As a young child, you may have heard these words from an angry parent: "What were you thinking?" (Perhaps with some colorful metaphors added, but you get the picture.) However, this statement was actually accurate. What we think makes us do what we do, and be who we are.

There was a three-year-old who shared his version of the Lord's Prayer with us: "Our Father, who does art in Heaven, Harold is his name."

Or, the four-year-old who said, "And forgive us our trash baskets as we forgive those who put trash in our baskets."

So, what do these two quotations have to do with this book? Nothing, really, we just wanted to put these sayings in here because "a merry heart does good like a medicine" (see Prov. 17:22). Any time we can have a laugh or chuckle, we are boosting our immune system!

However, trash in our thoughts does produce trash in our lives. It's that stinkin' thinkin'. When you go by a dump-site, what do you smell? And if our minds are stinky, our lives just may be too. In this book, we will be helping you take back your thoughts so that you produce a better and richer harvest in your life.

This title "What Was I Thinking?" causes us to imagine someone jumping out of a plane yelling, "What was I thinking?" Or someone who is clinging to the side of a mountain, looking down miles below crying out, "What was I thinking?" Places where we ended up, after making a conscious decision.

As we dive into the Scriptures and see what medical evidences we have that cause us to make decisions, whether good or bad, we will discover such things as why we think the things we do, where these thoughts come from, and if there is anything we can do about it. We are not doctors, but we do have some insight on these issues and have seen many people healed and set free, just by putting these simple principles into action. Combined with personal experiences and the Word of God, we hope this proves to be very helpful in teaching you how important your thoughts are and how they play an integral role in your life.

The Bible, the True Source

Before starting, we want to clarify the reason we use the King James Version (KJV) for our resource text when quoting Scriptures. Many of you are using a variety of versions, but here is something to think about. If your Bible is under copyright, then, as an author, you need approval to use any of the text for your materials, books, or other literature referencing it. Not so with the KJV. And keep in mind, a Bible is only under copyright because the translation is unique to that version. We use the KJV because it's been in use since the 1600s and has not changed since then; in the United States, it has passed out of copyright, and we find it the most reliable source today. It also lines up nicely with the ancient manuscripts.

In order to help you, we desire to use the most accurate text possible so that we share the whole truth. The Bible gives a very stern warning in the last chapter of Revelations that anyone who alters the Word of God is going to have some problems (see Rev. 22:18-19). Perhaps some of our problems are a result of the Bible version we are using. There was a man who realized that his version left out an important Scripture that caused him to be under great condemnation. It was found in Romans 1:1 *"There is therefore now no condemnation for those who are in Christ Jesus."* That was all his version said, but there was more. *"Who walk not after the flesh but after the spirit."* This gave him the reason he was feeling condemned and what he could do to get out of it.

Since he learned this, he has changed to the KJV where he is being fed the whole truth and nothing but the truth, resulting in his freedom.

Because we take this seriously and want to see you set free, we want to use the best resource available. Whether you use the KJV or another version is entirely up to you. But now you have something to think about, pray about, and decide for yourself. We suggest that you pick up a KJV and read it concurrently with your version for comparison. Where applicable, we look up the text in both Hebrew and Greek to get a full picture of what the Word says. We need to be Berean (good students of the Word).

The Bible tells us faith without works is dead. We will not make any observation that we cannot back up with Holy Scripture, and where applicable, we will also share with you what the medical community says about that particular subject.

The Word Heals

As you read this book, you will find that it's peppered with Scriptures because it's His Word alone that will heal and deliver you. It is all-powerful and mighty, and will give what you need to live a prosperous and healthy life.

Again, we do not have all the answers, but we have a desire to be used of the Lord each day as He leads. Our passion is to see people get into a right relationship with Papa God and healing and miracles are simply a by-product of that. Today, people of all ages, young and old are suffering from all kinds of sickness and disease that the Bible addresses. It is apparent that we are in the last days where God is going to pour out His Spirit upon all flesh, and we will see miraculous things happen.

> *And it shall come to pass in the last days, saith God, I will pour out of my Spirit upon all flesh: and your sons and your daughters shall prophesy, and your young men shall see visions, and your old men shall dream dreams: And on my servants and on my handmaidens I will pour out in those days of my Spirit; and they shall prophesy"* (Acts 2:17-18).

This is not a time to be lukewarm; our example is Christ Himself and He was called a radical. If we seem on fire for the Gospel's sake, so be it. Our prayer is that we decrease even more so that He may increase in us. We simply hate to lose anything to the devil; and want to reach out and help as many people get free as possible.

Please read the following prayer as a petition of your heart to the Lord, setting the stage to receive all Papa God desires to bless you with.

Opening Prayer

Papa God, I love You more than my words are able to express. I come today and give You all my praise and worship. I want to enter into Your gates with thanksgiving in my heart. I thank You for removing curses from my life as I line up with Your Word more and more each day. I thank You for the precious shed blood of my Lord Jesus of Nazareth that covers me now. I thank You for the Holy Spirit and Your Word, for the Gospel of Your Kingdom. Thank You that You want Your children healthy and well; You do not want me sick, walking about with a broken heart or broken life.

It is truly Your heart that I would prosper even as my soul prospers. So, Papa God, I want to come today with my whole heart; I am so grateful that it is by Your grace through faith; that it is a gift to those who belong to You; that I am not into legalism or perfectionism, but I do things that are pleasing in Your sight.

You are holy and righteous. Help me now to come and relate to You in knowledge and responsibility, to be in covenant with You and seek first Your Kingdom and Your righteousness. I trust that You will take care of all the rest of the details of my life. Jesus said it is Your pleasure to give us the Kingdom. Come have Your way with me, Lord, that signs and wonders would follow me now. I pray this in Jesus Christ of Nazareth's name. Amen.

Chapter One

OUR THOUGHTS AND HEART

There is a connection between our thoughts and our heart. You may already know this; however, we are going to address several aspects of the thought process and how it actually over or under produces chemicals in our body (which causes dis-ease) and other manifestations. By pointing out these aspects, we believe that you will be more equipped to handle successfully just about every single situation that comes your way.

We'll be talking a lot about relationships because that is the basis for all healing and restoration. By addressing our relationship with our Heavenly Father, with ourselves, and with others, we are well on our way to discovering why things happen the way they do and what we can do about them, as found in Matthew 22:37-40:

> *Jesus said unto him, Thou shalt love the Lord thy God with all thy heart, and with all thy soul, and with all thy mind. This is the first and great commandment. And the second is like unto it, Thou shalt love thy neighbour as thyself. On these two commandments hang all the law and the prophets.*

Planting Good Seeds

As we begin to be doers of the Word, cleansing our hands and purifying our hearts, the blessings of the Lord begin to overtake us and chase us down.

And all these blessings shall come on thee, and overtake thee, if thou shalt hearken unto the voice of the Lord thy God (Deut. 28:2)

When we draw closer to our Lord, He draws closer to us:

Draw nigh to God, and He will draw nigh to you. Cleanse your hands, ye sinners; and purify your hearts, ye double minded (James 4:8).

As we help to bear each other's burdens as we are taught in Galatians 6, we are fulfilling the law of Christ.

Brethren, if a man be overtaken in a fault, ye which are spiritual, restore such an one in the spirit of meekness; considering thyself, lest thou also be tempted. Bear ye one another's burdens, and so fulfill the law of Christ (Galatians 6:1-2).

Every day, moment-by-moment, what we do and think will affect our tomorrow and our future. We are going to reap what we sow. As we focus on God, His love, and His ways, we are sowing good seeds into our lives. Galatians 6:7 says, *"Be not deceived; God is not mocked: for whatsoever a man soweth, that shall he also reap."*

If we plant corn, we are not going to harvest lettuce. If we plant murmuring and complaining, then fertilize it with strife, come harvest time, what will we get?

Just as seeds germinate and produce a greater yield than what was sown, be careful what you plant in your life because you will be known by the fruit you bear:

Ye shall know them by their fruits. Do men gather grapes of thorns, or figs of thistles? Even so every good tree bringeth forth good fruit; but a corrupt tree bringeth forth evil fruit. A good tree cannot bring forth evil fruit, neither can a corrupt tree bring forth good fruit. Every tree that bringeth not forth good fruit is hewn down, and cast into the fire. Wherefore by their fruits ye shall know them (Matthew 7:16-20).

We want to plant good seeds and bring forth fruit that will last forever. Even when difficult things happen, we want to keep our peace and do what is pleasing in God's sight. But this passage tells us what happens if we don't plant good seeds. We want to plant good and healthy thoughts so that they produce good and healthy fruit in our lives, impacting our spiritual, physical and mental health.

As we look at the examples in the Bible about sowing and reaping, we see that we are going to have to work at it. There are times when we must pull weeds and times when we must water before we can reap the harvest, but we must not faint in our thoughts. If we start thinking of giving up, our body will follow. We'll stop doing what we have been doing and simply collapse; we could even fall into depression. We miss out because we've been deceived, believing that God isn't doing anything or isn't doing it fast enough. However, if we are walking in the Spirit, the Lord is going to pull us through our difficult circumstances.

> *Be not deceived; God is not mocked: for whatsoever a man soweth, that shall he also reap. For he that soweth to his flesh shall of the flesh reap corruption; but he that soweth to the Spirit shall of the Spirit reap life everlasting. And let us not be weary in well doing: for in due season we shall reap, if we faint not* (Galatians 6:7-9).

We need to wait. As the Scriptures say, having done all you know to do, now stand, or "wait" on the Lord to do His part (see Ephesians 6:13).

Really Knowing Christ

We've heard people say, "Yes, I know the Lord." Then we ask, "If you really know the Lord and follow His commandments, why are you holding on to all that bitterness and unforgiveness?" The Lord tells us He will not share us with devils. He is a jealous God. If our spouse was having an affair with someone else, we would have a very difficult time maintaining intimacy. When we put other things before God—be it television or a job or money or whatever is holding our attention—we are having an affair.

Here is another example. Let's say that you are traveling

abroad by yourself, carrying a lot of camera equipment. You find the perfect spot to take some video footage and spend a lot of time setting it up for that perfect shot when you realize that you left the battery in the hotel room. What do you do? Do you ask a stranger to watch your equipment? Of course not. But let's say you are traveling with a friend; you would trust them to watch your equipment, right? Your friend is someone you could trust with your most prized possessions. The Lord is saying this to you now: "Are you treating Me like a stranger or a friend? Are you trusting Me with your equipment or not?" This will help you see where you are in your relationship with Him.

When we really know Him, we trust Him and all that He has said. When we trust a loving friend and they ask us to do something, we do it without question because we know they have only good in mind. When we know Him, our fruit is that we act like it, in what we say, think, and do. We believe that He loves us through and through, no matter what. We believe that He is able to take care of us; we can even trust Him with our future and not have fear about it because we know God is going to take care of us.

Talk to God

If you've had difficulty trusting God in the past, today is a new day. Don't stay under guilt and condemnation; simply talk with Him about it. Say, "Papa God, I realize that I'm not leaving my valuables with You; I haven't really trusted You completely. Forgive me; I want to trust and believe You every single minute of the day with every breath I take. Help me to know You more. I want that intimate relationship with You as my Papa God. Help me to receive Your love. I want my fruit to demonstrate my love for You and Your love for me. Thank You, in Jesus Name, Amen."

It doesn't mean we won't still be goofy from time to time; it means when we are, we go to Him, not run from Him, for forgiveness and restoration.

God's Promises Are For Today

Has anyone ever sat in a Bible study or gone to a church

meeting and heard someone say, "Well, I do not believe that Scripture is meant for today."

2 Corinthians 1:19-20 rebuts all those foolish dispensational theories that try to steal believers' blessings.

> *For the Son of God, Jesus Christ, who was preached among you by us, even by me and Silvanus and Timotheus, was not yea and nay, but in Him was yea. For all the promises of God in Him are yea, and in Him Amen, unto the glory of God by us* (2 Corinthians 1:19-20).

All means *all* of God's promises. Every one that meets our needs is for us today! Over the years, a number of people have said that you can't take a promise of blessing or of punishment that God gave to Israel and apply it to us. They somehow think that certain things were just for Israel and the Israelites. Our response is usually 2 Timothy 3:16:

> *All Scripture is given by inspiration of God, and is profitable for doctrine, for reproof, for correction, for instruction in righteousness.*

If we pick just the Scriptures we like and reject the ones we do not, or claim they were not specifically written to Gentiles, then we would eliminate much of the Old Testament, which is there for our "instruction in righteousness." Our understanding of the Bible is that all the promises it contains are applicable to our lives. This is one reason they were preserved to be passed down to us from generation to generation.

Obeying the Word Brings Victory

James Chapter 1 says that we are to be doers of the Word of God. The main "Word" here (which fulfills all the laws and commandments) is to love God, ourselves, and one another.

> *Thou shalt love the Lord thy God with all thy heart, and with all thy soul, and with all thy mind. This is the first and great commandment. And the second is like unto it, Thou shalt love thy neighbor as thyself. On these two commandments hang all the law and the prophets* (Matthew 22:37-40).

When we keep this main commandment, we keep them all. This, dear friends, is the beginning of your healing and restoration and victorious living. Living, walking, and breathing in His love—and then loving everyone else—is really the answer.

The Power of Our Thoughts

All of our perceptions and the way we respond to them happen quickly. In fact, our reactions to any stressful situation are initiated during the first few seconds of a stress encounter. We all have to deal with a certain number of them each day in this present world. How we think affects how our bodies handle those encounters because how we think often dictates whether we keep our peace or lose our peace. If we lose our peace and our joy, we are opening a doorway for sickness and disease to enter in. If we learn to develop good habits to help us manage those difficult times we are all going to face now and then, we will help minimize any sickness and disease from entering in.

Isn't it amazing how powerful words can be? Let's say someone corrects you about something you said or did, and because you are still dealing with spirits of accusation and rejection, it could cause your day to be ruined if he or she says something that makes you feel bad. That's what this book is all about—teaching you to stay in peace in every situation that comes your way.

Perhaps you have been falsely accused of something or had a misunderstanding that resulted in something being blown up out of proportion. Often the words spoken will begin to try to torment you, keeping you up at night, or even manifesting in bodily symptoms.

> *For as he thinketh in his heart, so is he: eat and drink, saith he to thee; but his heart is not with thee* (Proverbs 23:7)

What we think does, in fact, matter. We need to understand that our thoughts matter more than we really even completely understand at this time. As we research into the brain and how it functions, more and more evidence is showing that thousands of chemical changes occur with every single thought, and we really only know about some of them. We need to know that our thoughts will manifest in good or bad actions—and in good or bad health in our bodies.

We are to take every thought captive to the obedience of Christ so that we display Christ! As we think Christ-like thoughts in our heart, we become Christ-like.

> *Casting down imaginations, and every high thing that exalteth itself against the knowledge of God, and bringing into captivity every thought to the obedience of Christ* (2 Corinthians 10:5).

Does this mean you can use your thoughts to get freed from health, family, and business problems? Yes, it does! John 8:32 says that when you know the truth, you can find freedom:

> *And ye shall know the truth, and the truth shall make you free.*

The Bible tells us there is a mind, body, and spirit-soul connection; science has also shown that there is a mind-body connection. For example, when you think about something stressful, your heart begins to pound, your body begins to sweat, you begin to pace, and have a number of other responses. Several diseases that you can read about in any medical book are derived from stress and anxiety, which is fear based. Stress is the politically correct word for fear, so anything that is stress-induced is what we are talking about here. These bodily manifestations begin in our thinking.

The Bible tells us in the Old Testament that when someone got sick he was to go to the priest. In the New Testament, he was to go to the elders of the church. Where do we go ourselves? Do we search the Internet? Go to the pharmacist? Look in a book? Or do we ask a friend? What does the Bible say? Are we going to be doers of the Word or go with what is popular?

Perhaps 95 percent of all sickness and diseases start with wrong thinking. So what do we do about it? We must begin to change our thinking. It takes about 28 days to correct our thought life, just as it does with any kind of a habit. But we can start to see some positive results in as few as three days. When something happens, think about where your mind goes. Are you allowing it to go down a pathway of destruction or a pathway to wholeness? If we want to see improvements in our lives, we may need to form new, positive habits. That is why the Bible advises that we wash our minds with the watering of the Word, conforming not to this world, but renewing our minds daily. Our Heavenly Father knew that our minds were going to be the battlefield. He wants to equip us with the truth so that we have what we need for clear understanding of His direction for us. Let's start exercising our mind to produce good thoughts for good results (fruit), just as the Lord said. By renewing our minds in God's truth, by forgiving everyone, whether we feel like it or not, we are sowing good seed. Learning to walk in love all the time is the only way to holiness, wholeness, and health.

We see that all behavior begins with a thought. There has to be someone, or something, to think it. We will discuss later that not every thought we have is our own. We can have thoughts from God or from Satan; the ones we choose to think on will produce fruit in our lives. It will be an act of our will, and the good news is that we can learn to control what we think about by taking every thought captive to the obedience of Christ.

> *And Samuel said, Hath the Lord as great delight in burnt offerings and sacrifices, as in obeying the voice of the Lord? Behold, to obey is better than sacrifice, and to hearken than the fat of rams* (1 Samuel 15:22).

Practical Application

We encourage you to take a moment and reflect on your own thought life. What were you thinking when you laid your head on your pillow last night? What conversation have you found yourself playing over and over again about things that have happened that day that you cannot change? Is it a peaceful experience or a tormenting and unsettling experience?

Take a moment and think of something that keeps nagging at you, something that causes you to get sad or lose your peace—some tormenting thought.

Make note of it, because the first step to freedom is recognition. In the following chapters, we will be discussing how to recognize a wrong thought and what to do about it.

It all starts in our thoughts because where our mind goes, our body follows—with or without us even knowing it. What we don't know, can hurt us.

So the next time you feel badly, stop and ask yourself what you were thinking. Many times we don't even realize we were thinking anything. The enemy is subtle; remember, he is a deceiver, a liar, a thief, and will creep into your thoughts unbeknownst to you. Don't let that happen any longer. Ask the Lord to help you recognize when your thoughts go astray. Ask for His forgiveness and then ask Him to teach you to take that thought captive and replace it with His truth. Ask Him to help you develop your mind to think like He thinks. After all, we do have the mind of Christ; we just have to appropriate the Word into our lives more fully.

> *For who hath known the mind of the Lord, that he may instruct him? but we have the mind of Christ* (1 Corinthians 2:16).

Chapter Two

OUR PHYSIOLOGY

Not only do we discuss the spiritual aspects according to the Bible, but we also talk about our physical bodies, and how they are connected to our spirit.

Pastor Henry[1] and Dr. Terri[2] teach quite a few things about how our hearts and bodies work, especially when Caspar was a "professional heart patient" back in 2000. Please believe me, it was no joke: I was suffering and afflicted with this disease. That was one of the most difficult times I ever experienced. So naturally, now I want to share what I discovered and help others be free so they do not have to suffer as I did.

A *disease* can be anything that takes away your peace and happiness. You can read about it in my book called, *"Nothing Is Impossible,"* about the ingredients it takes to get sick unto death and the steps to get to a place where the Lord could heal and perform a creative miracle.

Heart Rate Variations

There is a device called an electrocardiogram (better known as the EKG) that monitors the rate of each heartbeat. The normal heart does not actually beat at a constant fixed rate like a metronome does; a normal heart tends to fluctuate between two rates. For example, a normal heart will tend to beat a bit faster and a bit slower at times, averaging out at 70 beats per minute. It may go up to 75 beats per minute or slow down to 65 beats per minute.

The beat-to-beat pattern is called the "heart rate variability," or HRV in medical terminology.

That is a normal heartbeat. An unhealthy heartbeat has an erratic pattern, which appears to be the most accurate physiologic predictor of impending problems such as sudden death from heart attacks, according to medical studies by Doctor Michael Jacobson.[3]

What science is learning is that a person's emotional state is very much involved in all this. The Bible has told us that for thousands of years, as a man thinks, so is he (see Proverbs 23:7).

Numbers 13:33 also shows this truth. The Israelites saw themselves small as grasshoppers, and so they were already defeated in their minds. We have to see ourselves as bold, courageous, and able in the power of the Holy Ghost to face anything that comes our way. But that will depend on what we think of ourselves. Do we think we are bold and courageous—or wimpy and fearful? What you think of yourself others will think of you too.

> *And there we saw the giants, the sons of Anak, which come of the giants: and we were in our own sight as grasshoppers, and so we were in their sight* (Numbers 13:33).

If you are familiar with horses, you know that they can pick up on and respond to an individual's fear even from a significant distance. Dogs and other animals do the same thing. Your fear of them will cause them to respond. Then how much more do people need to deal with their fear of one another? The only thing that gets rid of fear is love and forgiveness. When we aren't feeling loved, fear is present because perfect love casts out fear and torment. And since there are no walls in the spirit these things can come and go as we give them permission. We give permission by not forgiving and loving one another! Then the cycle starts all over again because there are no walls in the spirit world and that yucky, fearful stuff in you wants to link up with the yucky fearful stuff in them. What a mess!

It's like not having any walls in your heart to prevent junk from coming and going.

> *He that hath no rule over his own spirit is like a city that is broken down, and without walls* (Proverbs 25:28).

> *For we wrestle not against flesh and blood, but against principalities, against powers, against the rulers of the darkness of this world, against spiritual wickedness in high places* (Ephesians 6:12).

There have been couples that married each other's "junk" (sins and iniquities). Because when you don't forgive each other, and love each other, we retain their sins into our lives! John 20:23 explains it clearly, that when we do not forgive others, we retain their sins, but if we do forgive them, their sins are returned to them and we remain clean: *"Whosoever sins ye remit, they are remitted unto them; and whosoever sins ye retain, they are retained."*

If these same individuals attended ministry and began getting free from their stuff, it may be that they find out they have to get to know each other all over again. Linda knew a lady that said she didn't want to change because she was afraid of what she was going to turn into. But then she explained that she'll be what God intended her to be from the foundation of the world. The truth is, we will change into the image of Jesus Christ. Isn't that what we all want to see happen? Don't we want to change into the image of Christ? Then let's get rid of that junky stuff in our hearts.

Healthy Heart

People who have a healthy heart rate are usually characterized as those who are compassionate, who care about others, and who can hold their peace. In contrast, people with unhealthy hearts often experience anger or frustration and are easily stressed about things that happen in their lives.[4]

Many of us have to relearn a lot of things because the enemy convinced our generation of the need to internalize issues, to have a "stiff upper lip." We just bottle up how we feel about things, instead of dealing with them in a healthy way. We mistakenly thought it was better not to express our real feelings. How many people, when you ask how they are doing respond with, "Oh, I am fine?" But you can visibly see they are not. They are really lying to you without realizing it; lying can actually complicate their health issues. Remember, it's the truth that makes us free, therefore, lying can put us into more bondage!

Individuals who can learn to change their emotional thoughts from negative to positive are able to dramatically reduce and improve their HRV patterns, thus reducing the chance of sudden cardiac death. Keep in mind that this affects people in all age groups.

Effects on the Human Immune System

Research has linked the emotions with other physiological effects as well. There is something called the IgA, which is an antibody secreted as the first line of defense against any invading infection. If you keep your peace, your immune system works the way God intended it and you will be less susceptible to infections and diseases. This is called "homeostasis."

What is really interesting is that if an individual experiences an episode of intense anger or frustration for just five minutes, the IgA level drops 55 percent in the first hour and remains below normal for over six hours. That means for six hours you are susceptible to any virus you come in contact with!

However, if you respond as a child of God and keep your peace, you are not in danger of this. If you experience an episode of deep appreciation or love for only five minutes, your IgA levels rise up to 40 percent above normal and stays elevated for over six hours. See, it is true that a hug a day keeps the devil away! Someone once said that we need a minimum of 12 touches a day—and not slaps or punches, either. It actually boosts our immune system.[5]

Proverbs 17:22 tells us that *"a merry heart does good like a medicine: but a broken spirit dries up the bones."* The word "medicine" literally means "cure," but a broken spirit dries up the bones. Could a broken spirit be the same as a broken heart? Sure it is. The Bible talks about the heart, and the more we study passages on the heart, we have discovered that our heart is interchangeable with the spirit:

> *And he that searcheth the hearts knoweth what is the mind of the Spirit, because he maketh intercession for the saints according to the will of God* (Romans 8:27).

> *Create in me a clean heart, O God; and renew a right spirit within me* (Psalm 51:10).

The sacrifices of God are a broken spirit: *a broken and a contrite heart, O God, thou wilt not despise* (Psalm 51:17).

There is a connection between your bones and a broken spirit (or heart). There is a connection between your spirit, soul, and body. These are pathways. The condition of the spirit is as important as the condition of your soul and body.

Research shows that people suffering with a severe spirit of heaviness are now considered major candidates for heart disease—possibly even more prone than people who smoke, or have high blood pressure, or a poor diet. Studies have shown that suffering with fear (which God did not give you, see 2 Timothy 1:7), produces high anxiety, worry, and insecurity, which are really just modern words for a spirit of fear. The findings indicated that there was six times the risk of sudden cardiac death for those who think negatively (coming from a spirit of fear) than for those who think positively (coming from faith and love).

In doing research for this book, we found a Science Daily article called "Brain Differences Found Between Believers in God and Non-believers." It says, "Believing in God can help block anxiety and minimize stress, according to new University of Toronto research that shows distinct brain differences between believers and nonbelievers."[6] It's quite amazing, but God knew this all along! The medical community is just coming on board.

It also seems that there are two types of "A" behaviors that have been associated with heart disease. One is a time-pressured kind, and the other is a hardworking kind. A type-A personality is someone who sets a lot of goals. The person who sets a lot of goals and meets most of them does okay and is not really at high risk. However, the person who sets goals and is easily overwhelmed, frustrated, and doesn't meet his/her goals continues in unresolved self-conflict (self-hatred) is a high risk for heart disease or other illnesses.

The person who entertains a spirit of anger, resentment, or bitterness toward others or himself is in great danger if he does not recognize that he has been had by a lie from an invisible kingdom whose goal is to steal, kill, and destroy.

Your Oscillating Heart

The Lord has designed you, and says you are marvelously and wonderfully made, and you are! In fact, your heart connects with an oscillating system that starts with your brain. We want to be sure to explain the word *oscillating* correctly so Linda asked her doctor friend, Craig Jace,[7] to confirm these findings. He explained it this way: *oscillating* simply means to go back and forth. As I thought about this, I realized I had been oscillating all my life and did not even know it. I've been rockin' and rollin' since I rode in a stroller!

Okay, back to the brain. This electrical activity can be measured with the EEG (electroencephalogram). The lungs are electrically triggered to inspire 12 to 16 times a minute, moving the blood along the arteries with a rhythmical pulse, which moves the intestines along with food and waste through rhythmic contractions.

Of all the oscillators, the heart seems the most powerful, with an average of 40 to 60 times the electrical strength, keep in mind that our bodies are electrically charged; that's why we know to drink electrolytes for various illnesses such as the flu. Because everything in our body is connected, it's important to understand something called entrainment.

Entrainment here means to draw along with, or to incorporate.[8]

Let's take a look at a pendulum—the one that has several weights hanging from a chain. When you hit the weights, they get all tangled, but pretty soon, one of the dominant balls begins to get things in order, and the pendulum begins swinging succinctly. Clearly, it is easier for the weights to flow together than to go against the flow. Have you ever tried to swim upstream in a river? It gets you nowhere.

That is what should be happening with us in our bodies and in the Body of Christ. Your heart is the strongest oscillator in the body, and it's going to set the pace for all the other parts. When you are in homeostasis, you have good HRV patterns, and all your inside parts are working well. The brain, the lungs, and the intestines are doing what they are supposed to be doing. Why are we told to try to stay calm in emergencies—to slow down, take a few deep breaths, and gather our thoughts before making a quick decision? We are taught to drop down and roll if we find ourselves in a fire. This is good advice. Staying calm in any given situation is what we are talking about here. Your heart is really part of your soul and is the seat of your intellect, emotions, and motives. God looks upon the hearts of men, which are our motives, and if it's filled with wrong thoughts and wrong teachings, you will not make good godly decisions.

> *Shall not God search this out? for he knoweth the secrets of the heart* (Psalm 44:21).

> *Therefore judge nothing before the time, until the Lord come, who both will bring to light the hidden things of darkness, and will make manifest the counsels of the hearts: and then shall every man have praise of God* (1 Corinthians 4:5).

> *And God saw that the wickedness of man was great in the earth, and that every imagination of the thoughts of his heart was only evil continually* (Genesis 6:5).

May We Help You Learn "A More Excellent Way?

Your owner's manual (otherwise known as the Holy Bible) contains all the information you need to walk in divine health and blessings. Why is it that so many ministers have not shared this truth? It's been there all along. We fellowshipped in churches for years and were even on staff and never heard anyone come close to what we learned at Pleasant Valley Church (PVC) under Pastor Henry Wright.

We have received letters and calls from people who have been converted and healed just by reading *A More Excellent Way* by Pastor Henry Wright; *Nothing Is Impossible* by Caspar McCloud[9] and "A Matter of the Mind" by Linda Lange.[10] All of these books show that there are conditions with every promise of the Lord and that we need to understand what those are so we can represent Him well on this earth. We have all been given this task to fulfill. Even the Lord's prayer says, *"Thy kingdom come, Thy will be done on earth, as it is in heaven"* (Matthew 6:10). We need to understand His will so we can bring Heaven to earth.

Many who claim to be believers are fellowshipping with devils and don't even know it. If you have unforgiveness or a spirit of fear, you are fellowshipping with devils. If you are constantly critical of your wife or husband, you are fellowshipping with devils. If you are constantly tearing down your spouse, you probably have a spirit of self-hatred because the Lord brings you together to become one flesh! We need to build each other up, not tear each other down. When you tear your spouse down, you are actually tearing yourself down, too. Ephesians 5:28 tells us a man who does not love his wife hates himself:

> *So ought men to love their wives as their own bodies.*
> *He that loveth his wife loveth himself.*

If a man does not love himself, he cannot possibly love his wife (or others). This would also be true for the wife: If she does not love herself, she cannot really love her husband (or others). And the interesting thing is that when a husband truly loves his wife the way the Lord intended, she will respond exactly with what he desires! A love relationship between a husband and a wife truly starts with the husband.

Most men do not think that they really have a problem until they are dying from it. Some have even been trained to harden their hearts. And many don't realize that when they don't love their wives by honoring them, their prayers are hindered!

Likewise, ye husbands, dwell with them according to knowledge, giving honor unto the wife, as unto the weaker vessel, and as being heirs together of the grace of life; that your prayers be not hindered (1 Peter 3:7).

Men need to be teachable and able to take reproof. They need to stop blaming everyone around them for their problems. This is one of the steps to freedom, taking responsibility for our lives and decisions.

When love is distorted, this is caused by what is referred to as an unloving spirit. There is an ungodly spirit that will not allow you to feel loved, or to give real unconditional love. It is a spirit that is self-centered rather than Christ-centered and full of condition. If the world will know that we are Christians by our love, then we need to build each other up, not tear each other down. If you are a child of God, you better act like one.

By this shall all men know that ye are My disciples, if ye have love one to another (John 13:35).

See that none render evil for evil unto any man; but ever follow that which is good, both among yourselves, and to all men"(1 Thessalonians 5:15).

When we live the Word, He keeps us by His Word

God said, *"If thou wilt diligently hearken to the voice of the Lord thy God, and wilt do that which is right in His sight, and wilt give ear to His commandments, and keep all His statutes, I will put none of these diseases upon thee, which I have brought upon the Egyptians: for I am the Lord that healeth thee"* (Exodus 15:26).

Some of our issues come from our own selves. Jeremiah 5:25 says that our own sins and iniquities prevent good things from happening to us.

Your iniquities have turned away these things, and your sins have withholden good things from you (Jeremiah 5:25).

We need to stop blaming God for our situations or health conditions; we must begin to take responsibility by taking our thoughts captive, replacing the wrong thoughts with godly thoughts so that we won't sin against Him! Again, it all starts in our hearts and minds. It's not God's fault when things go wrong in our lives. So whose fault is it? Could it be thoughts that you have entertained from that other kingdom? The Bible tells us that God can do anything for us but chooses not to when we have sins and iniquities in our lives. What do Isaiah 59 and Psalm 66 have to say?

> *Behold, the Lord's hand is not shortened, that it cannot save; neither His ear heavy, that it cannot hear: but your iniquities have separated between you and your God, and your sins have hid His face from you, that He will not hear* (Isaiah 59:1-2).

> *If I regard iniquity in my heart, the Lord will not hear me* (Psalm 66:18).

In preparation for our next chapter, this is something quite fascinating, how our brains are truly equipped to perceive and handle more than we ever imagined. See if you can read the following:

I cdnuolt blveiee taht I cluod aulaclty uesdnatnrd waht I was rdanieg. The phaonmneal pweor of the hmuan mnid, aoccdrnig to a rscheearch at Cmabrigde Uinervtisy, it dseno't mtaetr in waht oerdr the ltteres in a wrod are, the olny iproamtnt tihng is taht the frsit and lsat ltteer be in the rghit pclae.

The rset can be a taotl mses and you can sitll raed it whotuit a pboerlm.

Tihs is bcuseae the huamn mnid deos not raed ervey lteter by istlef, but the wrod as a wlohe.[11]

Were you amazed how easy it was to read? Why? We are marvelously and wonderfully made (see Ps. 139:14).

Practical Application

Is there something you can do to help turn things around in your life? Yes! It's up to you. Remember, we prevent good things from happening to us (see Jeremiah 5:25). What will you choose to think about? We challenge you to start meditating on heavenly things. There is an old hymn that says, "Turn your eyes upon Jesus, look full in His wonderful face, and the things of earth will grow strangely dim, in the light of His glory and grace."[12]

You won't be pulled to the left or to the right if you keep your mind fixed on Him. Keeping our eyes and mind on Him also produces peace. Have you heard the saying, "To be heavenly minded is to be no earthly good"? But that is a lie! Because to be heavenly minded is to be earthly good.

Always remember that Peter actually did walk on water as long as he kept his eyes on Jesus; the moment he took his eyes off the Lord Jesus and looked at his circumstances, the waves crashed in all around him, and he began to sink.

Remember Isaiah 26:3:

> *God keeps in perfect peace those whose minds are stayed on Him because they trust in Him.*

Endnotes

1. Pastor Henry Wright, A More Excellent Way (New Kensington, PA: Whitaker House, 2009); www.beinhealth. com.

2. Dr. Teresa Allen, DO, Internal Medicine Physician: 7047 Halcyon Park Dr., The Fit Centre, Montgomery, Alabama, 36117.

3. Dr. Michael D. Jacobson, The Word on Health, (Chicago, IL: Moody Publishers, 2000) and Co author of The Biblical Guide to Alternative Medicine. Board certified osteopathic family physician, holds an undergraduate degree in biblical studies. Pastor and founded Provident Medical Institute, and educational ministry dedicated to assisting Church leadership in effectively addressing health-care issues.

4. Mayo Clinic online database: http://www.mayoclinic. com/. This information is in any medical book, connecting stress to heart conditions.

5. Dr. Teresa Allen, DO, Internal Medicine Physician: 7047 Halcyon Park Dr., The Fit Centre, Montgomery, Alabama, 36117.

6. Science Daily, March 5, 2009: http://www.sciencedaily.com/releases/2009/03/090304160400.htm.

7. Doctor Craig Jace, Jace Medical, 10843 Magnolia Blvd. Ste 1, North Hollywood, CA 91601 (818) 505-8610.

8. Intelegen Inc. "The science behind audio based brain wave entrainment."

9. Caspar McCloud, Nothing Is Impossible (Gainesville, GA: Praxis Press, 2006); Caspar McCloud Ministries; www.pastorcaspar.com.

10. Linda Lange, "A Matter of the Mind" (Createspace.com 2000, ISBN# 9781463562809, Life Application Ministries Publications, www.truthfrees.org.

11. Liliana Marquez; sent through email.

12. See http://library.timelesstruths.org/music/Turn_Your_Eyes_upon_Jesus/.

Chapter Three

ANATOMY OF A THOUGHT

Your brain works with corresponding electrochemical reactions for every single thought you have. All sorts of chemicals are released and make their way down pathways throughout your entire body.

Types of Brain Waves

Electromagnetic waves are produced by your thoughts, and some have compared them to a fine symphonic work played by the most accomplished orchestra. Before going on, it's important to give a clear description of how this works.

Each brain wave has a various function, and you should know a bit about them to help you understand what is going on in your thoughts and how they work. We have already established that the brain is functioning as an electrochemical organ. Some researchers have actually speculated that a fully functioning brain can generate as much as 10 watts of electrical power.

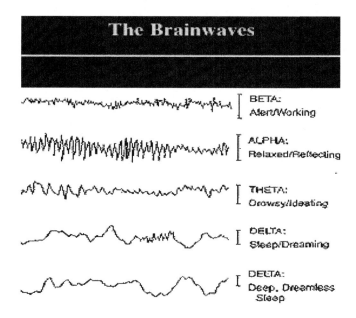

http://brain.web-us.com/brainwavesfunction.htm[1]

Some research suggests that if one could harness all 10 billion interconnected nerve cells and then have them all discharged at one time that a single electrode placed on the human scalp would record something like 5 millionths to 50 millionths of a volt.

If you could convince enough people to lend you their heads and could attach enough wiring to hook them all up in a row, you might actually be able to light up a light bulb. Now there's an idea!

Electrical activity that is emanating from the brain is recorded in different forms of brain waves. There are at this time four main categories of brain waves: beta, alpha, theta, and delta. The waves may vary, depending on the study and source, but they are all in close proximity to each other.[2]

When the brain is aroused and actively engaged in some mental activity, it generates what is known as beta waves. The frequency of the beta waves usually ranges from 15 to 403 cycles a second. Beta waves are characteristic of a mind that is very active. For example, if you were to record brain wave frequency when an individual is in the midst of giving a presentation, you would find that he or she is generating beta waves.

The next frequency would be alpha. Alpha waves have frequency ranges from 9 to 14 cycles per second, a slower rate. After someone has finished teaching and goes home to rest, he or she would then enter into the alpha state. A relaxed person who is meditating on the Word of God would also be in the alpha state.

Theta brain waves have a slower frequency range, normally between 5 and 8 cycles a second. People who are daydreaming would often be engaged in theta. Now theta is a very spiritual place, and this is good and bad news. When you enter into theta, you can hear from the Lord who is a Spirit. However, the Lord meant it for His use, but the enemy, since he has access to the same spiritual realm, is using it too, and it's really up to you to decide who gets that access. Many have tapped into theta as a form of meditating, connecting with their spirit, as you see in New Age movements. But God only intended it to be used to communicate with us, but since the enemy is spirit too, it has access to us in spirit. That is what this book is all about getting our mind, conscious, and subconscious working together to think in God's realm, not to be used of the enemy.

Scientists in Portugal have found a way to fly a drone by using brainwaves from a person on the ground.[3] If you think that is impossible, think again. Our brains have power more than we know, that is why we have power in the Name of Jesus, it's these brainwaves activating that communication with the God of the universe.

Then there are "Theta Healers." They actually have conferences that teaches you to use your brain to heal your body. Perhaps that works, but please hear us out, these individuals are seeking the wrong kingdom. God doesn't want you deceived (see Ephesians 4:14), just as He has told us to stay away from occultism, though it "appears" to be real, it is not. It bypasses His plan for you, His love, and His relationship with you. He wants you to know the truth so you won't perish for lack of knowledge (see Hosea 4:6). These individuals may receive healing, but what happens to them when they leave this earth? Our faith, hope and trust comes from the ultimate healer, God and God alone.

> *Bless the Lord, O my soul, and forget not all his benefits: Who forgiveth all thine iniquities; who healeth all thy diseases; Who redeemeth thy life from destruction; who crowneth thee with lovingkindness and tender mercies* (Psalm 103-2-4).

> *He healeth the broken in heart, and bindeth up their wounds* (Psalm 147:3).

The Lord Speaks

The Lord speaks to us through theta, and since this book is talking about our thoughts, that is why we emphasize it here. When people find out that the enemy uses theta to mess with us, they have asked if they could be prayed for so they don't go into theta at all. Well, that is not a good prayer, because that would mess with God's design for their lives and cancel hearing directly from the Lord God. We are simply showing you how all this works so you can indeed learn how to hear from God and to take every thought captive to the obedience of Christ.

> *That we henceforth be no more children, tossed to and fro, and carried about with every wind of doctrine, by the sleight of men, and cunning craftiness, whereby they lie in wait to deceive* (Ephesians 4:14).

> *My people are destroyed for lack of knowledge: because thou hast rejected knowledge, I will also reject thee, that thou shalt be no priest to me: seeing thou hast forgotten the law of thy God, I will also forget thy children* (Hosea 4:6).

Another example of theta brain waves could be when you are driving a long distance and the highway starts to look very similar as you travel. Your mind begins to process the driving as a very repetitious thing and starts to go into theta where your imagination takes you for an adventure. You are able to drive and function normally, but maybe you are not very conscious of the last ten miles or so, or if you had to step on the brake and slow down, or how many signs you passed along the road as you traveled.

When I used to teach art classes, I would often would tell my students this story: I read a quote in the adventures of Sherlock Holmes by Sir Author Conan Doyle where Holmes asks Dr. Watson how many steps led up to the flat at 221 Baker Street? Undoubtedly, Watson has gone up and down them countless times over the years. Watson replies, "I do not know." Holmes explains, "You see, Watson, but you do not observe."[4]

I used this excerpt to explain how important it is to observe! I would encourage my art students to examine something closely before attempting to draw or paint it. How is the light hitting the object? Where is the light source coming from? What is the texture like? Is it smooth or rough? Look at something you recognize with childlike eyes and see it for the first time. While an artist will go in and out of beta as he or she works, a driver in stop-and-go traffic would be primarily in beta in order to drive safely and defensively.

I recall getting some really good ideas as I traveled long distances in a state of theta. I would compose music or imagine some artwork that I would later paint or music I would record in my studio. Riding my horse down a trail in a forest would keep me in beta, as horses can spook at a moment's notice by anything that tends to move, such as deer or some shadow. It takes awhile to desensitize a horse so it trusts you and knows you will not allow anything bad to happen to it. Horses are a prey animal. They seem to be in a beta state most of the time, ready to go into a fight-or-flight mode.

The last brain wave state is delta, which is the slowest cycle. Delta typically has a range of 1.5 to 4 cycles per second. Brain waves that get down to zero generally indicate brain death. When you are sleeping and enter into a deep, dreamless sleep, you would be in the lowest frequency—usually two to three cycles a second. If you like to read in bed before falling asleep, you are likely to be in low beta state. Unless you are reading a book that you cannot put down, like this one hopefully, you should be able to start to drift off from a full day's activities. After you turn off the lights, you should be leaving beta, going in to alpha, then in to theta, and as you fall asleep, into delta.

Now as we sleep, most humans will dream in 90-minute cycles. As we start to dream, we enter into theta. Rapid eye movement (REM) a characteristic of this stage of active dreaming. Wonderful information can be released through dreams. The Bible has a number of accounts of the Holy Spirit giving revelation through dreams—the story of Joseph and Pharaoh is a good example (See Genesis 40-41).

When you wake up from a deep sleep, you will go through a number of brain waves that increase and adjust to what you must do or accomplish next. In other words, you will go from delta to theta, then to alpha, and finally, when the alarm goes off or someone wakes you, into beta.

If you are able to hit the snooze alarm button and fall back to sleep, you most likely will go back to a lower frequency, to a non aroused state, and possibly back into theta. Some may actually just go back to sleep and reenter delta. During this time when you are going to have to wake up soon, you may only stay in the theta state for a few minutes, perhaps five to ten.

I recall some artist friends who loved to have this type of experience (I being one of them because in this state you feel you are awake, yet you can still dream images and have a free-flowing stream of ideas). My wife after many years finally realized I was actually working when I would drift off like this before heading to my studio for the day's activities. I found this very useful before working on a message to present to my church fellowship.

You may find yourself receiving a fresh look at some recent events and getting clarity on how to deal with them, or you may begin to unravel some ideas for the day ahead. This can be a very productive time. But the enemy also knows this, and is now opening up our kids to a new fad called "I-Dosing" where the parts of the brainwaves are used! There is a letter to parents warning them of this deception. We spoke earlier on entrainment, and this is an example of what this looks like, as it pertains to technology used today:[5]

Dear Parents,

We wanted to make you aware of a concern we have with a new fad among young people called I-Dosing, also known as digital drugs. The trend involves downloading an MP3 that uses binaural brainwave technology. The technology works by using two tones in close frequency, one in each side of a set of headphones. To a listener, the different tones combine to create a beat frequency, which alters brainwaves. The apps can be downloaded, often for a fee, to many cell phones and MP3 players.

The administrators and nurse at Mustang High School became aware of the use of this technology this week. Sites promoting the binaural brainwave technology claim there are no dangers to listening to the "doses." However, some students who listened to one of these MP3s exhibited the same physical effects as if they were under the influence of drugs or alcohol, including increased blood pressure, a rapid pulse, and involuntary eye movements. Two students reported auditory and visual hallucinations.

Based on the physiological effects we are concerned about this phenomenon. Please talk to your child about the dangers around them, including the potential dangers from things that are promoted as being perfectly safe.

It is important to spend time with the Lord as ideas flow. Because then it will flow in the right direction and be used for His glory.

Each one of us experiences these different brain waves. If we use them to our advantage now that we understand them a little bit, it will make a difference in our lives.

An Orchestra for Good or Evil

The more we study and explore the Bible the more we realize we do not really know very much. But that is also an exciting thought to contemplate as we are going to spend eternity in one of two places. For those who are Heaven bound, we will be learning continually for all eternity, and it will be glorious.

Your body can actually be compared to a fine symphonic orchestra with all sorts of movements and themes, all the finely tuned instruments playing their parts perfectly on time. In this case, the many chemical reactions that a single thought can have affect your emotions and perception at any given moment.

Mind you, this raises the question: who is conducting your body's orchestra—the Lord or someone else?

You are a holy temple. God created you so that He can dwell within you:

> *Know ye not that ye are the temple of God, and that the Spirit of God dwelleth in you?* (1 Cor. 3:16).

Though God created you, your enemy knows how your body works, too. The devil was there in the Garden when the Lord God created Adam and Eve. He saw how it was done and knows how it works. The devil and his demons are still after one thing, and that is your blood. The life of the man is in the blood, and if he can get to your blood, he can get your life.

> *For it is the life of all flesh; the blood of it is for the life thereof: therefore I said unto the children of Israel, Ye shall eat the blood of no manner of flesh: for the life of all flesh is the blood thereof: whosoever eateth it shall be cut off* (Leviticus 17:14).

Did you know that your bones are filled with blood, and that if the enemy can dry up your bones, he can get to your immune system? That is why Proverbs 17:22 says that when we have a happy heart, it promotes good health, and when we don't have a happy heart, our bones are dried up. Read the following proverbs:

> *A merry heart doeth good like a medicine: but a broken spirit drieth the bones* (Proverbs 17:22).

> *A sound heart is the life of the flesh: but envy the rottenness of the bones* (Proverbs 14:30).

> *A virtuous woman is a crown to her husband: but she that maketh ashamed is as rottenness in his bones* (Proverbs 12:4).

The enemy's whole plan is to steal, kill, and destroy, especially relationships, because he knows that can compromise your immune system if we have broken hearts because of them—but God is greater than our hearts! See the passages below:

> *The thief cometh not, but for to steal, and to kill, and to destroy; I am come that they might have life, and that they might have it more abundantly* (John 10:10).

> *Ye are of God, little children, and have overcome them; because greater is He that is in you, than he that is in the world* (1 John 4:4).

> *Submit yourselves therefore to God. Resist the devil, and he will flee from you* (James 4:7).

> *For if our heart condemn us, God is greater than our heart, and knoweth all things* (1 John 3:20).

Chemicals Trigger Emotions

When you feel happy, there are specific types of chemicals or neurotransmitters called endorphins that are triggering emotions. The release of endorphins brings pleasurable feelings. My wife probably releases endorphins when she is invited to eat some decadent chocolate cake. This would not work for me as I no longer find sugar appealing. So for me, it is probably when I ride my horse. This is a form of exercise, even though my son thinks the horse is the one who gets the real workout!

Anyway, we have all heard that exercise releases endorphins, a natural antidepressant that can profit you somewhat, according to the Bible.

> *For bodily exercise profiteth little; but godliness is profitable unto all things, having promise of the life that now is, and of that which is to come* (1 Timothy 4:8).

Your brain releases different chemicals when you feel happy, sad, fearful, or are full of faith. Your brain is like a mini-factory producing all sorts of chemicals in a variety of emotions, depending on what you are experiencing at any given moment.

Now we must understand why the Lord tells us to take our thoughts captive, to think about what we are thinking about. Why? Because not every thought is your own and not every thought is good for you. Some thoughts are very harmful or toxic to your body—if you allow yourself to think about negative (toxic) thoughts long enough, they will become one with you.

When you do, you are making them "you." You are not a disease, but you have opened the door to a host of problems; they not only will create conditions for many health problems, but will set up situations in your life that will bring in curses and not blessings.

Fear is More Than An Emotion

Deuteronomy 28 lists blessings and curses. The first 14 verses speak of blessings, and verses 15 to the end of the chapter list the curses. The curses come because of disobedience to the Word. This has nothing to do with salvation; it has to do with sanctification and living in the Promised Land here and now. Linda had a great question: What **promises** are you trying to **land**? That's what this is all about. To live a life filled with peace, righteousness, and joy now. Jesus came to give us life abundantly, so what is our problem? It could just be our stinkin' thinkin', or "trash in our basket" like the little four-year-old said.

In our view, the principalities and powers we read and study about would be spirits like: unforgiveness, anger, rage, resentment, bitterness, and depression (which the Bible calls a spirit of heaviness), or anything that causes us to fall under a heaviness of heart is sin—and sin, in our understanding, is a spirit.

> *To appoint unto them that mourn in Zion, to give unto them beauty for ashes, the oil of joy for mourning, the garment of praise for the spirit of heaviness; that they might be called trees of righteousness, the planting of the LORD, that he might be glorified* (Isaiah 61:3).

Looking diligently lest any man fail of the grace of God; lest any root of bitterness springing up trouble you, and thereby many be defiled (Hebrews 12:15).

Let all bitterness, and wrath, and anger, and clamour, and evil speaking, be put away from you, with all malice (Ephesians 4:31).

Fear is in this category, yet fear is also a spirit unto itself. These spirits are very harmful if you invite them in and entertain them. We do that when we start thinking the opposite of what God thinks.

Fear is not just an emotion; Second Timothy 1:7 says that it is an evil spirit. Fear is the opposite of faith, and it is sin! That which is not of faith is sin, according to Romans.

"For God hath not given us the spirit of fear, but of power, and of love, and of a sound mind" (2 Timothy 1:7).

"And he that doubteth is damned if he eat, because he eateth not of faith: for whatsoever is not of faith is sin" (Romans 14:23).

It's your decision every day who you are going to serve. Will it be the Lord your God or the devil? Will you serve in the Kingdom of God or the kingdom of darkness? You may be saying, "Wait a minute, I serve God all the time." Well, let's take a minute and look at your thought life. Did you know that being angry is not from God? Who is it from? Did you know that thinking negatively is not from God? Then who is it from? Did you know that stretching the truth because of what others may think or do is not from God? We don't realize how much we may be serving that other kingdom. We hope by the time you finish reading this book that you will have a clearer understanding of how important our thought life is and how much it reflects on whom we trust and serve.

Where Are Your Thoughts?

As Joshua was talking to the tribes of Israel, he actually gave them instructions to serve God in sincerity and to put away the gods that their fathers served.

And if it seem evil unto you to serve the Lord, choose you this day whom ye will serve; whether the gods which your fathers served that were on the other side of the flood, or the gods of the Amorites, in whose land ye dwell; but as for me and my house, we will serve the Lord (Joshua 24:15).

Is this a command or a suggestion? Which will you obey? Again you may say, "But I don't serve any other gods, just God in Heaven." Again, where are your thoughts? Where your mind goes, your body follows. It is a moment-by-moment decision.

When Jesus asked His disciples who they thought He was, Peter spouted out, "You are Jesus, the Son of God." Then Jesus said that only God in Heaven could have revealed that to him. This tells you that you are able to hear directly from our Lord.

He saith unto them, But whom say ye that I am? And Simon Peter answered and said, Thou art the Christ, the Son of the living God. And Jesus answered and said unto him, Blessed art thou, Simon Barjona: for flesh and blood hath not revealed it unto thee, but My Father which is in heaven (Matthew 16:15-17).

Then just a few minutes later Jesus is telling Peter, "Get thee behind Me, Satan." Why? Because Peter began speaking from that other kingdom. The enemy tempted him in his thinking, and Peter spoke it out.

Then Peter took Him, and began to rebuke Him, saying, Be it far from Thee, Lord: this shall not be unto Thee. But He turned and said unto Peter, Get thee behind Me, Satan: thou art an offence unto me: for thou savorest not the things that be of God, but those that be of men (Matthew 16:22-23).

There are several other instances in the Bible that display a response from the thoughts of God or from the thoughts of Satan. Let's take a look at a few.

Thoughts Coming From Satan

Let's start with Judas Iscariot. The enemy has access to us through our thoughts, as discussed earlier by theta brain waves. He uses our weaknesses, lustful desires, and a number of other sins to get us to agree with him in thought.

That is why it is so important to get our thoughts and hearts cleaned up, so he doesn't have anything to use against us to tempt us to think like he thinks. He knows that we will "act" upon anything we dwell upon. In Judas' case, it was greed; his focus was on money. He opened the door for the enemy to enter when he rebuked Jesus for letting the woman pour the oil on Him, saying that the oil was being wasted and could have been sold for a lot of money. This came from his lust and greed for money.

It's interesting to note that all the disciples were indignant about this, but only Judas acted upon it! The enemy had 12 men to tempt, but because of Judas' heart of greed, pride, anger, jealousy, envy, and fear, he was prime bait.

> *But when His disciples saw it, they had indignation, saying, To what purpose is this waste? For this ointment might have been sold for much, and given to the poor....Then one of the twelve, called Judas Iscariot, went unto the chief priests, and said unto them, What will ye give me, and I will deliver Him unto you? And they covenanted with him for 30 pieces of silver* (Matthew 26:8-9;14-15).

This is how it worked. Satan put a "thought" in Judas because he knew Judas' heart condition.

John 13:2 says:

> *And supper being ended, the devil having now put into the heart of Judas Iscariot, Simon's son, to betray him.*

Satan then entered Judas. Yes, he entered Judas!

> *Then entered Satan into Judas surnamed Iscariot, being one of the twelve* (Luke 22:3).

Satan has an advantage over us when our hearts and thoughts are not conformed to God's heart and thoughts.

> *To whom ye forgive any thing, I forgive also: for if I forgave any thing, to whom I forgave it, for your sakes forgave I it in the person of Christ; Lest Satan should get an advantage of us: for we are not ignorant of his devices* (2 Corinthians 2:10-11).

After that, Judas came to his senses and realized that he had sinned.

> *Then Judas, which had betrayed him, when he saw that He was condemned, repented himself, and brought again the thirty pieces of silver to the chief priests and elders, saying, I have sinned in that I have betrayed the innocent blood. And they said, What is that to us? See thou to that* (Matthew 27:3-4).

The end of that story was that Judas ran out and hanged himself. Only a spirit of death can cause someone to kill himself or have another killed.

> *And he cast down the pieces of silver in the temple, and departed, and went and hanged himself* (Matt. 27:5).

That spirit that entered Judas had an agenda, and that was to kill Jesus. And if that wasn't enough, it caused Judas to kill himself. The thief (Satan) comes to steal, kill, and destroy (see John 10:10). And he will take you a little at a time if need be—just like the frog in a cold pot of water. He won't jump out as long as you slowly heat it up. Then before he knows it, he's been boiled to death. It's slow, but very effective.

We need to be wise; we need to know the enemy's wiles. He comes to us with small thoughts to tempt us, and then he brings in more and more. We have to recognize them immediately so we aren't cooking our own goose!

> *Lest Satan should get an advantage of us: for we are not ignorant of his devices* (or wiles/ways) (2 Corinthians 2:11).

What could have Judas done differently? Perhaps he could have read this book? Perhaps gone to a seminar and received ministry? Well, that's silly, of course. But he could have taken that thought captive and perhaps someone else would have taken his part in the betrayal of Jesus. Christ was going to die, but at whose hand? Because of what was "in" Judas, he was easily deceived and used.

So you may be asking this question by now: was Judas possessed? We'll answer it this way. He was led astray in thought by his own lust and desires. This allowed Satan free access to use him as a puppet. Who has access to you? What things reside in your heart that the enemy could use to tempt you to think and act like him? Perhaps it's time to ask God's help in identifying sins in your life that could be used by the enemy to get you to think like him. Perhaps it's time to repent about some iniquities and sins? These are the very things that keep the door open for wrong thinking. So the question really is does an evil spirit have a Christian?

Let's take a look at Adam. He opened the door for Satan when he listened to what Eve said the serpent (Satan) told her. He began to dwell on it, and it caused him to doubt God's Word and the command not to eat of the tree of knowledge of good and evil. So he disobeyed God and ate the fruit. Who was he listening to?

Then on another account after the fall of Adam, he realized he was naked. As he and God were talking, God asked him why he was hiding. Adam replied, "Because I am naked." And God asked him, "Who told you, you were naked?" Those thoughts came to his mind. No physical being told him he was naked. So where did that thought come from? Through theta brainwaves that the enemy has access to. It's up to us to pay attention to what our minds are thinking... because they just may not be your own!

The enemy's job is to cast doubt on God's Word. Have you found yourself in unbelief? Have you found yourself doubting? It wasn't you doing it; it was that other kingdom, the thoughts coming from the enemy to tempt you to doubt God. To tempt you to believe a lie. To tempt you to think things that are not lovely, honest, pure, holy and good. We need to recognize when this happens and then do something about it. We have been given the power and ability to overcome the enemy. Let's start taking our role seriously as believers and use the resources God has given to us.

Thoughts Coming From God

As mentioned earlier, Simon Peter heard from God, but there were others who did as well. What about the Bible as a whole? It was written by inspiration of the Holy Spirit. How did the Holy Spirit inspire? Through thought!

> *All scripture is given by inspiration of God, and is profitable for doctrine, for reproof, for correction, for instruction in righteousness* (2 Timothy 3:16).

What about Paul? The Lord spoke to Paul in a dream, telling him not to fear but to speak boldly (see Acts 18:9-10). The Spirit spoke to Paul (see Acts 21:4). How did the Spirit speak? He spoke through inspiration and thought.

> *Then spake the Lord to Paul in the night by a vision, Be not afraid, but speak, and hold not thy peace: For I am with thee, and no man shall set on thee to hurt thee: for I have much people in this city* (Acts 18:9-10).

> *And finding disciples, we tarried there seven days: who said to Paul through the Spirit, that he should not go up to Jerusalem* (Acts 21:4).

How about Jesus' voice? John 10:16 says that His sheep "hear" His voice. Do we hear Him audibly today? More frequently, His voice comes to us through reading the Word, praying, and our conscience.

> *And other sheep I have, which are not of this fold: them also I must bring, and they shall hear My voice; and there shall be one fold, and one shepherd* (John 10:16).

> *Having a good conscience; that, whereas they speak evil of you, as of evildoers, they may be ashamed that falsely accuse your good conversation in Christ* (1 Peter 3:16).

Spirit-Soul Connection

We have discovered through research of various medical books and documentation that 80 percent of all diseases are spiritually based. There are some that say it's higher. We have seen some medical research that claims it is as high as 87 percent. This research attributes 87 percent of disease to our thought life and 13 percent to diet, genetics, and environment *(see bibliography)*. So it is not so much what you eat, but what is eating you!

"Capiche?" Got it?

In other words, your thought life can be heavily contributing to problems and diseases in your life. Now, science will call them "lifestyle diseases." Personally, we call them by the evil spirits that are behind them. We know what is behind things like migraines, hypertension, and heart problems. We (ministry team) are becoming experts in the field of helping people get free of allergies and diabetes.

So much of this begins when you allow the Lord Jesus to come and mend your broken heart (We address this in a later chapter). The things that we share with you have now been accepted by many physicians; yet, they've been in the Bible all along.

What and how you think does affect your emotional and physical state. It will affect the course of your life! Proverbs 26:2 tells us the curse cannot come without a cause.

> *As the bird by wandering, as the swallow by flying, so the curse causeless shall not come* (Proverbs 26:2).

The enemy cannot just mess with you anytime he wants without a reason (cause). You are the one who gives him his reason. Many wonder about Job in the Bible. He was a righteous man but yet was attacked by Satan. How could this be? We need to read the whole story of Job, because Job had a spirit of fear. What was it that he feared? He feared that his children weren't being obedient to God and so Job decided to sacrifice for them almost daily. So what happened? The very things he was "trying" to save, he lost. He lost all his children, family and possessions. The things he feared the most came upon him. There is a saying that the thing you fear the most controls you. And this was true in Job's life.

See, Job had fear before Satan had access to him. Satan had every right to him, and that is the only reason God gave him permission! There are times even in our life where we wonder what happened, where is God. The Bible says that He sometimes turns us over to Satan for the destruction of the flesh for the saving of our soul (see 1 Corinthians 5:5).

But in the end, Job got right with the Lord, and the Lord blessed his obedience again more than all the sacrifices he had made.

"For the thing which I greatly feared is come upon me, and that which I was afraid of is come unto me" (Job 3:25). Remember, to obey is better than sacrifice!

> *I know that Thou canst do every thing, and that no thought can be withholden from Thee. Who is he that hideth counsel without knowledge? Therefore have I uttered that I understood not; things too wonderful for me, which I knew not. Hear, I beseech Thee, and I will speak: I will demand of Thee, and declare Thou unto me. I have heard of Thee by the hearing of the ear: but now mine eye seeth Thee. Wherefore I abhor myself, and repent in dust and ashes* (Job 42:2-6).

Job recognized that God knew his heart and thoughts, as we see in the New Testament writings.

> *For the word of God is quick, and powerful, and sharper than any two-edged sword, piercing even to the dividing asunder of soul and spirit, and of the joints and marrow, and is a discerner of the thoughts and intents of the heart* (Hebrews 4:12).

We also want to add that Job not only repented, but he prayed for those who accused him, his very friends! This has significance to the outcome of his story—that the Lord gave Job twice as much as he had before.

> *And the Lord turned the captivity of Job, when he prayed for his friends; also the Lord gave Job twice as much as he had before* (Job 42:10).

How many people can you think of who were going along healthy and happy when some stressful event took place in their life, and then "zap!" Soon they had all sorts of health problems on top of the already-difficult issues that they were facing.

Someone goes through a bitter divorce, and suddenly he or she is dealing with heart problems or cancer. Can you recall a time in your life when someone personally wounded you with words or a traumatic event took place, and soon afterward you became ill? It was not just some coincidence.

People who are dealing with happy occasions can get stressed out, too. As a matter of fact, the same chemicals that run through your body when you are excited about something good run through your body when you get anxious and fearful; it's all about what is going on in the mind at the time that dictates the outcome. However, sometimes even good things cause us to fear, and that could result in a bad body response. Just ask anyone who has gone through taking part in a wedding. Did they get stressed (fearful)? Did they end up with a cold or the flu soon after the event? How many performers in the show business world can attest to this? There are quite a few.

Emotions and Your "Magic" Memory

A neuroscientist named Dr. Candice Pert has demonstrated that there is a biomolecular basis for our emotions. Dr. Pert's conclusions are very compelling for the medical community because she shows there are biological components establishing a crucial link between the mind and body. She calls these biochemicals "molecules of emotion." That is also the title of her book. The information molecules carry a literal photocopy of the thought formulated in the depths of the memory networks of your brain.[6]

Another doctor, Dr. Marion Diamond, has done some ground-breaking work in brain research. She calls these memory networks the "magic trees of the mind," which is also the title of her book. Basically, both doctors are saying that these networks create copies of your "thought life." These networks also carry the emotions which are the chemicals traveling throughout your bloodstream. It's called photosynthesis, a process in which our brain takes pictures of life events, through this chemical, which are then permanently ingrained in our minds.[7]

It is almost like having our own "information super-high-way" that can be accessed in a moment's time. Information molecules are then able to cause changes at the cellular level. They can actually reconstruct the DNA on the inside and the cell's makeup on the outside. This is how the enemy is able to bring diseases into your body if you have had trauma or repeated verbal abuse.

Even what you experienced as a child will show up years later. You will have all the thoughts associated with those experiences, which will release negative chemicals upon recall. These chemicals travel throughout your body and can change the shape of the receptors on the cells, and illness can quickly begin.

However, the opposite is also true if you were repeatedly given praise and encouraged. Positive chemicals are released and distributed throughout your body, which makes positive changes to your cells and DNA. This boosts your immune system and enhances your ability to build memory and develop intelligence.

This is why we see so many people today who have all sorts of emotional and physical issues, who were not loved properly by godly fathers and mothers. Negative reinforcement releases over-under secretion of chemicals, and positive reinforcement releases proper chemical amounts.

Now let's look at those magic memory trees of the mind. First, we want you to know that your thoughts actually look like trees under a microscope. The Bible talks about strongholds. There are strongholds where you have been programmed in your mind. Strongholds are things such as addictions, bitterness, rage and anger, depression, relationship problems, where people get stuck in their thoughts like getting stuck in the mud. There are feedback loops that release biochemicals such as endorphins, enkephalins, and serotonin. These bring, at the proper level, a state of well-being. This is where your intellect can flourish, and with it, mental and physical health.

If you are taking your thoughts captive to the obedience of Christ, you will be in peace and make good decisions. If not, you will not be in peace and will make foolish decisions. The Lord tells us to choose this day who we will serve. We get to choose each day, moment-by-moment.

Remember, as a man thinks in his heart, so he is (see Prov. 23:7). But before you can think yourself well, you need some more insights into the actual thought pathways by which blessings or curses come.

Stress and the Spirit of Fear

We asked several personal friends, who happen to be doctors, what their patients come to see them about. Amazingly, their answers are comparable to conclusions reached by the American Institute of Stress. Approximately 80 to 90 percent of all visits to a primary care physician result from stress-related disorders. In others words, a spirit of fear, which God did not give them, contributes significantly to our health problems.

In human anatomy, a region in the brain called the hypothalamus secretes a hormone called CRH, which is an emotion hormone. It acts like the brain of your endocrine system, and how much CRH is released is dependent on what you are thinking.

The Word on Health by Dr. Michael Jacobson, says that autopsies on suicide cases have shown that 10 percent more CRH (corticotrophin-releasing hormone) is present in the brains of people who committed suicide than in those who die of natural causes.[8]

CRH races into the pituitary gland, which is located in the brain and stimulates the release of another stress hormone called ACTH. ACTH races down to the adrenal glands on top of the kidneys and easily convinces them to release the biochemicals cortisol and adrenaline. That is not real good news! An over secretion of cortisol breaks up your T cells, and that busts up your immune system when this occurs over a period of time.

Remember, you get to choose what thoughts you think about. Are they thoughts from the Kingdom of God or the other kingdom?

For example, cortisol and adrenaline begin to have an adverse effect on the cardiovascular system when you repeatedly entertain ungodly thoughts.

That can bring about high blood pressure, which is the result of taking thought for tomorrow, which the Lord said not to do.

Looks like a commandment to us, the way we read it in Matthew 6:34 is this:

> *Take therefore no thought for the morrow: for the morrow shall take thought for the things of itself. Sufficient unto the day is the evil thereof* (Matthew 6:34).

Taking thought (or being anxious) for tomorrow can bring on heart palpations, aneurysms, or even strokes.

When you take thought for tomorrow, you are letting this stuff attack your immune system, making it harder to do what it is designed to do: protect you from infections and diseases. Next, these adverse hormones start affecting your ability to remember and think creatively, causing memories to literally shrink. If you do not "get a grip," you are headed down a destructive pathway that leads to a total breakdown, bringing illnesses and even premature death. What are you going to do? Believe the Word of God or some other kingdom?

God does not need you in Heaven helping to build mansions. He needs you here; besides, those mansions are not built with human hands anyway. He has work for you here to do to help bring in the harvest.

> *Then saith he unto his disciples, The harvest truly is plenteous, but the labourers are few;* (Matthew 9:37).

We are His hands and feet and mouth on this planet. He needs us here to do His will! We need to get a hold of this powerful truth! The Lord has given us His power to use.

> *Verily, verily, I say unto you, He that believeth on me, the works that I do shall he do also; and greater works than these shall he do; because I go unto my Father* (John 14:12).

Your hypothalamus responds to your emotional state, and that is the reason negative thoughts can affect your emotional and physical state. The hormones it releases can destabilize your brain and create a bunch of broken feedback loops, disrupting the natural flow and balance of chemicals in your brain. In other words, you lose your homeostasis. Homeostasis is when the chemicals in your body are perfectly balanced, producing health. It's like the peace of God running through your veins. You will be calm and collected as you trust in the Lord and lean not on your own understanding. You can let go of the stress and live in His perfect peace.

> *And the very God of peace sanctify you wholly; and I pray God your whole spirit and soul and body be preserved blameless unto the coming of our Lord Jesus Christ* (1 Thessalonians 5:23).

The Fall of Satan

We need to also understand what happened when Satan was cast out of heaven. Scriptures say he was thrown out for rebelling against God, taking 1/3 of the angels with him (See Revelation 12:4). So we have a question. What exactly happened when Satan landed on planet earth? This is what we believe took place. He cannot love, because when he was separated from God, he was separated from God's love. What remained is what Satan ended up with. See, his rebellion was inside him while he was in heaven, otherwise how could he have rebelled? That is why we are on this earth. God is wanting us to choose Him from our own free will. He doesn't want anyone going to heaven that doesn't want to be with Him. He doesn't want someone ending up being cast out of Heaven like Lucifer was. God wants us to make our choice while on earth so that when we do go to heaven, we won't want to rebel.

Satan's sentence was swift and eternal. He can never be saved. He can never show love. He can never be merciful. He will never have any characteristics or nature of the Lord God. He is the exact opposite. If God is love and faith, Satan is hate and fear. See, God creates, and Satan corrupts. Scriptures say that Satan is a liar and the father of it (see John 8:44). That is who he is and that will never change. Just as God is who He is, and He never changes.

If we continue listening to lies and negativity, or even choose not to forgive our neighbor, we are submitting to Satan and his kingdom here on earth! We have to "know" our enemy and quit putting all responsibility on God. That is why Jesus came, not only to save us from our sins but to equip us to defeat the enemy. What does Revelation 12:11 say? *We overcome the enemy by the blood of the Lamb and the word of our testimony.* Do you know what this is saying? It is saying that our testimony (what God is doing in our lives) is just as important as the Blood of the Lamb. How do we know this? Because it's in the same sentence! When we share the goodness of God we are tearing down the kingdom of darkness. But if we walk around complaining, gossiping, not forgiving, being angry, hateful, even depressed, confused and fearful, etc., we are keeping the kingdom of darkness alive.

A Fallen World

Because of the fall of Satan, we now live in a fallen world. And because Satan can never know peace, guess what he's doing to this planet? Perpetrating chaos. So we can be sure we will have some stressful things to go through. But, remember, the earth is the Lord's and the fullness thereof (see Psalm 24:1). So you can also expect good things to happen here on planet earth, too.

We were not designed to take on an avalanche of stress, or a constant stream of it. Look at it this way: life is like an obstacle course, and how we "go through" it depends on what we believe. This time on earth is a test of our hearts, to see who we believe. Will it be the Lord, or will it be Satan?

Lucifer had free will just as we have free will. The Lord did not make him a robot, and neither did He make us robots. We have freedom to choose.

As an equestrian, I know that pulling the reins of a horse does not always mean the horse will obey. They are very powerful creatures and have the strength to be very stubborn; they may refuse to turn their head and hearts to do what is being asked of them. The same is true with us. Who is pulling your reigns? Life is one long test, and it is an open book test. You will need a Bible to pass this test.

Examine me, O Lord, and prove me; try my reins and my heart (Psalm 26:2).

Every day we need to decide who is pulling our reins. Statistics show most people who commit suicide will do it around holidays more than at any other time. Why? Because the enemy brings thoughts to them of past holidays of being alone.

During the holidays, my daughter was helping me hang some of my old paintings after repainting the dining room. We were talking about how to help someone who seemed to be having such a difficult time over the holiday season and was so lonely.

As my daughter handed me the stud finder, she said, "Dad we should shoot a commercial for lonely women saying, *"If you call right now we will throw in the amazing new stud finder, all you do is go up to any single man you are interested in and place the stud finder over his forehead; if the red light comes on you have found your stud; call now—operators are standing by."*

Remember, the enemy's whole plan is to "kill you off"! His plan is to separate you and isolate you, making you think you are all alone. Again, who are you listening to? Who is pulling your reins? The Bible is all about relationships—and the enemy knows it and targets all relationships!

The same passage says that God's plan is to give life and more abundantly (see John 10:10). We need to consider what we are thinking about, especially during these times.

We want to pose a question. Let's say you just bought a new refrigerator. As it was being installed, you realize that the cabinets hang too low so the refrigerator won't fit. What do you do? Blame someone? Get mad? Kick the refrigerator? Or do you take responsibility, stay in peace, and work the solution? The enemy wants you to lose your peace. And it's the everyday things we are talking about here, *"the little foxes that spoil the vine"* (see Song of Sol. 2:15).

Think about the last time something happened in your life that wasn't good. How did you respond? Our responses are manifestations of our thought life. It's not time to fall under any kind of guilt or condemnation; it's time to recognize our own heart condition and cooperate with God. We can be delivered from the thoughts that plague us and promote disease. Our definition of a disease includes anything that causes you to experience discomfort in any way—dis-ease. What does Peter say? Not to get stressed out when things happen, as it's just a trial:

> *Beloved, think it not strange concerning the fiery trial which is to try you, as though some strange thing happened unto you* (1 Pet. 4:12).

Can you see now how our lives are by-products of our own thinking? Yes, things do go wrong from time to time; the enemy is still at work; we still live here in a fallen world, but you don't have to fall to pieces when they happen. By getting your thoughts lined up with the Word of God, you will have what you need to be strong and courageous through any obstacle.

> *Have not I commanded thee? Be strong and of a good courage; be not afraid, neither be thou dismayed: for the Lord thy God is with thee whithersoever thou goest* (Joshua 1:9).

Instead of seeing that thing as an "attack of the enemy," look at it as an opportunity to exercise faith and see God work.

It may be time to take that frown and turn it upside down. A smile a day helps keep the devil away.

Submitting to God is the Key

James 4:7 is the key to taking every thought captive. How do we submit to God? Believe all He represents, receive His perfect love, trust Him with our lives, and keep our minds fixed on Him. The Bible says that He will keep those in perfect peace whose minds are stayed on Him.

> *Thou wilt keep him in perfect peace, whose mind is stayed on thee: because he trusteth in thee* (Isaiah 26:3).

Submit yourselves therefore to God. Resist the devil, and he will flee from you. (James 4:7)

How do we resist the devil? By keeping our mind on the Lord. And how do we do that, by trusting Him and His Word. It's all in this passage. But what we find is that people are not trusting the Lord. Why? Because they don't really know Him. To the degree we trust God is the degree we believe Him. So instead of fearing God in the proper way of respect and reverence, we fear the enemy. We need to stop fearing the enemy. Did you know that when we fear for any reason, we are making the devil greater than God? That alone should cause us to stop and change our thinking!

Let's say you had a traumatic experience and you saw the Lord working in that situation. Once it was over, your mind begins to process all that took place; it may be later that night, the next day or next week, but you will eventually process what happened.

This is where you will be a victim or a victor. As we have taught already, our mind is the battlefield. See, that circumstance starts replaying the details, but what happens is our mind intensifies the events beyond what actually happened. We start to think of all the "what if's" associated with it, which is all fear based. But, when you submit to God, you choose to think like He thinks, to trust He was there through it all and is still with you. When you believe God is greater, when you put your faith and confidence in His Word, you will be able to resist the devil. God is greater than anything, even what we "think" in our heart.

For if our heart condemn us, God is greater than our heart, and knoweth all things (1 John 3:20).

Resisting the devil is to choose not to dwell on that incident, the feelings, the "what if's," etc. This is how PTSD is formed. By not leaving that incident in the past where it belongs, but keeping it in the present. And we do that by allowing those thoughts to replay. We are entertaining devils when we do this. We resist the enemy by choosing not play the "past" over in our mind.

The Lord is always a gentleman, and He is not going to force you to do the right and proper thing. If you bow down to an evil kingdom, then the Lord will let you. He will step aside and let you have it your way until you finally have had enough and run back to the Lord your God. The Lord cannot bless you in your sins; you will have to turn away from your sins if you want Him to bless you.

The Lord's prayer even addresses our thought life! *"And lead us not into temptation, but deliver us from evil"* (Matt. 6:13). In a traumatic situation, we see that a person can be tempted to keep reliving (rethinking) all that happened as though it's happening again, and with all the bodily manifestations. But we can be delivered from evil when we keep our thoughts on Him!

Who's Your Daddy?

The Bible talks about various individuals who listened to the voice of God or to the voice of the enemy. We also need to ask ourselves which voice we are listening to. Because whoever you listen to, you will end up serving.

Are we listening to ourselves or talking to ourselves? Are we just going with the flow in our thinking, not really paying much attention, or are we attentive to our thoughts, telling ourselves the truth when a wrong thought comes? Are we replacing those thoughts with God's thoughts, or are we going to allow the lies of the devil to enter into our thoughts? Are we thinking victory or defeat? Because if we are thinking like God thinks, defeat isn't an option. And Jesus even said we better take a moment to see whom we are listening to.

Linda recalls in the movie, "Anne of Green Gables" Anne and Murilla were having a conversation. Anne said she was in the depths of despair. So she asked Murilla if she was ever in the depths of despair? Murilla responded, "No I have never been that way, to despair is to turn your back on God."

That is about right. We can't be in despair (hopeless) if we truly believe God!

Jesus said unto them, If God were your Father, ye would love Me: for I proceeded forth and came from God; neither came I of Myself, but He sent Me. Why do ye not understand My speech? even because ye cannot hear My word. Ye are of your father the devil, and the lusts of your father ye will do. He was a murderer from the beginning, and abode not in the truth, because there is no truth in him. When he speaketh a lie, he speaketh of his own: for he is a liar, and the father of it. And because I tell you the truth, ye believe Me not (John 8:42-45).

Have you ever heard people say, "Talking to yourself is a sign of being crazy"? Of course, people nowadays don't really see that as odd anymore because of the cell phones they have plugged into their ears. But in biblical times, perhaps it did look a bit crazy to people. The Bible says that David encouraged himself in the Lord. How would he do that if he didn't talk? Maybe he talked to himself all day long. Maybe he talked to the flocks of sheep he took care of. But the enemy used fear of being crazy so that you wouldn't tell yourself the truth. It's an okay thing to do at times. You may sometimes have to help motivate yourself by grabbing the back of your trousers and pulling them up saying, "get up, get going, and carry on." Take the time to tell yourself the truth.

Personal Insights

Linda remembers walking through a department store just talking to herself. It may have seemed silly to others, but because she had a good relationship with herself, it wasn't strange to talk to herself from time to time. She said that whoever coined the phrase that talking to oneself is a form of insanity did us an injustice. That was the enemy distoring something that could have saved so many from wrong thinking.

The relationship she developed with herself, because of the love of God she learned to receive personally, was one key to her healing and freedom—combined with forgiving—resulted in what she had sought after for so many years.

Years ago, I (who can actually joke about it now) thought myself as a "professional heart patient." The doctors basically gave me a death sentence telling me to get my affairs in order. Every time I took some heart medicine—which the medical community told me I would be on for the rest of my life—I would make a proclamation out loud so both invisible kingdoms heard as well as convincing my own mind and body, "I will not take this medication the rest of my life. I will not die, but I will live and be healed and proclaim the Kingdom of my God. I will believe the report of the Lord."

The result was that I was completely healed in 2001— which is medically documented—because I learned to agree with the Word of God. The Lord performed a miracle, and I have taken any heart medication since and have been walking in rather good health since that time. Not only that but a number of people have been healed of all sorts of things through this ministry of what I learned from the Holy Bible —to live the more excellent way. (You can also read about this in my book *"Nothing is Impossible."*)

> *My son, attend to my words; incline thine ear unto my sayings. Let them not depart from thine eyes; keep them in the midst of thine heart. For they are life unto those that find them, and health to all their flesh* (Proverbs 4:20-22).

Your Body Follows Thought

Have you ever said to yourself, "What Was I Thinking?" If you took a few minutes to identify what you were thinking about, you may find the answer. Remember, where your thoughts go, your body follows.

It's okay to admit you have been listening to the enemy; being honest is the first step to freedom. When we admit this, half the battle is won. See, the enemy doesn't want you to address these thoughts. He's telling you that if you say it out loud it gives him more power. That is a bold-faced lie! When you say it out loud, he loses his power! The Bible clearly says we are to confess our faults one to another, and pray for each other so that healing can come. That means we have to say something out of our mouth, not just think a thought!

> *Confess your faults one to another, and pray one for another, that ye may be healed. The effectual fer-*

vent prayer of a righteous man availeth much (James 5:16).

It is so refreshing to get before the Lord and repent of those things in your life which should not be there. When you take a shower, afterward you feel so fresh and clean. It's the same when you ask the Lord to forgive you and accept His forgiveness, you will feel like you just took a shower, washed and cleansed from all your sins. Today is the day of salvation. This is not the day the devil made; this is the day the Lord has made—let us rejoice and be glad in it!

Practical Application

Let's unravel this mess, showing you from the Holy Bible how the devil has been able to bring such diseases and devastation into our lives and what steps we can take to stop him in his tracks. We want to become doers of the Word, walking in all God's benefits, His blessings.

> *Beloved, I wish above all things that thou mayest prosper and be in health, even as thy soul prospereth* (3 John 1:2).

Researchers internationally have conceded for many years that when you participate with the emotions of fear, stress, anxiety, anger, depression, etc., it plays a major part in causing mental and physical health problems. You can find this in any medical book that talks about fear and the manifestations. The medical community's solution has been, for the most part, to give you a pill. The pharmaceutical companies are getting very wealthy as people are being destroyed from lack of knowledge as found in Hosea 4:6: *"My people are destroyed for lack of knowledge."*

If our minds produce various chemicals, what chemicals are your thoughts creating? Take a moment to think about the following questions.

- Did someone hurt you when you were a child?
- Did you go through a horrible experience alone?
- Are you still trying to get love from an unloving parent?

- Do you hear voices in your head telling you that you are worthless? If so, who's voice?

- Are you living with someone who doesn't understand you?

- Did you say or do something that you still feel guilty about or have regrets?

- Is there anyone in your life that you cannot and will not forgive?

If you were able to answer these questions affirmatively, then your mind is producing harmful chemicals. It means you have unforgiveness in your heart. The number one block to any healing, deliverance and restoration is unforgiveness.

This is a serious problem that needs immediate attention because if you do not forgive others, including yourself, God says He will not forgive you.

> *For if ye forgive men their trespasses, your heavenly Father will also forgive you: but if ye forgive not men their trespasses, neither will your Father forgive your trespasses* (Matthew 6:14-15).

Have you ever asked yourself, "How did I end up here?" If so, what were the circumstances surrounding it? Who were involved? What were you thinking at the time? All good questions to ask, then you will see the truth that can actually bring your freedom.

If you are still hurting from a past experience, and you begin thinking about it, you will produce chemicals harmful to your body. You are creating your own toxins. That is why Philippians 4:7-8 gives instruction on what to think on; love and forgiveness are good in every situation because you are producing perfect chemicals to bring health into your body.

> *And the peace of God, which passeth all understanding, shall keep your hearts and minds through Christ Jesus. Finally, brethren, whatsoever things are true, whatsoever things are honest, whatsoever things are just, whatsoever things are pure, whatsoever things are lovely, whatsoever things are of good report; if there be any virtue, and if there be any praise, think on these things* (Philippians 4:7-8).

Our thoughts plague us at times because unforgiveness is mingled with them. We need to forgive every person who has offended us in word or deed, that is why we need to see who was involved in all our hurtful times. Because resentment keeps a record of wrongs done and plays it over and over. No one can change what has happened, but we can change our thoughts. When we read and meditate on God's Word, and forgive those who have wronged us, our thoughts are being changed, our hearts are being changed, our health improves and we are being transformed more into His image. Then those things that happened to us become a thing of the past (where they should remain), and your life is new in Him, as Ephesians 5:26 says:

That He might sanctify and cleanse it with the washing of water by the word.

So what are you going to do? Decide today to face that thought, take responsibility, repent and receive forgiveness for your part, forgive all those associated with that situation, forgive yourself, and then thank God for His forgiveness, restoration, and unconditional love. If you do this each time a thought surfaces that causes you pain, you will start to experience more joy, peace, and freedom. You will begin to see results very quickly as you practice thinking what you are thinking about and then doing something about it.

By recognizing who's voice you are listening to is half the battle, because then you can do something about it.

Let us hear the conclusion of the whole matter: Fear God, and keep His commandments: for this is the whole duty of man. For God shall bring every work into judgment, with every secret thing, whether it be good, or whether it be evil (Ecclesiastes 12:13-14).

Endnotes

1. http://brain.web-us.com/brainwavesfunction.htm.

2. W. J. Freeman, How Brains Make Up Their Minds (New York: Columbia University Press, 2000).

3. Drones: www.bbc.co.uk, or GPSworld.com

4. Sir Author Conan Doyle, A Scandal in Bohemia (First published 1892).

5. "MHS Students Report Hallucinations after Using 'Digital Drugs,'" Mustang Times, 3/11/10; Mustang High School publication for parents of Mustang Public School Students. From Superintendent Bonnie Lightfoot, Mustang, Oklahoma. http://www.mustangpaper.com/content.aspx?module=ContentItem&ID=167181&MemberID=1586.

6. Dr. Candice Pert, Molecules of Emotion (New York: Touchstone, 1999).

7. Dr. Marion Diamond, Magic Trees of the Mind (New York: Penguin, 1999).

8. Dr. Michael Jacobson, The Word on Health (Chicago: Moody Press, 2000).

Chapter Four

HOW THOUGHTS BECOME THOUGHTS

Learning to take your thoughts captive to the obedience of Christ is like traveling down the highway of sanctification. It's a journey that brings us to an eternal place eventually. While on this planet, we have two choices. We will either follow after the Kingdom of God or that other kingdom—and you get to make the decision.

 We say it this way: If we really believe with our whole heart, mind and soul, every Word of God is true, we would act differently. Now this isn't to bring you under condemnation, it's to get you to see what is really going on in your thought life so you can do something about it. As long as you have breath, you can do something about it. Don't forget the scripture that says we are to cleanse ourselves from all filthiness of the flesh AND spirit (see 2 Corinthians 7:1).

Thought Trees

By understanding how our thoughts work, we are better equipped to do something when our mind falls into thought traps.

Thoughts under a microscope apparently look very much like a tree with a trunk and many branches—like a tree in wintertime when all the leaves have fallen off. The more branches, the more intelligent and accessible the thought will be. Each thought is made up of cells called neurons; they are the electrically excitable cells that make up those trees of the mind.

There are perhaps 100 trillion thought trees in your brain, and each one may grow over 70,000 branches. According to researchers such as Dr. Caroline Leaf,[1] you can store approximately three million years worth of information. So then after the three million years are filled up, do you do something like disk clean-up and get rid of files that are just collecting dust? Just wondering?

At the end of each neuron tree are branches called dendrites. Dendrites are specialized for receiving information and form synaptic contacts with the terminals of other nerve cells to allow nerve impulses to be transmitted. These highly complex structures are involved in processing information via the five physical senses—touch, smell, hearing, taste, and sight. They are continually integrating this information as it is translated into electrical impulses and transported across synapses, which are small chemical gaps between neurons that form interconnected neural circuits.

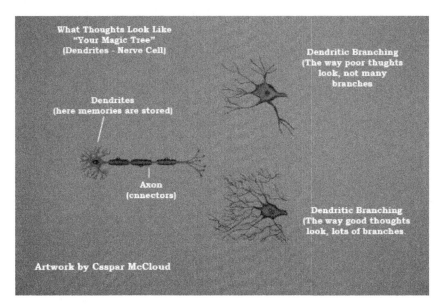

Neuroscientists can devote entire conferences to the study of dendrites. Basically, the brain builds a double memory of the content of every thought. Both sides of your brain are working together but have different functions. For example, when you are doing math, the left side of the brain sees it as $2 \times 2 = 4$. The right side sees it as $4 = 2$ groups of 2.

Artwork by Caspar McCloud

Both sides of your brain work together in synergy, providing perspective on every thought. The more you think, the more you understand. The more you are focused and aware of what you are thinking about, the more you grow out those branches on your treelike neurons, and they get firmly attached.

Those who are experienced on horses may find that when horses approach a scary object, they may get a bit jumpy. However, once they conquer the obstacle, they settle down. But it's always a good idea to go back the other way to that same obstacle. Is the obstacle scarier? No, but it will be seen through another part of the brain! That is why, when training horses, you need to have them jump from both sides of the obstacle, to get both sides of the brain in balance.

When Forgetfulness is Healthy

Glial cells are little vacuum-type cleaners that prune off those thought branches. It allows you to forget about stuff while you sleep, much like the "honey do" list your wife gives you. You did not really hear her when she spoke this list because you were watching the big game or something along those lines, and said, "Yes, Dear, I will do it later. Go! Go! Run, man! Did you see that play! Did you say something, Dear?"

Simply put, when you stop thinking about something, whatever it is, it will eventually be cleaned out. So let's be sure the wrong thoughts are being cleaned out, not the good ones.

You have 50 times more glial cells than those 100 trillion neurons running about your brain, so they must be as important as the dendrites.

Glial cells are essential to brain functioning, and without them the neurons could not do their job. They are the support team that provides all the backup as well as the nourishment and protection your neurons need. Basically, the glial cells help sort out your thinking.[1]

Now, let's put this together in laymen's terms. Those nasty negative thoughts, which are toxic to you, will interfere with the free flow of these important electrochemical processes in your brain. That will mess up and diminish the quality of stored memory so that your memory becomes distorted and harmful. The opposite would also be true. If you dwell on good things, as the Bible says in Philippians 4:7-8, the electrochemical processes of your brain won't be hindered, but will work properly, resulting in better health and better decision making.

Keeping Your Mind on God

If we are going to learn to be attentive to what we are thinking about and take every thought captive to the obedience of Christ, we need to understand some of this stuff. As we practice every day keeping our mind on God, the fruit of that will be perfect peace:

Thou wilt keep him in perfect peace, whose mind is stayed on Thee: because he trusteth in Thee (Isa. 26:3).

Let's look at what this passage really says, as it is a key Scripture to acquiring peace—which will, in turn, balance out our chemicals and produce good health.

This passage indicates that we don't have to make ourselves be at peace. Peace comes when we keep our "minds" on Him. And it gets better than that! It tells us how to keep our mind on Him: it's when we trust Him completely with our whole mind, soul, body, and strength—that sounds like obedience to us! It reminds us of an old hymn: "Trust and obey, for there is no other way to be happy in Jesus, but to trust and obey."[2]

Let's take a look at how the body responds to thought. The glial cells are working to help clear out the stress of modern life so we can practice Isaiah 26:3. When you enter into theta you are able to really receive communication from the Lord. Because theta opens you up to the spiritual side of things, however, that also means the devil can try and speak with you as well.

This is why you really need to take every thought and examine it against the Bible. The Lord loves you more than you can possibly understand, and He wants you to stay in peace. If you are not experiencing peace, then it usually comes down to the level of your trust.

To the degree you trust Him, is the degree of your peace.

Remember the account of three young men in Daniel 3 who decided to trust the Lord and not bow down to any ungodly idols. The king in this story was about to throw them to their deaths in a fiery furnace, but these three men said they would trust the Lord to deliver them—and even if the Lord did not deliver them, they would still not bow down.

They were all thrown into the fiery furnace and lived to testify about it because the Lord honored their faith. They trusted Him. This is not a parable but an actual account of a real event and we serve the same God today as they did. He is still able to rescue you even out of certain death.

If you have been giving in to a spirit of fear and are having difficulty trusting Papa God, now is a good time to repent, confessing your doubt and unbelief towards Him. Fear robs you of peace and could be the block hindering your healing, health, or whatever it is you desire of the Lord. Because, frankly, how can you receive something from God when you don't really trust or believe Him? Oh, you may say, "I trust God," but if you are honest, there are areas in your life where you clearly don't. Let's just get to the bottom line; be honest with God because He knows all your heart and intents anyway.

> *For there is nothing covered, that shall not be revealed; neither hid, that shall not be known* (Luke 12:2).

We stay in constant communication with Him by praying. The Bible teaches us to pray without ceasing. How do we pray without ceasing? We continue to keep Him in all we think or do. Talk to Papa God, every single minute. We can accomplish this, not by kneeling all day long in a prayer position, but by keeping our minds fixed on Him, which produces homeostasis.

> *Pray without ceasing* (1 Thessalonians 5:17).

We are to set our affections (our minds) on things above not on things of the earth.

> *Set your affection on things above, not on things on the earth* (Colossians 3:2).

And it doesn't mean to keep asking Him for the same things over and over again, but to ask Him with a thankful heart, believing that He has heard you the first time. The enemy would want you to think God has not heard you, but what does the Scripture say? We must believe that He exists, and that He will reward those who seek Him. Do you believe this?

> *But without faith it is impossible to please Him: for he that cometh to God must believe that He is, and that He is a rewarder of them that diligently seek Him* (Hebrews 11:6).

When you understand the process of controlling your thoughts, you create conditions in which your neuronal cells, dendrites, and glial cells can do their work in perfect harmony. By thinking about what you are thinking, you can then exercise your right as a believer and cast out anything that does not line up with the Word of God. This is a good way to keep yourself out of the snare of the devil who can take you at his will when your thoughts are out of control.

> *And the servant of the Lord must not strive; but be gentle unto all men, apt to teach, patient, in meekness instructing those that oppose themselves; if God peradventure will give them repentance to the acknowledging of the truth; and that they may recover themselves out of the snare of the devil, who are taken captive by him at his will* (2 Timothy 2:24-26).

We have the power to have self-control (temperance); it is one of the fruits of the Spirit.

> *But the fruit of the Spirit is love, joy, peace, longsuffering, gentleness, goodness, faith, meekness, temperance: against such there is no law* (Galatians 5:22-23).

When we don't have self-control, our lives become ruined.

> *He that hath no rule over his own spirit is like a city that is broken down, and without walls* (Proverbs 25:28).

Which Pathway Will You Choose?

Fear and faith are not just emotions. Fear is a spirit that God did not give you, and faith is His power in you to believe things you can't figure out or see.

> *For God hath not given us the spirit of fear; but of power, and of love, and of a sound mind* (2 Timothy 1:7).

> *Now faith is the substance of things hoped for, the evidence of things not seen* (Hebrews 11:1).

It is our considered opinion—after studying the Bible now for many years—that every thought we have either goes down a pathway of faith or fear. You decide moment-by-moment which invisible kingdom you will obey. We are all dealing with a spiritual force whether we want to or not and this spiritual force comes with chemical and electrical representation in our body.

This directly impacts the way your body will function. Your attitude is a place in your mind that dictates a reaction and causes your behavior. It appears that all the negative emotions come from that spirit of fear which God did not give you. However, God designed all of us with a measure of faith, which produces the fruit of the Holy Spirit: love, joy, and peace in the Holy Ghost. Your faith can increase, as you read and hear the Word of the Lord (see Rom. 10:17).

A spirit of fear will cause you to feel anxiety, anger, and rage, which are also spirits. They will connect you to spirits of resentment, frustration, impatience, and irritation. This is not good news, brothers and sisters: behind many diseases and problems, there is a direct link to a spirit of fear.

Science is now able to demonstrate these links through imaging techniques and technology, which we discuss later in this book. Proverbs 23:7 says,

> *For as he thinketh in his heart, so is he: Eat and drink, saith he to thee; but his heart is not with thee.*

The Midwest Center for Anxiety and Stress, Inc.,[3] has related anxiety and stress to fear. It uses imaging techniques to bring a calm state of mind, helping you deal with those stressors in your life that come from fear. They recognize the real battle is in the mind, just as the Bible has said all along. Though this program does work, it costs hundreds of dollars to learn, and becomes a maintenance plan, and not really freeing because it doesn't base it's "meditation" on the Word. Jesus came to set us free, not put a maintenance plan on it, and it doesn't cost you a cent!

You may have noticed in your life that there have been many pathways of fear that it was not easy to walk in faith; there were doorways of fear all along your pathways of thought. There could have been a trauma, or reoccurring traumas, difficult places, relationship problems, and the like. The experiences are not truly the problem: our thoughts about those issues cause our problems—which the world calls "negative emotions." These include fear, stress, anxiety, envy and jealousy, bitterness and unforgiveness.

All these chemicals are rushing through the pathways of arteries, veins, and marrow, and as we shared earlier, the first place they go to is the heart.

Scientists are finding that if your heart and your brain are not in congruency, you cannot replace those old fear-based patterns. Dr. David J. Abbott[4] says that a positive operating system is positively congruent. Your mind, heart, and head will move in the same direction. Your intellect, emotions, and will speak with one voice. Your head selects a positive destination, your heart enjoys the trip, and your will takes you there.

All three parts of who you are move congruently in the same direction. Sometimes your head leads the way, and at other times it's your heart and head (will) that are out in front showing the way. It doesn't matter which leads as long as all three come along for the ride. And these scientists are not always taking into account the spiritual implications.

As believers, we have been blessed with the Word of God, and He does not want us perishing from lack of knowledge (see Hosea 4:6 and Matthew 18:32-35).

We are to be led by the Holy Spirit, who comes to teach us all of the things we need to know. We are learning the truth that will make us free.

> *But the Comforter, which is the Holy Ghost, whom the Father will send in My name, He shall teach you all things, and bring all things to your remembrance, whatsoever I have said unto you* (John 14:26).

Bitterness and Unforgiveness

Unforgiveness is a spirit and goes along with a spirit of bitterness. The Bible tells you to not go to bed angry because a spirit of bitterness could spring up and even affect others.

Be ye angry, and sin not: let not the sun go down upon your wrath (Ephesians 4:26).

Looking diligently lest any man fail of the grace of God; lest any root of bitterness springing up trouble you, and thereby many be defiled (Hebrews 12:15).

When these toxic thoughts are allowed, they are like weeds in a garden. If you do not pull them up by the roots, they will strangle the plants and kill the garden. Did you ever have problems with dandelions? They have a root system, but if you go around picking off the plants, they just grow back. You have to remove the complete root system; otherwise, you'll be fighting with those little plants forever. Those bad thoughts will do the same to your neuron trees. Allowed to go unchecked, they will continue to grow and bring disease. But once you take the time to locate the "root" of those thoughts, —repent of these thoughts and replace them with the truth— you are being a "doer" of the Word and all the blessings will follow.

Our Thoughts Produce Fruit

Whether your thoughts, emotions, and attitudes are positive or negative, they represent two systems in your body: the endocrine system and the nervous system. We also need to explore the limbic system, which influences the endocrine system.[5] It is like this chemical factory deep in the middle of your brain waiting for your instructions on what to produce.

Everything that concerns thought, both good and bad, travels up and down this connective pathway. The limbic lobe, hippocampus, amygdala, and thalamus all play a vital role in how thoughts grow and how they produce emotions and physiological responses in your mind. You need to guard your eyes and ears, because they are windows of your soul.

Practical Application

What can you do to guard your heart and mind? Pay attention to what you are paying attention to. Be selective in the movies and television programs. Be discerning about the radio, books, Internet, and people with whom you associate. You are responsible for your health, spiritually, physically, and emotionally. You can use a journal to write down all your activities and your thoughts about those activities. You will begin to see that perhaps some of your own dis-eases and circumstances are a result of these thoughts and associations. Whatever we feed our minds ends up manifesting in our actions and our health. Whatever we sow, we will reap. It's really up to you.

The following Scriptures reflect what we are talking about here. Please take a moment and study them. They show us that we can keep ourselves from so much harm when we pay attention to what we see, hear, speak, or keep company with. Do you know the saying, "Hear no evil, speak no evil, see no evil"? Well, it was in the pages of the Bible long before someone came up with that statement.

The sinners in Zion are afraid; fearfulness hath surprised the hypocrites. Who among us shall dwell with the devouring fire? Who among us shall dwell with everlasting burnings? He that walketh righteously, and speaketh uprightly; he that despiseth the gain of oppressions, that shaketh his hands from holding of bribes, that stoppeth his ears from hearing of blood, and shutteth his eyes from seeing evil; he shall dwell on high: his place of defense shall be the munitions of rocks: bread shall be given him; his waters shall be sure (Isaiah 33:14-16).

Touch not; taste not; handle not; which all are to perish with the using (Colossians 2:21-22).

Endnotes

1. Dr. Caroline Leaf, Who Switched Off My Brain? (Nashville, TN: Thomas Nelson, Inc., 2009).

2. See http://library.timelesstruths.org/music/Trust_and_Obey.

3. Lucinda Bassett, Attacking Anxiety and Depression (New York: Midwest Center for Anxiety and Stress, Inc., 2006).

4. Dr. Dave Abbott, M.D. zerotolerancetonegativethinking.com.

5. Wikipedia.com, http://en.wikipedia.org/wiki/Limbic_system.

Chapter Five

UNDERSTANDING BRAIN FUNCTION

Whatever you see, hear, touch, smell, and taste—whatever you are experiencing—will become information from your senses that converges on the lower part of the cortex. That is the pink, fleshy part of the brain underneath the front of the temporal lobe, which is the side of your brain. It's like a doorway into the brain where your five senses pass information about.

The Thalamus—the Relay Station

Information passes into the relay station of the brain, which is the thalamus. The thalamus relays the information to the cortex where the memories are kept. This is the first place where attitudes begin. It's like a breeze comes through and moves some of those neuron trees to shake, rattle, and roll.

Now you are not particularly aware of this entire process going on inside you as it is, but it is important to understand it, nonetheless. The kind of attitude you are falling into will determine what emotional responses are relayed back to the thalamus. It travels to your hypothalamus, which activates the release of chemicals to build your emotional state.

The Hypothalamus—the Feeling Releaser

The main gland of the limbic system is the hypothalamus, often called the brain of the endocrine system. When you have a tension headache, you rub the back of your head and neck. That is where the hypothalamus gland is—situated in the third ventricle at the top of your neck. Your hypothalamus will respond to your thought life. This is very important; it can only produce chemicals in response to what is going on with you deep within your soul and spirit.

The feelings you are entertaining, be it peace, happiness, and joy in the Holy Ghost, or fear, anger, greed, and jealousy, which are not from the Holy Ghost, will produce and release the chemicals from the hypothalamus gland that correspond to that emotion.

You need to understand that fear, anger, greed, and jealousy, etc., are not from the Lord but are characteristics from your enemy. You may agree with us or not, but we see these things that people call "emotions" as spirits who whisper in your ear; then, as you agree with them in thought, they become one with you in your thinking. You think it's just you having these thoughts and feelings. You may have even said, "That is just the way that I am." But the truth is, it may not be your thoughts at all. This is why it is so important to think about what you are thinking about. As a man thinks, so he is. All this information then goes into the amygdala. Who names this stuff anyway?

The Amygdala—the Library of Long-Term Memory

The amygdala is an almond-shaped structure of your brain that stores and files all your emotional experiences. Inside your amygdala is where the library of your life is kept. Every time you build a memory, you are stimulating emotions, because your endocrine system is releasing all those chemicals that build up to help those memories. This is the mind, body, spirit, and soul connection and they are inseparable. That part of the brain does not understand words and cannot be communicated to with spoken or written language. It responds only to smell. That is why when you smell apple pie you remember your grandmother's kitchen. Or smell petri-oil, it reminds you of the 70's. The Lord designed us this way, utilizing all of our five senses to live our lives full and vibrantly. Anyone who says we were created with a big bang, this alone discounts that. Our minds are the biggest computer ever built. It's designed to never run out of memory, because each strand of DNA (100 trillion cells) is capable of storing up to six gigabytes of memory.[1]

Once you get hold of this, you will understand that you do not need to give in and be afraid anymore. You do not have to look at symptoms and ever be concerned. They are a lie, just like bait on the end of a hook for a fish. If the enemy can get you to take your eyes off the Lord and onto the symptoms, you are in for a struggle to get free.

Proverbs 4:20 can change your life forever!

My son, attend to my words; incline thine ear unto my sayings. Let them not depart from thine eyes; keep them in the midst of thine heart. For they are life unto those that find them, and health to all their flesh (Proverbs 4:20-22).

Now this passage does not say God will heal some of your flesh, sometimes. It says health to all your flesh. This is really good news; the Gospel means "good news." You are no longer alone in this battle; if the Lord is with you, who can come against you?

What shall we then say to these things? If God be for us, who can be against us? (Romans 8:31)

And all this assembly shall know that the Lord saveth not with sword and spear: for the battle is the Lord's, and He will give you into our hands (1 Samuel 17:47).

When you have a broken heart, you have a spirit of fear messing with you. You do not feel safe. You go to church, get filled up with the gospel truth, and then you leak all the way home. The next day you try to deal with the problems of your life, but you feel trapped.

If you are dealing with a broken heart, you cannot even use the truth you have. There is a saying, "If you have a broken heart, you cannot trust it." In other words, when we try having relationships with others with a broken heart, it will distort that relationship and cause all kinds of problems. It's so important to allow the Lord to heal our broken heart.

We need to create a safe place where we can confess our sins to one another, pray for one another, so that we may be healed.

> *Confess your faults one to another, and pray one for another, that ye may be healed* (James 5:16).

We are not here to build up the darkness of this world, but to tear it down, and to let our light shine before all men:

> *Let your light so shine before men, that they may see your good works, and glorify your Father which is in heaven* (Matt. 5:16).

Everything that concerns thought travels up and down this connective pathway (limbic system). We've got stuff like the mimic lobe, hippocampus, amygdala, and the thalamus, which are brain areas supporting cerebral cortex function playing vital roles in the production of thoughts, emotions, and physiological responses.

All these cerebral parts come together and create a biochemical representation of a thought. Building memories, both good and bad, will help to structure the emotional and physiological parts of our life.

This is why it is so important to think in "faith" and not entertain fearful thinking. Fearful thoughts long-term will put you into fight or flight mode. Scripture says that anything that is not of faith is sin (see Rom. 14:23). And as believers, we only want to walk in faith, right? So what do we do when we don't? We repent, and we are instantly restored in our hearts and minds to the Lord. That, my dear, is faith at work!

Your thoughts generate chemicals that are playing with your emotions. Maybe a doctor told you, "Your chemicals are out of balance." As long as your mind is thinking positively and continues being washed by the Water of the Word, it will produce balanced chemicals, but if you are dwelling and thinking on anything contrary, it will produce unbalanced chemicals such as oversecretion or undersecretion. We are chemical beings, and if we understand how these information molecules work, we may be able to help control how we think and get rid of the stinkin' thinkin', which will negatively affect your health and well-being, as well as your life circumstances.

People think life is just a bunch of facts and events, which make up the tapestry of your life. But, the truth is, it's not really about those events but how you handled those events either negatively or positively—is the glass half-full or the glass half-empty mentality. You can't see the negative or positive thoughts, but you do see what they produce! It's like the wind that you cannot see, but you can see the effects of it when it blows on something. The enemy of your soul wants to blow storms into your life, just as he tried to sink the boat Jesus was sleeping in when the disciples panicked and woke Him up thinking they were about to die. And as Jesus commanded the wind and waves to stop (see Matthew 8) you can also command the storms of thought to stop that have been blowing endlessly through your mind.

What you allow yourself to think about will affect every chemical in your body. When negative and depressing toxic thoughts gain entrance, it's like a cyclone of negativity and it will bring you into fear, because a spirit of fear is behind them much of the time. That brings in a spirit of heaviness that we call depression today, and it will sweep through you and affect your life.

However, if you fill your mind with positive thoughts good and holy thoughts as the Bible instructs us to do, you will experience fair winds of thoughts that will help steady your course, guiding you through harmoniously with His Spirit— congruency.

> *Finally, brethren, whatsoever things are true, whatsoever things are honest, whatsoever things are just, whatsoever things are pure, whatsoever things are lovely, whatsoever things are of good report; if there be any virtue, and if there be any praise, think on these things* (Philippians 4:8).

Remember, as discussed earlier in Chapter 3, there are electromagnetic charges that carry a photocopy of memories that affect our whole being positively or negatively, creating balanced chemicals or in-balanced chemicals. The Lord understands all of this because He is the one who created this memory process to be used for your good—before sin even entered into the picture. Unfortunately, our enemy was there when the Lord God created us, and so he knows your make-up, too. That is why we have a battle now. The enemy knows that by getting you to think like him, your chemicals will get out of balance! He is looking for those who don't have their minds fixed on God, because they are easy prey! (See 1 Peter 5:8.)

The Effects of Past Thoughts

From the time you were in your mother's womb, you have been building memories that help form your perception of things. While in the womb, your spirit might hear your earthly father tell your mother that this is not a good time to be pregnant. A spirit of rejection and abandonment will enter in that child, and some children may develop asthma. Sources come from case studies and testimonies from "A More Excellent Way."[2]

Dr. Stephen Paine said, "Asthma is a hypersensitive state of the airways. It is associated with an imbalance in the immune system and the nervous system."[3]

When there is a narrowing of the airways, the result is a build-up of mucus and carbon dioxide. In this state, air can be freely inhaled but is blocked from being exhaled. When a person resolves fear of losing a parent (being abandoned), the cause is removed of the hypersensitivity that caused airway blockages.

When you were a child in school, did you have a teacher who told you that you would never be any good at math? Guess what?—you will struggle with math because every time you have to do a math problem from then on that library in your mind will replay the feeling associated with that negative experience. It will tell you, "This is just too hard; I will not be any good at this," even before you begin.

The opposite is also true if you were blessed by parents and teachers who encouraged you in a particular area: you will excel in that area for the rest of your life. Parents have been entrusted with children, a gift to them, to bring them up in the ways of the Lord so that when they grow older they will not fall away from Him.

> *Train up a child in the way he should go: and when*
> *he is old, he will not depart from it* (Proverbs 22:6).

Parents who truly understand this passage will encourage and help a child to be all they can be, not make them into what they want them to be. Psalm 127 goes on to say that children are a blessing!

> *Lo, children are an heritage of the Lord: and the fruit*
> *of the womb is his reward. As arrows are in the hand*
> *of a mighty man; so are children of the youth. Happy*
> *is the man that hath his quiver full of them...* (Psalm
> 127:3-5).

The Bible also says not to provoke your children to anger. Why? Because God knows it could break a child's spirit. Children don't have the maturity yet to deal with such things, and we are to care for them as Papa God cares for us.

> *Fathers, provoke not your children to anger, lest they*
> *be discouraged* (Colossians 3:21).

Let's take a look at the emotions that come from the amygdala. These can also be strong enough to override even the positive elements because of a spirit of fear. This happens because there is more information being transferred from the amygdala to the cortex than from the cortex to the amygdala. This prevents your natural reasoning from exerting its influence.[4]

The Apostle Paul said it this way:

> *For that which I do I allow not: for what I would, that*
> *do I not; but what I hate, that do I. If then I do that*
> *which I would not, I consent unto the law that it is*
> *good. Now then it is no more I that do it, but sin that*
> *dwelleth in me* (Romans 7:15-17).

Still there is hope, brothers and sisters, as we begin to unravel this mess and start to see that not every thought is our own. The real concern is that first we learn not to continue in habitual sins, but to come to the Lord, repent of them, and receive His forgiveness. Second, we must forgive ourselves and everyone else.

> *Be careful for nothing; but in every thing by prayer and supplication with thanksgiving let your request be made known unto God. And the peace of God, which passeth all understanding, shall keep your hearts and minds through Christ Jesus* (Philippians 4:6).

It goes on to say in verse 11 to be content in whatever state you happen to be in. Again I say, rejoice! That's Philippians 4:4, a good Scripture to memorize.

The Hippocampus—the Short-Term Memory

At this point, information travels from the amygdala into the hippocampus, a tube-shaped structure that extends in a circle around the center of the brain. It basically holds your short-term memories for about 48 to 72 hours (which may explain why a couple days after the test, students do not remember much of what they studied to pass an exam).

Your five physical senses are feeding information to the hippocampus, so it is building memory and releasing emotional molecules. That is, until your free will either accepts the information or rejects it. Interestingly, science is telling us now that we do, in fact, have free will[4]. The Bible tells us that all along. Look at the wrong choices Adam and Eve made because they had free will. Just look at the choices we have made. We rest our case.

If you were sailing on a ship and told a sailor he looked seasick, chances are, his hippocampus would reject it. He might even laugh at the suggestion. If you told someone sailing for the first time that he looked seasick, you can pretty much watch him soon come down with seasickness just at the suggestion of it. Are you starting to see how susceptible you are to words? This is why we will be held accountable for every idle word we speak.

But I say unto you, that every idle word that men shall speak, they shall give account thereof in the day of judgment (Matthew 12:36).

Proverbs 18:21 says that words are containers for life and death:

Death and life are in the power of the tongue: and they that love it shall eat the fruit thereof.

Words are powerful and by our words we can even defeat the enemy.

Behold, I give you power to tread on serpents and scorpions, and over all the power of the enemy: and nothing shall by any means hurt you (Luke 10:19).

The Corpus Callosum—the Agent of Free Will

You also have a structure called the corpus callosum that connects the two sides of your brain together. It's about the size of your thumb and integrates memories and perspective. The corpus callosum helps analyzes all the information coming from the five physical senses, as well as information that is activated in the neuron trees of your mind.

Professor David Suzuki,[5] a geneticist at Columbia University, claims to have identified a genetic code for free will. According to Suzuki, there are genes in your body that give you the ability to change behavior in response to environment—what is now recognized as free will. Life is about choices. The Scriptures even back this up when it says, *"You reap what you sow"* (see Gal. 6:7). Our life is really a result of reaping and sowing. Whether your ancestors sowed something that you are reaping, or you are reaping something you sowed yesterday, this life is truly about reaping and sowing. Perhaps we need to start paying attention to what we are sowing? Just sayin'.

Your genes provide a blueprint, but they also give control to your brain. Because we each make choices based on our thoughts and attitudes, we all create responses that differ from one another. Remember, you were fearfully and wonderfully made. Papa God has a unique plan and purpose for each person, and it is a good plan to prosper and bless you. Before you were ever formed in your mother's womb, He already knew you.

> *I will praise thee; for I am fearfully and wonderfully made: marvelous are Thy works; and that my soul knoweth right well* (Psalm 139:14).

> *For I know the thoughts that I think toward you, saith the Lord, thoughts of peace, and not of evil, to give you an expected end* (Jeremiah 29:11).

> *By Thee have I been holden up from the womb: Thou art He that took me out of my mother's bowels: my praise shall be continually of Thee* (Psalm 71:6).

> *Before I formed thee in the belly I knew thee; and before thou camest forth out of the womb I sanctified thee, and I ordained thee a prophet unto the nations* (Jeremiah 1:5).

The corpus callosum and frontal lobe area are the part of the brain involved in free will processing. Genetics may be a predictor in intellectual development, but as you now can understand, the brain is capable of assimilating unlimited amounts of information and then making choices based on that information. That is why it is so vital to know what the Word of God says.

A good way to learn a coping skill is to know what the Lord says about being content in all things. This way you can then obey what the Lord said because it is His strength that helps you do it.

> *Not that I speak in respect of want: for I have learned, in whatsoever state I am, therewith to be content. I know both how to be abased, and I know how to abound: every where and in all things I am instructed both to be full and to be hungry, both to abound and to suffer need. I can do all things through Christ which strengtheneth me* (Philippians 4:11-13).

The Peptides—Emotional Music

Your emotions regulate what you experience as reality, and the peptides are, in effect, molecules of emotions. Because your emotions affect your perception, like a glass half empty or half full, in every situation we face, our emotions dictate reality.

But then your cells also have a memory, which means that, because of the information being sent all over your bodily systems, your body will literally reflect your thought life.

Peptides are your body's music, of sorts. Dr. Leaf said, "The peptides working alongside the building of thought into memory provide the mechanism through which health and diseases are created."[6] As peptides trigger receptors on cells, they initiate many cellular processes and changes. They are working on building thoughts into memories, which provide the mechanism for health or diseases.

For example, peptides do a very good job of helping the immune system kill tumors. The fact is that we all have cancer cells floating through our bodies all the time. But your immune system recognizes them as enemy cells and destroys them. Any destabilizing of the psychosomatic networks disrupts the peptide flow, which reduces apoptosis (cell death). This could create conditions where cancer cells can lead to a formation of a tumor. Another example are viruses that attach themselves to receptors. Your emotional state will affect how your body is able to respond to a virus. If you are stressed, the peptides will change the cells receptors to be more permeable. Any virus that happens to be hanging about will seize its chance to slip into the cell and make you sick. That is how you are able to catch a cold or the flu. The Bible tells us there are infirmities common to man. Still, if we are walking in His peace, we can walk away from these things.

Battlefield of the Mind

One of the best things you can do is meditate on the Word of God. Your mind is truly where the battle is being fought. There is an ongoing war between the good thoughts and the bad ones. Those bad thoughts come to deplete your body of energy and health. *The devil comes not but to kill, steal, and destroy* (see John 10:10).

The battlefield of the mind is located in the memory networks, the amygdala, hippocampus, and corpus callosum, as well as in the genetic code for free will. Again there are a number of issues to consider here. Like it is not so much what you eat, but rather what is eating you. This is where the real battle begins for most issues we have to deal with.

Are we going to stay in faith and trust in the Lord to show us the way that leads to peace in our life? Or will we bow down to the enemy in fear that is the opposite of faith?

Often we find that people have been set up, programmed by the enemy to respond to everyday situations in a negative way. The Bible tells us about familiar spirits, and to stay away from them. These demons gain access to lives through divination, transcendental meditation, visualization, necromancy, witchcraft, drugs, and alcohol. Instead, we are to be filled with the Holy Spirit, with love, with joy, and with the fullness of life that comes from Jesus Christ. We are to be on guard *"for our struggles are not with flesh and blood, but against the rulers of darkness and spiritual forces of evil"* (see Eph. 6:12). They have every right to be there until they are found out and commanded to go and have their assignment canceled in the name of Jesus Christ of Nazareth.

Familiar spirits are often what is behind the sins of the fathers and being passed on to the third and fourth generations, until someone finally gets spiritual and repents to the Lord. And that is you, dear saint! You can stop this progression.

> *Thou shalt not bow down thyself unto them, nor serve them: for I the Lord thy God am a jealous God, visiting the iniquity of the fathers upon the children unto the third and fourth generation of them that hate me* (Deuteronomy 5:9).

But people don't know they have the power of the Holy Spirit, being a child of God, to stand up and stop this from continuing in their generations.

> *My people are destroyed for lack of knowledge: because thou hast rejected knowledge, I will also reject thee, that thou shalt be no priest to me: seeing thou*

hast forgotten the law of thy God, I will also forget thy children (Hosea 4:6).

There is now a wealth of scientific evidence to support what Philippians 4 advises us to think upon:

> *Finally, brethren, whatsoever things are true, whatsoever things are honest, whatsoever things are just, whatsoever things are pure, whatsoever things are lovely, whatsoever things are of good report; if there be any virtue, and if there be any praise, think on these things* (Philippians 4:8).

Also, notice what 2 Corinthians 10:5-6 tells us about our thoughts:

> *Casting down imaginations, and every high thing that exalteth itself against the knowledge of God, and bringing into captivity every thought to the obedience of Christ; and having in a readiness to revenge all disobedience, when your obedience is fulfilled* (2 Corinthians 10:5-6).

If you are taking your thoughts captive to the obedience of Christ, you will be in peace and make good decisions. If you do not take your thoughts captive, those other thoughts—which are not even your own—will take you captive. The Lord tells us to choose this day whom we will serve, and it starts in our thinking.

You can literally build new, healthy memories over the old, toxic, negative ones as you begin to line up with the Word of God. But again, no matter how many facts or proof of something you may have, you will not believe it unless your brain's limbic system allows you to receive it is truth. Just ask any atheist. Atheists are programmed not to receive even when they have all the facts. It's like showing someone the sun on a cloudless day—and they deny it is there. The Lord said that a fool in his heart says there is no God (see Ps. 14:1). But, we also have to interject here that even an atheist can be saved when they choose to seek the Lord God.

Practical Application

Here is an exercise that Linda teaches through her book called *"Discovering the Truth that Makes You Free"* [7] that helps to identify when we are doubting God. Sometimes we just don't know what we are thinking any more, not realizing our thoughts are causing a breach between us and God. Scriptures say that we are to "believe that He is." And this is a great way to determine if we are believing He is in everything or not, and what we can do to be restored in that area of our thinking.

Get out a piece of paper and draw a line down the middle of the page. Write at the top of the left side, "God Isn't," and on the right column write, "God Is." Then begin to write in the first column all the areas in your life that you don't trust God with. Things that cause you to have doubt and unbelief toward Him. Things you can't seem to let go of. Things you worry about. Even things you think God won't give you or is holding back from you. And on the right side, write things that you do believe and trust Him with. Now take the "God Isn't" stuff and confess these to the Lord. These are your sins about your thoughts toward God, and need to be repented of. Because truthfully, God IS in all your life, issues, and situations, and when we "think" He's not, well, that's when we get into trouble. We are saying that God doesn't really love us or care for us. We are saying that God isn't really there. Remember, we must believe that He is.... (see Hebrews 11:6). We are accusing God of not being good (see Mark 10:18).

Anything that we dwell on or say contrary to the Word is sin. So let's just get on with the program and take some responsibility, repent for not trusting God and receive forgiveness. Don't let another day go by. These are the very things preventing good things from happening to you!

> *We prevent good things from happening to us because of our sins and iniquities* (Jeremiah 5:25).

Then finally, thank the Lord for all the blessings He has done for you and thank Him for what He is going to do for you. A thankful heart is a receiving heart.

And let the peace of God rule in your hearts, to the which also ye are called in one body; and be ye thankful (Colossians 3:15).

Endnotes

1. Healing Oils of the Bible, by David Stewart PHD, (2003, Care Publications)

2. Henry Wright, A More Excellent Way (New Kensington, PA: Whitaker House, 2009).

3. Doctor Stephen Paine, http://lifepurposehealth.com/index.php/memories/overcoming_fear_and_asthma/ (accessed April 17, 2010).

4. Dr. Caroline Leaf, Who Switched Off My Brain? (Nashville, TN: Thomas Nelson, Inc., 2009).

5. Professor David Suzuki, Columbia University.

6. Leaf.

7. Discovering the Truth That Makes You Free - Workbook. www.truthfrees.org.

Chapter Six

BREAKING DOWN THOUGHT PATTERNS

The Lord created our minds to work for us, not against us. But guess who else was there when we were created? Lucifer. He watched Papa God mold and make us in His image, and so he knows your anatomy too, far better than even the world's smartest scientists! That means we need to know it as well so that we aren't taken for a ride every time we turn around. We need to know that we can do something about it.

Hosea 4:6 says that we perish for lack of knowledge. We find ourselves in messes because we just don't know. But we hope that what we share in this book is changing all that so you don't perish for lack of knowledge, but use the knowledge to keep yourself "out" of the enemy's snare.

> *And the servant of the Lord must not strive; but be gentle unto all men, apt to teach, patient, in meekness instructing those that oppose themselves; if God peradventure will give them repentance to the acknowledging of the truth; and that they may recover themselves out of the snare of the devil, who are taken captive by him at his will* (2 Timothy 2:24-26).

Pathway of Fear or Faith

As we have already taught, every thought you have will go down either a pathway of faith or a pathway of fear. Most people have been trained by the enemy for so long to look for fear. Your brain picks up on it and says, "Hmm, that looks like fear." Then it goes down that familiar fear pathway.

But if you begin to do as the Bible instructs us and look for faith, you will begin to trust in the Lord with your whole heart and mind. You then will begin to have thoughts that travel down the faith pathway. You must start training yourself to practice walking and thinking and speaking in faith. If you can just start practicing this for about three days in a row, you will begin to reap some of the benefits. Remember, this life is full of reaping and sowing. If you want to reap good things, then start sowing good thoughts now. It's never too late. You can start sowing good seeds now to reap a harvest tomorrow.

A new growth of faith thoughts will begin to override the old fearful ones. You will cut off that old pathway and begin to blaze a new trail going down the faith way. Perhaps you have noticed that in your life there have been many pathways of fear, and that it was not easy to walk in faith; there was a doorway here and a doorway there of fear along your pathways of thoughts.

Linda remembers a time when she was having difficulty with a reoccurring health issue. She decided to put into practice what we're talking about here. She changed her thought pathway on purpose. As you know, it's easy to think a negative thought; you don't even have to try, but it takes effort to think a God thought. Since this was the case, the battle was on. Imagine how easily the wheels of a car fall into a rut in a road. Well, that's what happens in our thinking unless we do something about it. In her case, when this health symptom came, her mind went down that same rut, and the results were the same—dis-ease. What she did was imagine that rut she was in, and on purpose pulled herself out of the rut as she changed her thinking.

Isn't that what the Bible says to do? Recover yourself from the snare of the devil who have taken us captive? (see 2 Timothy 2:26).

She recovered herself from the pit. She didn't have a whole truck load of Christians come and scoop her up... she chose to believe the Word and do something about it. What thoughts did she change, you ask? The truth that God loves her and wants her well. That He has good plans for her, and there is nothing too big for Him. That He is in control, and that her life was in His hands. She began thanking Him for loving her, for His presence, for His help, for healing her, for saving her soul. She thought on Scriptures that pertained to her situation, such as, "God has not given us a spirit of fear, but power, love, and a sound mind." "The plans for us are for good not for evil." And as she meditated on these things, a new pathway was created that brought her peace. It took effort on her part to change that rut; it's also up to you to do the same. We are creatures of habit, so let's form some new ones today! And by the way, that dis-ease never returned.

Whenever there is a trauma, reoccurring traumas, or illnesses in your life, all those chemicals from your thoughts about these things are being released throughout your body causing what the world calls "emotions and attitudes."

All these chemicals are rushing through the pathways of arteries, veins, and marrow, and the first place it goes to is the heart.

Forgiveness Breaks Old Patterns

Research shows us that your heart has over 40,000 neurons. It's like your heart has its own brain, if you will, which checks for congruency between the heart and the head.[1] That is why Matthew 18:35 states very clearly that we need to forgive each other! *"So likewise shall My heavenly Father do also unto you, if ye from your hearts forgive not every one his brother their trespasses."* It's important for our relationship with God, and our blessings of good health. *"But if ye forgive not men their trespasses, neither will your Father forgive your trespasses"* (Matt. 6:15).

If you are trying to replace an old memory pattern by saying with your lips "I forgive them," when your heart is not in it, you are performing lip service, and it simply will not work.

This people draweth nigh unto Me with their mouth, and honoureth Me with their lips; but their heart is far from Me (Matthew 15:8).

Let's say you decide to forgive your mom or dad; that forgiveness thought starts to cascade through the blood, and then the heart picks it up and says, "Wait a minute, that's not the way I feel!" Although previously unknown, neuroscientists have now discovered that there are over 40,000 nerve cells (neurons) in the heart alone, indicating that the heart has its own independent nervous system sometimes called the brain in the heart.[2] Research on this is being done by numbers of individuals, so this information is available for anyone searching for it. So if your thoughts are congruent, then we can begin to start healing and mending that place in the heart that was broken.

And his lord was wroth, and delivered him to the tormentors, till he should pay all that was due unto him. So likewise shall my heavenly Father do also unto you, if ye from your hearts forgive not every one his brother their trespasses (Matthew 18:34-35).

There is torment that comes when we do not forgive from our hearts.

Jesus came to mend the brokenhearted and restore their hope and faith in Him as King of kings and over all things, both visible and invisible.

For by Him were all things created, that are in heaven, and that are in earth, visible and invisible, whether they be thrones, or dominions, or principalities, or powers: all things were created by Him, and for Him (Colossians 1:16).

That is why Jesus tells us in Matthew 18:28 that the Lord of that servant was moved with compassion, and loosed him, and forgave him the debt (see Matt. 18:27).

To "release" means to separate that person from their sin (or separate yourself from your own sin). In this passage, he forgave the servant, which loosed the servant from the debt. As long as we stay in unforgiveness, we are not "loosed." We are not free! As a matter of fact, we are still tied to the person we have not forgiven, which is called soul-ties. When we forgive, we also break these ungodly ties. Let's take a look at Romans 7.

> *For we know that the law is spiritual: but I am carnal, sold under sin. For that which I do I allow not: for what I would, that do I not; but what I hate, that do I. If then I do that which I would not, I consent unto the law that it is good. Now then it is no more I that do it, but sin that dwelleth in me. For I know that in me (that is, in my flesh,) dwelleth no good thing: for to will is present with me; but how to perform that which is good I find not. For the good that I would I do not: but the evil which I would not, that I do. Now if I do that I would not, it is no more I that do it, but sin that dwelleth in me. I find then a law, that, when I would do good, evil is present with me. For I delight in the law of God after the inward man: but I see another law in my members, warring against the law of my mind, and bringing me into captivity to the law of sin which is in my members. O wretched man that I am! who shall deliver me from the body of this death? I thank God through Jesus Christ our Lord. So then with the mind I myself serve the law of God; but with the flesh the law of sin* (Romans 7:14-25).

This passage clearly shows a struggle within Paul. The same struggles we have today, but he found the secret. He realized that what was "in" Him was not him but the sin in him. That is why he wrote a large passage on being content, because he learned to live with himself and not have self-hatred for what he saw (see Philippians 4:11). We need to do the same. This is called "separation." Separating our who from our do. It's like when our child disobeys. We don't say, "You are such a bad boy." We say, "I love you son, but what you did was not a good choice." Well, we hope that's what parents are saying anyway.

When we can do this, we can actually be at peace with ourselves. We will be able to love ourselves. Because many who don't love themselves is because of all the junk they see in their lives. But if we can separate that junk (sin) from ourselves, and see it for what it really is, we may find our freedom. And remember Matthew 22:37-40 says we cannot love others until we love ourselves.

In order to have compassion toward the individual who offended or hurt you, or release the person from his or her debt, you first need to confess your heart to God about the matter. Get what is inside of you cleaned out, then you will be able to see clearly to love and forgive others. (see Matthew 7:1-4)

This brings the congruency that is needed for healing to begin. Having compassion for someone changes your heart! Remember Job? He also forgave his friends, and afterward twice as much as he had before was restored to him!

You can tell if you have not forgiven from your heart: the pain will still be there or the offense will keep playing over and over in your head, no matter how hard you try to cast those thoughts out. No matter how hard you try to think of something else. It keeps coming up. God doesn't want us to continue with those painful thoughts. What we need to do is forgive those involved in that thought. If you keep hearing Aunt Margie's voice in your head telling you that nothing you do will ever turn out to be good, then you need to forgive Aunt Margie for defiling you with her words. When you truly forgive her from your heart, that person's words no longer cause pain because the emotions attached to it is removed through forgiveness! There is nothing holding it to you any longer. The pain associated with that memory leaves. It's not really that difficult; we just don't know how.

John 20:23 says to forgive, or else we will take on that person's sins! Now not only do we have to contend with our own sinful stuff, but now we have more added!

If we forgive someone quickly, we are stopping any pain and added sins in our lives. To get rid of the past pains and hurts, we need to take each one of those sins we retained from that relationship to the Lord and confess them. These are the very sins keeping you in bondage, in pain, and unable to forgive from your heart because you are filled with these offenses. How can we forgive someone when our heart is far from it—in other words, filled with bitterness, anger, and resentment toward that person? We need to get rid of what is in our heart first, those sins we took on, before we can even attempt to forgive them properly. Then we can forgive from a clean heart. That is what God looks upon, our heart. Because He knows that whatever is in our heart will be what we become. Whatever we think, we are! Remember to take the beam out of your own eye first!

> *Either how canst thou say to thy brother, Brother, let me pull out the mote that is in thine eye, when thou thyself beholdest not the beam that is in thine own eye? Thou hypocrite, cast out first the beam out of thine own eye, and then shalt thou see clearly to pull out the mote that is in thy brother's eye* (Luke 6:42).

Truly, when you get rid of your own sinful stuff, their stuff isn't even a problem for you anymore! Why? Because you aren't looking at them through your junk. When you have a clean heart, you will see them as God sees them. And it could be that they just need a hug!

Faith or Fear

Our prayer should be, "Help me, Lord, to line up with Your Word." If our minds are not operating in faith all day long, we are giving place to the enemy and giving in to a spirit of fear that God did not give you. You will dwell in one or the other all the time: in faith or in fear. The absence of one promotes the other; that is why we are to "pray without ceasing." God knew our minds could be a vacuum of wrong thoughts if we do not set our minds on Him all day long.

Sometimes you have repented, and you still need to join together in faith with the Lord. Sometimes you might have to tell yourself, *I have repented, and I have forgiven, and I know the Lord has forgiven me because that is in His Word. I am not going to back down. You can stand me up against the gates of hell, but I won't back down!*

We need to work on this by saying, *"I am going to live in faith today!"* This is where the battle is! And you are in this battle whether you want it or not. We live in a fallen world this side of Heaven. Now as you study your owner's manual—your Bible—you begin to see faith everywhere throughout the Word. Stay in faith, no matter what! How? By the renewing of your mind and by the washing of the Water of the Word. Every thought has to choose a pathway of faith or fear.

That He might sanctify and cleanse it with the washing of water by the word (Eph. 5:26).

I was riding my horse in a full gallop when something went wrong; I fell off! Immediately thoughts started to grow in my brain. Those magic trees began asking, "Am I Okay? Am I hurt? Is my back Okay? What about my neck?" But then I changed my thoughts by saying, "I believe my God can do anything, and that He can totally heal me if I am hurt." Which pathway did he choose? In this instance, I got up, brushed myself off, and got back on my horse.

As children, we have always been taught that if you fall off your horse, you get right back on and keep riding; otherwise, you may never get on a horse again. What happens? A spirit of fear comes to steal your joy about that experience. Some of you need to get back on your horses and ride off into the sunset (figuratively speaking, of course, unless you do have a horse)!

Now the first thing that happens when you allow yourself to walk hand-in-hand with a spirit of fear is that you release stress molecules that trigger responses through the hypothalamus, releasing chemicals into your body. If your thoughts are long-term fear driven, you are going to have some health problems. But if you lose your peace and then take those thoughts captive, those chemicals will go back to homeostasis and will not wreak havoc in your health. Did you know there is a disease called "Broken Heart Syndrome?" Hmmm.

If you entertain the spirit of fear, the first target is your heart; your heart is very sensitive to what you think and feel, and that is why your thoughts impact your health. This can literally and spiritually break your heart. Your heart stops and evaluates the wisdom of these thoughts and tries to keep all rash and impulsive thinking under control. So if you get overwhelmed by the spirit of fear, it damages you emotionally. That's where the statement "scared to death" comes in. We can literally die from fright! In some cases we have heard of, people have died of fear or loneliness. They die prematurely, and the cause is a broken heart!

The stress chemicals affect your heart by increasing blood flow and narrowing the arteries. High blood pressure is the result of taking thought for tomorrow. Remember, the Lord said very clearly not to do that. Just be here now; deal with today.

> *Take therefore no thought for the morrow: for the morrow shall take thought for the things of itself. Sufficient unto the day is the evil thereof* (Matthew 6:34).

Not surprisingly, if you allow yourself to keep thinking this way, you are not giving your body what it needs to recover itself. (See 2 Timothy 2:23-24.) The longer the situation is allowed to continue, the worse it will affect your health.

The body is a system of electrochemical feedback loops that are continually running, and any disruption to this shows up as physical symptoms. This may give us some insights into why we sometimes hear of a young man in the prime of life dying of a heart attack. We have heard of men only 30 years old dying prematurely this way. The Bible tells us men's hearts will fail them because of fear.

> *Men's hearts failing them for fear, and for looking after those things which are coming on the earth: for the powers of heaven shall be shaken* (Luke 21:26).

You have cells that are constantly communicating with other cells through the release of chemicals called neuro-peptides that join with receptors. The receptors are little lock-type mechanisms on the outside of the cell that allows certain cells to come in—provided they have the secret password. *"Swordfish?"*—no, just joking. But receptors are very discriminating and only allow their own kind in, the ones that match their shape.

This is important because when you are stressed and entertaining a spirit of fear, that stress hormone can actually get in and corrode the shape of those receptors. Then they allow foreign neuro-chemicals or viruses to come into the cell, which can bring about health problems and diseases.

Cells basically are talking to other cells; they are having all sorts of interesting chats with one another. After a cell receives a signal, that cell feeds back into those peptide-secret-ing cells. Here a squirt, there a squirt, everywhere a squirt, squirt! They tell how much of the peptide to secrete.

When you are in peace, there is a smooth and steady flow of information available to your bodily systems. The opposite is also true. If you are not in peace, those fearful thoughts become toxic and start interrupting the communications in your bodily systems. You then have a communication breakdown.

Staying in the Lord's peace is the only way to really do this. First John 4:18 says that there is no fear in love, but perfect love (God's perfect love in you) will cast out all fears and torment. When we love each other, most of the time it is conditional. God's love is unconditional, always, and it's that unconditional love that will do the work. If we have any fear whatsoever, it is evidence that we aren't receiving God's perfect love.

> *There is no fear in love; but perfect love casteth out fear: because fear hath torment. He that feareth is not made perfect in love* (1 John 4:18).

If you know who you are in the Lord, then you do not need to ever question if you are truly loved. You do not need to listen to any more lies of the devil. Papa God sent His only begotten Son Jesus Christ of Nazareth just to get you and take your place on the cross, to die the most horrible death imaginable so you can inherit eternal life. The apostle Paul said, "Who can deliver me from the body of sin?" Ahhh... Jesus Christ can and did. We need to believe that all our sins are covered by the blood of the Lamb. But the more excellent way is not to allow wrong thoughts in the first place. But if they do come in, we need to know what to do about them.

> *O wretched man that I am! Who shall deliver me from the body of this death? I thank God through Jesus Christ our Lord. So then with the mind I myself serve the law of God; but with the flesh the law of sin* (Romans 7:24-25).

We fall into doubt and unbelief because we forget that we have been purged of our old sins.

But he that lacketh these things is blind, and cannot see afar off, and hath forgotten that he was purged from his old sins (2 Peter 1:9).

Applying These Truths

As writers of this book, both of us have something to say to you that may help you apply the principles of taking thoughts captive in your own life.

Caspar's insight: When you have a yucky thought, a tormenting one that wants to keep you focused on something unpleasant, the more you feed that negative thought, the more it grows thorns on the tree of that thought. But the moment you decide to stop dwelling on that unpleasant, negative thought and instead turn away from it and forgive everyone and everything concerned, those thorns start to fall off the tree. Then you cover over that old thought tree with a new, pleasant positive thought pattern. Over time, that new positive thought will overrule and replace the old nasty one. You will gain freedom from it. You cannot erase the old thought completely; it is part of your memory, but you can overwrite the old, bad memories with new, positive ones. That is good news, brothers and sisters! The Gospel means good news. The Lord's way is always the best way. As soon as you forgive, you enter into holiness! As you think, so you are.

For all the wonderful things that have happened in my life, I have also had some really difficult things happen. Like the time I received a telephone call a few hours after my first child was born, informing me that my father had been murdered. Not understanding much of this back then and being sort of a baby Christian, I unknowingly let it break my heart literally, emotionally, physically, and spiritually. Proverbs 13:12 says that when hope is lost, it makes the heart sick.

Years later, after I began to understand some of these basic biblical truths, I received ministry through Pastor Henry Wright and his staff at Pleasant Valley Church. We talked about the trauma of the day my father was killed that I thought was long forgotten. But I still needed ministry for it. They broke the power of the unclean spirits in Jesus' name, that were holding me captive through memory, which was behind the heart disease and other assorted health problems.

Amazingly, the painfulness of that traumatic event left me. I still have the memory, but the trauma behind that memory is now gone. I could not even talk about it for years, but now I can talk about it as a matter of fact. The anguish and pain of it has left me as I've learned to apply the Word of God in my life.

That day was the beginning of my walking out of certain premature death by heart disease, which is considered incurable by the medical community. I was soon released and restored back to health.

We cannot erase our memories, but we can rule over them. Because of what Jesus Christ of Nazareth did for each one of us on the cross, we can indeed have that more abundant life He wants us to have. We can walk in peace and health and happiness. We have the choice to obey the Lord and do as He has instructed us, and we can be made free. For nothing is impossible with the Lord God Almighty.

> *Hope deferred maketh the heart sick: but when the desire cometh, it is a tree of life* (Proverbs 13:12).

> *The thief cometh not, but for to steal, and to kill, and to destroy: I am come that they might have life, and that they might have it more abundantly* (John 10:10).

As we mentioned earlier, this is our beta brain waves at work. Throughout this book, we reference 2 Corinthians 10:5, which speaks of taking every thought captive. But it also says to cast down all imagination that exalts itself over God. It's clear then that God did create us to use our imagination, but not for evil.

Our minds were made for the Lord, not for the enemy. Let's start practicing this every day. Colossians 3:2 says, *"Set your affection on things above, not on things on the earth."*

Let's start thinking how to love each other. Perhaps think of ways to help our neighbor, bring them a meal, or visit someone who is sick. These are all things that start with our thinking. God made us in His image. If He is the creator, wouldn't it be natural that we would be creative too? We need to realize that when we design something or make something we are the chip off the ole' block! We're God's kids, and we take after Him and His creativity. Take a look at the world around us. He certainly has a colorful and vivid imagination, don't you think?

Personal Insights From Linda: While helping Caspar with this book, something happened to me that this book actually helped me with. I experienced a home invasion that could have been deadly, but my husband was able to intervene and apprehend the intruder. Yes, that in itself was pretty traumatic, and that's exactly what we are talking about here. Some bad things do happen, but the question is, what are we going to do with it from then on in our thinking? Even though a home invasion isn't likely to happen again, my thoughts continued replaying all the "what-if" scenarios, and was bringing me into great fear. I was having a hard time simply trying to think on something else. It did work for a moment, but I soon found my mind wondering back to that situation. I fell into that "rut" again. It was messing with my life. My thoughts began taking me down to a place I didn't want to go. Finally after recalling some of the teachings in this book, I prayed through it. The Lord gave me Ephesians 5:26: *"That He might sanctify and cleanse it with the washing of the water by the word."*

God taught me how to use my imagination to defeat the enemy that day. And that's how that Scripture came to mind, *"Washing of the water by the Word."* He had me imagine a bucket filled with all kinds of words from the Bible. Things like, "God is good' God is love, there is no fear in love; perfect love casts out fear; Jesus wept; this is My beloved Son in whom I am well pleased... all kinds of "words" of God. It was filled to the brim. Then when that tormenting thought came back, I poured that bucket of "Words" right on top of my head. And lo and behold, that tormenting thought actually washed away, right out of my mind. I was replacing the old thoughts with God thoughts, by washing the old away with the Word of God.

The Lord helped me to practically apply the Word of God to my life and He used what He created in me to do it, my imagination. As we mentioned earlier, this is our beta brain waves at work. Throughout this book, we reference 2 Corinthians

10:5 which speaks of taking every thought captive. but it also says to cast down all imagination that exalts itself over the knowledge of God. It's clear then that God did create us to use our imagination, but not for evil.

I came across an article that says when you use your imagination it actually strengthens your mind and memory; promoting good health.[3] You can exercise your mind as you would exercise your body. This article made this suggestion: Imagine yourself skiing down the Aspen slopes, or sky-diving or ice-skating like a pro. I have done this from time to time, and it's actually quite fun. I'm not sure what it really does yet for my health and memory, but if I'm to think on things that are lovely and good, this counts too, don't you think? I have even imagined what my home was like in Heaven. A big picture window, blowing white curtains overlooking the crystal sea. I have often imagined what the new earth will look like, the colors that will be there in the trees and landscapes. Imagine what it will be like to be in the presence of Jesus Himself? It is quite exhilarating, to say the least!

Let's start using what God has given us. Our minds were made for the Lord not for the enemy. Let's start practicing this every day. Colossians 3:2 says, *"Set your affection on things above, not things on the earth."*

A scripture comes to mind, 1 Corinthians 2:9 *"But as it is written, Eye hath not seen, nor ear heard, neither have entered into the heart of man, the things which God hath prepared for them that love him."* It's awesome to know that even if we think of the most amazing things through our imagination, there is far more that God has for us above that! So lets start imagining some good things for our lives and stop allowing the enemy to use our imagination to keep us in bondage.

An Experiment

Start counting backward from 100; please go ahead and start now: 100, 99, 98, 97... Now at the same time, start saying the ABCs. It cannot be done though many, even you, have tried. Which is precisely our point, and neither can you entertain a holy good thought and an unholy bad thought at the same time. You must choose one or the other. God gives you the freedom to choose moment-by-moment.

When a tormenting thought tries to come against you, start thinking about something good instead. Start thanking the Lord for all the blessings in your life; you will find you cannot count that high. He has blessed you with every breath you take, and as Scriptures say, let everything that has breath praise the Lord (see Ps. 150:6). Scriptures also say to pray without ceasing (see 1 Thess. 5:17). This will truly keep your heart and mind occupied with the things of the Lord so there is no room for the other kingdom to get a foothold.

You have the power and authority to take back your mind by keeping it on things above. We encourage you to put into practice what we've shared so far. Faith without works is dead (see James 2:17), and so by taking God at His Word and applying His truth, your faith will be established.

When your mind is on faith, love, goodness, and the like, you cannot think fearful things. You have to think on things above purposefully. Fearful thoughts come a dime a dozen; they just fall into our thinking, but we have to put our minds on Him. Fearful thoughts will try and come all day long; every thought you have has to go down a path of faith or fear, and you get to decide which path to take. The spirit world is constantly trying to invade our thinking, and spirits of fear will try to get you to grab hold of one of them so that more can enter. However, there is a better way; we have to put our minds on Him. Put is an action word, and that's what we need to do. Perfect peace comes to those whose minds are stayed on the Lord. You cannot live in fear and faith at the same time, nor can you think fear and faith at the same time. There is no room for fearful thoughts if your thoughts are on truth. Just as this experiment showed us, you cannot count and recite the alphabet at the same time.

We need to replace fearful thoughts with the "washing of water by the Word."

Practical Application

Earlier we spoke of ruts in our thinking. We hope you take the time and purposefully began thinking good thoughts to replace those old, rutty thoughts. Take a moment to write down some of your old thoughts that have caused you to go down that same miserable pathway. It's like going around the same mountain, always ending up where you started.

So the next time you find yourself thinking something that you have thought before, stop for a moment and pay attention to that thought. Is it the same thought you had before? If so, change it. If so, forgive. If so, repent. You have the power to do these things. Open your Bible and read, quote out loud a memorized Scripture, turn on some praise music, or do whatever it takes to get you to snap out of that rut! It's a fight for your life.

But there is good news. After you do this a few times and get your mind to habitually think of God thoughts, it will become easier and easier. Pretty soon, it's just who you are. Isn't that the goal here—not to have to work so hard at it, but finally get to a place where you see fruit? That, my friend, is true peace.

To review, these are the steps you can apply to help recover yourself from the snare of the devil who is trying to mess with your thought-life:

1. When that thought comes up, stop and look at it. Don't turn or run any longer. Sometimes we "feel" something bad before we realize our thoughts caused it. So it's important to stop and take time to ask ourselves, "What Was I just Thinking?"

2. If the thought torments, you have to come to the conclusion that it is coming from fear. By recognizing this, you are half way home to freedom. It could be fear of man, fear of being wrong, fear of displeasing God, fear of rejection, fear of being hurt again, fear of not pleasing someone. If you need help with this, ask God to show you all involved in that thought. And hands down, there is always a relationship issue.

3. Forgive all involved in that thought, including yourself, and even God! When we don't forgive, that keeps the door open for the enemy to torment our minds. See, we cannot erase that thought completely, but we can get rid of the pain that keeps it alive, and that comes through forgiving everyone involved. When we confess our sins to God, He is faithful to forgive us and to cleanse us from all unrighteousness (see 1 John 1:9). When we do our part, God will do His.

4. Then praise God for working with you even if you haven't seen any results yet. When the Israelites went out to battle, they sang songs of praise before they fought! There is a principle here. It means you are believing God for the victory. You are believing before seeing. This is your faith at work.

5. Then get a renewed mind. Begin thinking on the Word of God. Begin to speak songs and hymns and spiritual songs, making melody in your heart toward the Lord (see Eph. 5:19). Put your mind on things above (see Col. 3:2).

Endnotes

1. Mayo Clinic online database: http://www.mayoclinic.com/.

2. Virginia Essene, Heart and Brain: How are your Heart and Brain connected to God? Association for Prenatal & Perinatal Psychology & Health. http://www.birthpsychology.com.

3. Lumosity, "Reclaim your brain," www.lumosity.com/k/brain-exercises.

Chapter Seven

MOTIVES OF THE HEART

Many doctors have a heart to help, serve, and do good. The apostle Luke was a physician. A doctor can tell you what is going on in your body with scientific data and research to back up his or her statements. But the thing we want to do then is go back to the Bible and find out what the roots of the problem are so we can get right with the Lord God, in Jesus' name. He gives us a measure of time to get right with Him because it is His desire to always heal us; that is what is called mercy.

All ministry involves building up the Kingdom of God, putting back what God intended, and tearing down the kingdom of darkness and strongholds of this world. We tear them down by trusting God and abiding in His Word. Interestingly enough, the word abiding means to dwell.[1] And as we dwell (abide) continually in His presence, our light will shine and glorify God.

> Let your light so shine before men, that they may see your good works, and glorify your Father which is in heaven (Matthew 5:16).

A woman who was pregnant received a bad report that she was losing the baby. The couple did not deny this was happening; they saw the ultrasound picture and could see there was a real problem. Instead of saying, "We are not receiving this bad report," they both came together and dealt with the sins

116

and generational iniquities that were behind losing a baby. They spent several hours lying bare each other's issues. They went before the Lord and asked Him to search their hearts and show them what they should do. They repented; they changed the way they did some things and thought about some things. Then the Lord blessed them in their obedience, and they received a healthy, happy baby. The doctor must have thought it was a miracle. This couple did the Word; they tore down the kingdom of darkness by getting into the light! We as believers should be expecting this breakthrough in our situations as we line up with the Word of God.

We all need to address our issues. The Bible says that we all have fallen short of the glory of God. If we say we have not sinned, the Bible says we lie and make God a liar!

> *For all have sinned, and come short of the glory of God* (Romans 3:23).

> *If we say that we have not sinned, we make Him a liar, and His word is not in us* (1 John 1:10).

We are in a body, and have a mind, spirit, and soul. We communicate through our spirit with our Lord. Our souls give us our personalities, which allow us to communicate with each other. Our physical body is our holy temple, which keeps us. What you do in the spiritual is going to affect what happens in the natural.

> *And the very God of peace sanctify you wholly; and I pray God your whole spirit and soul and body be pre-served blameless unto the coming of our Lord Jesus Christ* (1 Thessalonians 5:23).

> *Forasmuch as ye are manifestly declared to be the epistle of Christ ministered by us, written not with ink, but with the Spirit of the living God; not in tables of stone, but in fleshy tables of the heart* (2 Corinthians 3:3).

> *For the word of God is quick, and powerful, and sharper than any twoedged sword, piercing even to the dividing asunder of soul and spirit, and of the joints and marrow, and is a discerner of the thoughts*

and intents of the heart. Neither is there any creature that is not manifest in His sight: but all things are naked and opened unto the eyes of Him with whom we have to do (Hebrews 4:12-13).

There is nothing that can hide from Papa God, visible or invisible.

Keep Your Eyes on the Lord

We probably have the best chance of having pure motives of the heart when we are focused on the Lord and esteeming others better than ourselves. That is being Christ-like.

Let nothing be done through strife or vainglory; but in lowliness of mind let each esteem other better than themselves (Philippians 2:3).

When we get self-centered, we are taking our eyes off the Lord and will most likely get into trouble by allowing evil thoughts to be entertained. Our hearts will either be led by the Holy Spirit or by evil spirits. We get to choose moment by moment.

Hebrews 11:6 says that without faith we cannot please God!

But without faith it is impossible to please Him: for he that comes to God, must believe that He is, and that He is a rewarder of them that diligently seek Him (Hebrews 11:6).

This is someone who doesn't really believe "in" Him or believe that He exists! Many say they do believe, but their fruit doesn't demonstrate that. We need to recognize where we are in our belief system, and whatever doesn't line up with God, we need to confess as sin. Remember the exercise we did earlier? "God is God Isn't? It applies here.

So if a "believer" doesn't "believe," what more is there? Repentance? Yes, repent for our lack of faith and trust. If we don't come back in line with the Scriptures, we won't "receive" anything of the Lord.

For let not that man think that he shall receive any thing of the Lord. A double minded man is unstable in all his ways (James 1:7-8).

Believing and Receiving

Let's say you do believe God. After all, the Bible said it, you believe it, and that settles it for you—or does it? Anyone can believe. The devils even believe and tremble (see James 2:19). The real issue isn't whether you believe it or not; it's whether you believe it and receive it for yourself. When we receive, that is when we start changing. When a person is saved, they are saved by believing what Jesus did and receiving Him into their heart and life. See, the devils believe, but they can't receive.

Often, we can believe that God loves others, but have a hard time receiving His love for ourselves. This is a major block that can cause you to be in fear and torment because it's His perfect love in you that casts out all fear and tormenting thoughts. We have to believe God, and then receive what He has said. He wants to give good things to you. It says He rewards (that means we receive something) those who diligently seek Him. How many are really diligently seeking Him? We believe we can see how much we truly seek Him by what rewards we have received. This isn't to bring you under any guilt or condemnation; it's to get you to see where you are so you can repent and be forgiven. Then restoration and healing can come.

Remember to seek first His Kingdom and His righteousness and all the things you need will be given to you (see Matt. 6:33).

The Importance of Emotions

Your heart can think as well. The heart is a highly intelligent system that plays a more important role than most people seem to understand. It helps dictate our perceptions, as well as our mental and emotional balance.

That ECG (electrocardiogram) is a device that does a test that measures the electrical activity of the heart. The electrical impulses made while the heart is beating are recorded and usually shown on a piece of paper. This is known as an electrocardiogram, and records any possible problems that may be going on with the heart's rhythm, and the conduction of the heartbeat through the heart, which may be affected by some underlying heart disease.

There is really a spectrum of feelings that are being dealt with here that are often overlooked like faith versus a spirit of fear, because as we have already tried to explain your emotion may dictate your perception of reality and that triggers a chemical reaction in you that either opens you up to diseases or keeps you in homeostasis—perfectly balanced health.

It is important to be able to feel your feelings but also to know how to deal with them according to the Word of God. The Scripture does not criticize feelings except when we do not have any—like Pharaoh with his hardness of heart or those who are just believers in appearance on Sundays only.

God created us to experience feelings; we need to make a choice to live fully for Him. Then we will be on fire for the Lord! Someone who just "gets through a day" may have some confessing to do. We need to be "hot," not lukewarm; there is a penalty for being lukewarm.

> *I know thy works, that thou art neither cold nor hot: I would thou wert cold or hot. So then because thou art lukewarm, and neither cold nor hot, I will spue thee out of My mouth* (Revelation 3:15-16).

If you can't say amen, say ouchy!

Joshua 24:15 says you need to choose today whom you will serve. The choice is to serve or not serve—middle ground is as appetizing to God as room-temperature milk.

In the book, *'Healing the Cancer Personalities'* [2] it describes individuals who do not allow their emotions out, which is very detrimental to their health. Did you know that when we are not honest with our feelings, we are actually lying? Remember, it's the truth that makes us free.

In past generations, many were taught not to share their feelings. Those who hold things in are more prone to dis-ease than those who find an outlet, friend, prayer, or confession to share their hearts and emotions with. It is okay to feel people, God created your feelings, so use them. The feelings displayed actually shows you what is in your heart. if your feelings are not good, then something needs to be addressed. If the feelings are good, then enjoy them. Allow your feelings to help you find your freedom. Forgive those who hurt you. Forgive those who rejected you. Have you ever said, "they hurt my feelings?" Then forgive them, so your feelings are restored and in proper condition to be used by God. Our feelings were made for God's use, for enjoyment and for love. The only way that can happen is if we remove the unforgiveness that is in there, that is what produces "hurt feelings." Scriptures tell us by keeping the commandments, you won't feel any emotional pain.

What is the greatest commandment? To love God, ourself and others. The degree we have pain in our hearts is the degree we are obeying the commandment to love and forgive.

> *Whoso keepeth the commandment shall **feel no evil thing:** and a wise man's heart discerneth both time and judgment.* (Ecclesiastes 8:5).

Practical Application

If you have seen things in yourself that don't line up with God's thoughts or actions, tell Him. If you are not serving God like you want to, then just confess it to Him. Ask Him to help you see the motives of your heart: are they good or not so good? Are your motives pure? Are you touchy? Do you get hurt feelings all the time? Right now is a good time to ask the Lord to help you discern your own heart and motives.

The One who created you loves you and wants the best for you, but it can only come about as we cooperate with Him. Isaiah 1:18 says, *"Come now, and let us reason together, saith the Lord..."* We need to participate in our sanctification process. Philippians 2:12 advises us to work out our salvation with fear and trembling. This means to work with God on your "stuff."

If you find that your heart is not where it should be, then just tell Him. He sees it anyway; we might as well be honest with ourselves.

Take a moment and tell Him you want more of Him. Tell Him that you desire to follow Jesus every step of the way, but that you need help with your thought life. That is where the rubber meets the road. If you don't believe God loves or cares for you, guess what? It will "seem" like God doesn't love or care for you because you're not being open to Him. And whatever you believe you will have, good or bad.

Let's ask another question. Do you believe He loves you exactly as you are right now in your life? Oh, you can believe He loves others, but what about you? You have to get your mind straight about this. God is love and can do nothing else. He loves you without condition. He is good all the time. He wants you to be hot for Him, not cold or lukewarm; He wants you to be happy and excited about your eternal future.

Take what you see to the Lord and have a little chat with Him. He is waiting.

Endnotes

1. American Heritage Dictionary, http://education.yahoo.com/reference/dictionary/entry/abide, s.v. abide.

2. Healing the Cancer Personality by Barbara Carroll (published by Life Application Ministries Publishing, printed by createspace.com

Chapter Eight

Knowing the truth Makes you Free

We need to believe what the Lord is showing us here: it is not enough to accept a truth with our minds; we must know it in our hearts as well.

Knowing truth will "make" you free. But that's where the trouble starts. We need to understand that *make* is an action word, and so we are "in process" of becoming free. Just saying that may have just freed some of you! Anyway, "knowing" the truth is evidenced by our lives. Do you have hope? Are you at peace? Are you learning to believe and trust Him for everything? These are evidences that we "know" the truth.

We are not to bend our idea of what is true to match our feelings, we must change our thoughts to match the truth, which will then change our feelings. Like we said earlier, where your thoughts go your body follows. In the Gospel of John, Jesus said that whatever you ask in His name, He will do:

> *If ye shall ask any thing in My name, I will do it"*(John 14:14).

And in 1 John 5:15, it says:

> *And if we know that He hear us, whatsoever we ask, we know that we have the petitions that we desired of Him.*

1 John 5:14 also says that we are to ask according to His will. That's what I've been talking about all along—getting your thoughts to match up with His thoughts so that when you pray, you do so according to His will!

Our thoughts have to line up with the whole truth, not just the parts we like. Hebrews 4:12 says that the Word of God is a discerner of our thoughts, intents, and motives. So we need to be sure they are pure and clean before the Lord. But if they aren't, what happens? 2 Timothy 3:8 says, *"Now as Jannes and Jambres withstood Moses, so do these also resist the truth: men of corrupt minds, reprobate concerning the faith."* Ouch!

God's Will

We want to take a moment to look at "God's perfect will versus His permissive will." Throughout the Bible it clearly defines the direction for our lives, and when we apply them to our lives, we are in His perfect will, thereby resulting in dwelling in the promises of God, entering into His rest and His protection. Permissive will is when we make choices that are not in line with Scripture, and there is always some sort of negative consequences. Sometimes people feel like God has abandoned them, but He hasn't, they have abandoned His Word. Confusion comes out of "permissive will." It's when people don't want to do what the Bible says to do, simple as that! They make all kinds of excuses what the Word says, and so they are stuck. We have to take the Word for what it says, and just do it (James 1:22). Frankly, the bottom line here is that people just don't want to do "it" and that is to love and forgive unconditionally (see Matthew 22:37-40).

Matthew 5:48 says that we are to be "perfect" even as our Father in Heaven is perfect. We need to define "perfect." The Scriptures say to be perfect is to love (see John 17:23; John 4:12; Colossians 1:28-29). We won't do everything right, that is why we have a Savior, but we can do our best and love each other through the power of the Holy Ghost. Did you know loving is an act of our will? That is God's perfect will for you too—to love. Matthew 22:37-40 wraps up all ten commandments into two—we are to love the Lord God completely, and love others as much as we love ourselves.

So in our view, permissive will is an excuse not to take responsibility for what the Bible says—to blame God somehow for the outcome of the choices we make. God has given us free will, and based on our will, determines the outcome. Truth is not determined by your feelings; either it is true, or it isn't. There is no real in-between. Like the Word says, say either yea or nay; otherwise, we get into trouble.

> *But let your communication be, Yea, yea; Nay, nay: for whatsoever is more than these cometh of evil* (Matthew 5:37).

If you take an honest look around, you will notice that believers and non-believers alike have the same sicknesses, diseases, broken relationships, and business struggles, etc. The difference is that a believer can apply the Word of God and repent (turn away) from the things that could be causing their problems. It appears many people don't realize that their sins and iniquities (generational sins) are behind many of the issues messing with their life today. Jeremiah 5:25 says that we prevent good things from happening to us because of our sins and iniquities.

Permissive will says, "I don't really know God's will, so I'll just do what I want, and I'll get away with it because I'm under His grace." But what does Romans 6:12-15 say?

> *Let not sin therefore reign in your mortal body, that ye should obey it in the lusts thereof. Neither yield ye your members as instruments of unrighteousness unto sin: but yield yourselves unto God, as those that are alive from the dead, and your members as instruments of righteousness unto God. For sin shall not have dominion over you: for ye are not under the law, but under grace. What then? shall we sin, because we are not under the law, but under grace? God forbid* (Romans 6:12-15).

We need to stop and define what the word *grace* really means. The word *grace*, for those who accept those modern Bible translations, says that it is "unmerited favor." You are given favor where you don't merit it; the concept that none of us in the human race deserve to be saved because we are all wretched sinners. But because of what happened on the cross, we are able to enter Heaven. If you want to live a life on earth in the promises of God, you now have to take that step of faith to believe why he died on the cross. You have to apply the principles of the Word to your life. We're not talking about salvation at this point, but there is a connection. The Bible says, *"Work out your salvation with fear and trembling"* (Phil. 2:12). That means, live every day the best you can, and when you mess up, have a heart-to-heart talk with Papa God. Ask for forgiveness, receive that forgiveness, and keep on moving forward. To put it simply: Grace means God is talking to us, helping us see the truth, and working with us; Mercy is time to figure out what He said.

1 Thessalonians 5:18 makes it very clear on how to be in His perfect will: *"In every thing give thanks: for this is the will of God in Christ Jesus concerning you."*

It also lists other commands:

- *Quench not the Spirit;*
- *Despise not prophesyings;*
- *Prove all things; hold fast that which is good;*
- *Abstain from all appearance of evil. And the very God of peace sanctify you wholly; and I pray God your whole spirit and soul and body be preserved blameless unto the coming of our Lord Jesus Christ. Faithful is He that calleth you, who also will do it.*
- *Brethren, pray for us.*
- *Greet all the brethren with an holy kiss.*
- *I charge you by the Lord that this epistle be read unto all the holy brethren.*

So, putting this all together, we can be perfect this side of Heaven, when we believe the Word and apply it to our lives by loving, forgiving, confessing, being thankful, staying clean before our Father in our heart, soul, mind, and spirit (see James 4:8).

The grace of our Lord Jesus Christ be with you. Amen

(1 Thessalonians 5:19-28).

Truth

The spirit of accusation likes to take the truth and distort it. It's like Adam telling God after he and Eve sinned that if He had not given him the woman, none of this would have happened. Adam was really blaming God for his own disobedience.

Truth is unchanging. We may think we know the truth, but we better think again. The very things we are thinking on could be our downfall. Proverbs 16:25 says, *"There is a way that seemeth right unto a man, but the end thereof are the ways of death."*

The heart needs to always test itself by a standard, and that, of course, is the Word of God. Linda has written a book called, *"Nothing But The Truth So Help Me God."*[1] Because we need God's help to know the truth that can make us free.

Scriptures say:

> *Examine yourselves, whether ye be in the faith; prove your own selves. Know ye not your own selves, how that Jesus Christ is in you, except ye be reprobates?* (2 Corinthians 13:5)

> *[1]Lord, who shall abide in thy tabernacle? who shall dwell in thy holy hill?[2]He that walketh uprightly, and worketh righteousness, and speaketh the truth in his heart. [3]He that backbiteth not with his tongue, nor doeth evil to his neighbour, nor taketh up a reproach against his neighbour.* (Psalm 15:1-3)

> *By mercy and truth iniquity is purged: and by the fear of the Lord men depart from evil.* (Proverbs 16:6)

Hardened Hearts

When the Lord speaks to you about something and you decide not to obey Him, you are fellowshipping with devils the moment you disobey the Lord. If you persist in doing that, it will not take long to develop a hardened heart.

> *But I say, that the things which the Gentiles sacrifice, they sacrifice to devils, and not to God: and I would*

not that ye should have fellowship with devils. Ye cannot drink the cup of the Lord, and the cup of devils: ye cannot be partakers of the Lord's table, and of the table of devils (1 Corinthians 10:20-21).

O come, let us worship and bow down: let us kneel before the Lord our maker. For He is our God; and we are the people of His pasture, and the sheep of His hand. To day if ye will hear His voice, harden not your heart, as in the provocation, and as in the day of temptation in the wilderness (Psalm 95:6-8).

We also need to understand what sin is. People do not think that entertaining a spirit of doubt and unbelief is sin, but that can harden your heart through the deceitfulness of it.

Take heed, brethren, lest there be in any of you an evil heart of unbelief, in departing from the living God. But exhort one another daily, while it is called today; lest any of you be hardened through the deceitfulness of sin (Hebrews 3:12-13).

Moses allowed divorces because of the hardness of people's hearts.

He saith unto them, Moses because of the hardness of your hearts suffered you to put away your wives: but from the beginning it was not so (Matthew 19:8).

It seems pretty obvious that God's wrath is being stored up for that day when He is going to deal with those hard and unrepentant hearts. As a matter of fact, He puts the responsibility on us. The more we know of the Word; the more we are accountable for. The Bible says that His people are inexcusable for judging each other as this causes condemnation.

Therefore thou art inexcusable, O man, whosoever thou art that judgest: for wherein thou judgest another, thou condemnest thyself; for thou that judgest doest the same things. But we are sure that the judgment of God is according to truth against them which commit such things. And thinkest thou this, O man, that judgest them which do such things, and doest the same, that thou shalt escape the judgment of God? Or despisest thou the riches of His goodness and forbearance and longsuffering; not knowing that the goodness of God leadeth thee to repentance? But after thy hardness and impenitent heart treasurest up unto thyself wrath against the day of wrath and revelation of the righteous judgment of God; who will render to every man according to his deeds (Romans 2:1-6).

Do you ever feel condemned? Perhaps you need to stop and take a look to see if you have been judging your neighbor? What do you think of your boss? How about the family with the new car next door? What about the preacher's sermon? Are you taking communion with anger in your heart? It may be that you are bringing on your own condemnation. Just get right with God. Confess your judgment, forgive yourself, and keep on keeping on.

But let a man examine himself, and so let him eat of that bread, and drink of that cup. For he that eateth and drinketh unworthily, eateth and drinketh dam-nation to himself, not discerning the Lord's body. For this cause many are weak and sickly among you, and many sleep. For if we would judge ourselves, we should not be judged. (1 Corinthians 11:29-31)

The Bible tells us we are to be compassionate and not harden our hearts toward those in need. Individuals who have been hurt in the past have hardened hearts, making it difficult to trust anyone; they fear people so they don't help those in distress. We need God to heal our broken hearts so we are ready and willing to help those in need, without fear.

If there be among you a poor man of one of thy breth-ren within any of thy gates in thy land which the Lord thy God giveth thee, thou shalt not harden thine heart, nor shut thine hand from thy poor brother: But thou shalt open thine hand wide unto him, and shalt surely lend him sufficient for his need, in that which he wanteth. Beware that there be not a thought in thy wicked heart, saying, The seventh year, the year of release, is at hand; and thine eye be evil against thy poor brother, and thou givest him nought; and he cry unto the Lord against thee, and it be sin unto thee. Thou shalt surely give him, and thine heart shall not be grieved when thou givest unto him: because that for this thing the Lord thy God shall bless thee in all thy works, and in all that thou puttest thine hand unto (Deuteronomy 15:7-10).

Jesus Christ of Nazareth is our leader and the one we are to follow by His example. Thankfully, He did not harden His heart against us. He loved us in our mess because He looked past that mess and saw us.

But when He saw the multitudes, He was moved with compassion on them, because they fainted, and were scattered abroad, as sheep having no shepherd (Matthew 9:36).

And there came a leper to Him, beseeching Him, and kneeling down to Him, and saying unto Him, If Thou wilt, Thou canst make me clean. And Jesus, moved with compassion, put forth His hand, and touched him, and saith unto him, I will; be thou clean (Mark 1:40-41).

Forgiving Others

When someone offends you or hurts you in some way, it is pretty easy to listen to the lies of the devil. You get angry and want to retaliate; you may just harden your heart against that person, or persons. But let's face it: we have all fallen short of the glory of God. We are told to forgive those who cause us grief; if we don't, we fall into the enemy's snare ourselves.

But if any have caused grief, he hath not grieved me, but in part: that I may not overcharge you all. Sufficient to such a man is this punishment, which was inflicted of many. So that contrariwise ye ought rather to forgive him, and comfort him, lest perhaps such a one should be swallowed up with overmuch sorrow. Wherefore I beseech you that ye would confirm your love toward him. For to this end also did I write, that I might know the proof of you, whether ye be obedient in all things. To whom ye forgive any thing, I forgive also: for if I forgave any thing, to whom I forgave it, for your sakes forgave I it in the person of Christ; lest Satan should get an advantage of us: for we are not ignorant of his devices (2 Corinthians 2:5-11).

Our Lord Jesus tells us we must instead forgive those who offend us, and forgive them from our hearts. We must not keep a record of wrongs done to us. What are our minds to be focused on?

So many Christians make the mistake of thinking they have forgiven someone simply by saying, "I forgive you." But inside they are still filled with spirits of anger, rage, resentment, and bitterness. They go out of their way to act cold to that person they said they forgave.

So likewise shall My heavenly Father do also unto you, if ye from your hearts forgive not every one his brother their trespasses (Matthew 18:35).

It seems that there is good and bad in each of us. Why not focus on the good? If you truly forgive someone, you will have positive feeling toward them. If you say you forgive but your feelings toward them are still not good, then you haven't truly forgiven from your heart.

The Bible tells us to give no place to the devil. You must tell the devil and his demons there is no room for him in your holy temple or in your life. The Lord has given you power over the devil, so use it.

And grieve not the Holy Spirit of God, whereby ye are sealed unto the day of redemption. Let all bitterness, and wrath, and anger, and clamour, and evil speaking, be put away from you, with all malice: and be ye kind one to another, tenderhearted, forgiving one another, even as God for Christ's sake hath forgiven you (Ephesians 4:30-32).

But the fruit of the Spirit is love, joy, peace, longsuffering, gentleness, goodness, faith, meekness, temperance: against such there is no law. And they that are Christ's have crucified the flesh with the affec-

tions and lusts. If we live in the Spirit, let us also walk in the Spirit (Galatians 5:22-25).

But without faith it is impossible to please Him; for He that cometh to God must believe that He is, and that He is a rewarder of them that diligently seek Him (Hebrews 11:6).

Forgiving From Our Heart

This portion is gleaned from Linda's book called, "Forgiving From Our Heart"[2] which goes into more detail on this topic.

As you have noticed, we talk a lot about forgiveness because it is the main KEY to our health. In this segment, you will learn "how" to forgive from your heart. The Lord commands us to forgive. And it also says that if we don't forgive others, He won't forgive us. This is pretty serious. This could be the very thing that is preventing your healing, preventing your success.

As an example, let's take a look at Lynne, who says she has forgiven a church acquaintance, Kate. But did Lynne remove Kate from her address book? Did she say, "I forgive you, but I never want to see you again?" Does she still hurt when she thinks of what Kate did? Does Lynne avoid meeting Kate at church meetings or other settings? Does she talk about Kate behind her back? These are indicators that there is unforgiveness. When we truly forgive, it is as though the offense never happened.

So you ask, how do I forgive from my heart? Before we can forgive others, we need first to be forgiven. Many are trying to forgive others with spirits of bitterness, resentment, anger, fear, and the like still in their hearts. That all has to be cleansed out before a person can truly forgive from a clean heart. Take a moment to identify someone who you think you forgave, yet you still have pain associated with that memory. Or someone you have vowed never to forgive. It's a good idea to get some paper... and write down what he or she did that caused your hurt. Once you have done this, take that list and begin to list things that you became because of this person. Your list should look something like this: angry, fearful, depressed, confused, resentful, unworthy, ashamed, rejected, bitter, betrayed, etc. These are the very things that prevent us from forgiving from our heart. These are sins that are retained from that relationship. We said it before, but we'll say it again. If you don't forgive another person, you will end up retaining their sins!

> *Whose soever sins ye remit, they are remitted unto them; and whose soever sins ye retain, they are retained* (John 20:23).

Once you have recognized what you are carrying around in your heart, you can take it to the Lord and repent. 1 John 1:9 says, *"If we confess our sins, he is faithful and just to forgive us our sins, and to cleanse us from all unrighteousness."* By faith, we believe He does this. Then there is nothing holding you back, preventing you from forgiving. See, it's not what they did that is the issue; it's what you retained from that relationship that is the issue. Get rid of that, and you have made yourself free to forgive from your heart.

You will discover that each time you do this, more peace will be apparent in your life. You may even feel lighter. I've heard some say they feel like a great weight was lifted. Now, we can't always trust our feelings, but it's good when we do get to feel that freedom when it comes. After all, God made our feelings to be used for good. Let's stop letting the enemy use our feelings for his purposes.

In Matthew 18 Jesus tells us the story of the unforgiving servant who was forgiven a great debt by his king whom he simply could not repay. He then goes out and treats a fellow servant very badly and refuses to forgive him of a small debt he owed him. The end result was that the king was very angered by this when he found out and reneged on the deal, sending the unforgiving servant to debtor's prison until he paid back all he originally owed. In England, most people who went into debtor's prison never got out again. And not only that, they went into prison to be tormented by the tormenters!

> *And his lord was wroth, and delivered him to the tormentors, till he should pay all that was due unto him. So likewise shall My heavenly Father do also unto you, if ye from your hearts forgive not every one his brother their trespasses* (Matthew 18:34-35).

Trusting God

When you went to sit in a chair, you did not have to test the chair before you had the faith to sit in it. The same is true with your faith in the Lord. You need to know He is strong enough to hold you up no matter what you are going through.

For example, let's say you need to go minister and pray for a family in a poor or rough section of town. Maybe you are going to bring them a meal because they are disabled or something along those lines. You are headed there, and on the way you learn there was a murder that took place in that particular neighborhood the night before.

You start singing, "Jesus loves me, this I know," or reciting to yourself all of Psalm 23:

> *Yea, though I walk through the valley of the shadow of death, I will fear no evil: for Thou art with me; Thy rod and Thy staff they comfort me* (Psalm 23:4).

Or Psalm 27:1:

> *The Lord is my light and my salvation; whom shall I fear? The Lord is the strength of my life; of whom shall I be afraid?*

All the while as you are going forward, the sky turns dark and stormy, and you remember Second Timothy 1:7, which says, *"For God hath not given us the spirit of fear; but of power, and of love, and of a sound mind."*

Okay, let's face the facts here: Even though you are reciting these verses and keeping your mind stayed on Him; quite honestly, most people would be feeling afraid. We need to discern if this is a feeling caused by an evil spirit of fear or not. Your mind is saying one thing, but your heart is saying something else, and that is double-mindedness.

> *But let him ask in faith, nothing wavering. For he that wavereth is like a wave of the sea driven with the wind and tossed. For let not that man think that he shall receive any thing of the Lord. A double minded man is unstable in all his ways* (James 1:6-8).

This people draweth nigh unto me with their mouth, and honoureth me with their lips; but their heart is far from me (Matthew 15:8).

If God is the one who really sent you, then He will see to it that you are taken care of and provide you with everything you need to complete the mission. You can go into scary situations with a peaceful heart, without sweaty palms and accelerated heart beats, because you trust Him completely, with your mind, body, and spirit. The Bible says to worship Him in spirit and in truth. They have to go hand in hand. To do both, we need to believe Him completely. John 4:24 says, *"God is a Spirit: and they that worship Him must worship Him in spirit and in truth."*

What is the worst thing that can happen to a believer? You die, go to be with the Lord, and on the day of resurrection, you get a glorified body.

If you have a hard time staying in peace during these times, you need to first confess that to Him. Just say, "Father God, Papa, I am not trusting You right now. Forgive me and help me to receive Your perfect love because that is what will cast out all my fear." We need to confess our lack so He can fill us. He knows it already; we just need to ask. He said that we have not because we ask not. We need to know what to ask for, too, out of a right heart and motive.

When we struggle in this area, we need to seek His love even more. It's His perfect love that casts out the fear, when that perfect love is working in us.

Ye lust, and have not: ye kill, and desire to have, and cannot obtain: ye fight and war, yet ye have not, because ye ask not. Ye ask, and receive not, because ye ask amiss, that ye may consume it upon your lusts (James 4:2-3).

There is no fear in love; but perfect love casteth out fear: because fear hath torment. He that feareth is not made perfect in love (1 John 4:18).

We are all absolutely dependent upon our Lord for every breath we take in this present world.

There is a song that says, "You are the air I breathe." It's very true. We can do nothing without Him, even breathe.

> *I am the vine, ye are the branches: he that abideth in Me, and I in him, the same bringeth forth much fruit: for without Me ye can do nothing* (John 15:5).

> *For in him we live, and move, and have our being; as certain also of your own poets have said, For we are also his offspring* (Acts 17:28).

Remember, He breathed life into Adam, and he became a living soul.

> *And the Lord God formed man of the dust of the ground, and breathed into his nostrils the breath of life; and man became a living soul* (Genesis 2:7).

We need to remain in faith knowing that He is King of kings and Lord over all things both visible and invisible; that He has given us power to complete the work on this planet; that we are able to do even greater things than He did.

> *And Jesus came and spake unto them, saying, All power is given unto Me in heaven and in earth. Go ye therefore, and teach all nations, baptizing them in the name of the Father, and of the Son, and of the Holy Ghost: teaching them to observe all things whatsoever I have commanded you: and, lo, I am with you always, even unto the end of the world. Amen* (Matthew 28:18-20).

> *Verily, verily, I say unto you, He that believeth on Me, the works that I do shall he do also; and greater works than these shall he do; because I go unto My Father* (John 14:12).

As we cooperate with Him, He will mold us and make us in His image. He will change our heart and give us a new heart. We can take that spiritually or physically, whichever applies.

> *A new heart also will I give you, and a new spirit will I put within you: and I will take away the stony heart*

out of your flesh, and I will give you an heart of flesh. And I will put My spirit within you, and cause you to walk in My statutes, and ye shall keep My judgments, and do them. And ye shall dwell in the land that I gave to your fathers; and ye shall be My people, and I will be your God (Ezekiel 36:26-28).

The purpose is so that we can live in the abundance Jesus came to give and in turn help others who are hurting and lost find that same abundance.

The Spirit of the Lord is upon Me, because He hath anointed Me to preach the gospel to the poor; He hath sent Me to heal the brokenhearted, to preach deliverance to the captives, and recovering of sight to the blind, to set at liberty them that are bruised, to preach the acceptable year of the Lord (Luke 4:18-19).

There are times we may face sorrow or accidents, and grief, even moments that can seem unbearable. We see the apostles had these moments, too.

The victory of Christ over the world and the victory of born-again believers through His victory are one of our favorite battle cries. We shall overcome! However, the disciples seemed to go back and forth from moments of brilliance when they made bold statements in faith and saw answered prayers to moments of weakness and confusion when they did not know what to do next. If we didn't have things to face, we wouldn't be overcomers or victorious!! Without trials we won't develop patience. And my friends, patience will defeat the enemy at any level.

My brethren, count it all joy when ye fall into divers temptations; Knowing this, that the trying of your faith worketh patience. But let patience have her perfect work, that ye may be perfect and entire, wanting nothing (James 1:2-4).

We aren't to run from these things, but turn and face them to get the victory! There are some of you who's pasts are chasing you. Choose today to stop this by turning around and facing them. You will find that thing chasing you is really nothing. But as long as you don't face it, it will remain strong and powerful and controlling of your life. We are to recover ourselves from the snare of the devil, and this is one we we do that. By exposing him. (see 2 Timothy 2-24-26).

Jesus rebuked them at times for their lack of faith. For example, the disciples showed their lack of faith when they couldn't heal the boy with a deaf and dumb spirit. Or the time they abandoned Jesus in the Garden of Gethsemane, and in their lack of faith were also afraid to stand with Him at his trial. Only the apostle John is recorded as standing there at Calvary while the rest of the disciples ran and locked themselves up in their rooms.

It's the truth, isn't it? We do not like to consider those aspects of the apostles. They're a lot like some of us. Unfortunately, it's true that sometimes we mix our faith with a spirit of doubt and unbelief instead of mixing our faith with our gifts and the Gospel. So in order to come clean before the Lord, just confess your doubt and unbelief. We need to simply be honest about our heart. We all have issues to deal with, but the first step to being made free is to admit them. Let's just be honest with our Lord. We would do well to plead like the boy's father in Mark 9:24, *"Lord, I believe; help Thou my unbelief."* Isn't that truly the real issue here? God wants us to see through a heavenly perspective!

We become overcomers when we know the truth that makes us free.

Sometimes we allow evil spirits to give us their thoughts of doubt and unbelief, which then releases all sorts of chemicals into our blood stream down the pathway of fear, causing our hearts to faint.

Some of you may be saying, "Wait a minute here, the Lord Jesus assured us that He has overcome all our enemies already." Jesus tells us in Luke 10:19, *"Behold, I give unto you power to tread on serpents and scorpions, and over all the power of the enemy: and nothing shall by any means hurt you."* So why do we ever entertain spirits of doubt and unbelief? Because we enter into a lack of faith. That is what this book is all about: to help you develop your faith in God and trust Him in every area of your life so that you will be strong in faith. The Bible says to keep our affections on things above. This will help you to entertain only God thoughts, rather than open yourself up for doubt and unbelief. The fact that Jesus has indeed overcome this world should always strengthen us in our time of need.

Satan's whole job is to get us to think about ourselves 24 hours a day; this way he will take our mind off Him—this is pride. God's desire is that you think of Him all day, taking your mind off of yourself—this is humility. The only way we will have complete peace no matter what is going on around us is when we stop putting ourselves in the equation. We overcome by keeping our mind on Him and Him alone.

Scriptures tell us to pray without ceasing. That way our minds are always fixed on Him. God knew where our battle was going to be, in our mind, so He made a way for us to keep it on straight! Through prayer.

Pray without ceasing (1 Thess. 5:17)

Let's look at the following verses:

> *They are of the world: therefore speak they of the world, and the world heareth them. We are of God: he that knoweth God heareth us; he that is not of God heareth not us. Hereby know we the spirit of truth, and the spirit of error. Beloved, let us love one another: for love is of God; and every one that loveth is born of God, and knoweth God. He that loveth not knoweth not God; for God is love* (1 John 4:5-8).

So we need to overcome by keeping our eyes on the Lord Jesus.

> *He that hath an ear, let him hear what the Spirit saith unto the churches; to him that overcometh will I give to eat of the tree of life, which is in the midst of the paradise of God* (Revelation 2:7).

> *To him that overcometh will I grant to sit with Me in My throne, even as I also overcame, and am set down with My Father in His throne* (Revelation 3:21).

> *I write unto you, fathers, because ye have known Him that is from the beginning. I write unto you, young men, because ye have overcome the wicked one. I*

write unto you, little children, because ye have known the Father. I have written unto you, fathers, because ye have known Him that is from the beginning. I have written unto you, young men, because ye are strong, and the word of God abideth in you, and ye have overcome the wicked one. Love not the world, neither the things that are in the world. If any man love the world, the love of the Father is not in him. For all that is in the world, the lust of the flesh, and the lust of the eyes, and the pride of life, is not of the Father, but is of the world. And the world passeth away, and the lust thereof: but he that doeth the will of God abideth for ever (1 John 2:13-17).

And I say also unto thee, that thou art Peter, and upon this rock I will build My church; and the gates of hell shall not prevail against it. And I will give unto thee the keys of the kingdom of heaven: and whatsoever thou shalt bind on earth shall be bound in heaven: and whatsoever thou shalt loose on earth shall be loosed in heaven (Matthew 16:18-19).

We are going to do all we know to do, and then we are going to keep standing because that's when we get the victory. We have the ability through Jesus to overcome all obstacles in our lives.

In this world, there are good times, and there are those times when we face challenges, sometime life-changing events. Sometimes we may even feel all alone, without anyone to comfort and encourage us through those difficult times. Nevertheless, our Savior the Lord Jesus gives us this awesome promise in Matthew 28:18-20.

And Jesus came and spake unto them, saying, "All power is given unto Me in heaven and in earth. Go ye therefore, and teach all nations, baptizing them in the name of the Father, and of the Son, and of the Holy Ghost: teaching them to observe all things whatsoever I have commanded you: and, lo, I am with you always, even unto the end of the world." Amen.

"*I am with you always, even unto the end of the world,*" pretty much sums it up, so you cannot be alone even if you feel that you are. God is still watching over His Word to per- form it.

Let us enter into His rest now and stop all the striving. Let's trust the Lord and not try to figure everything out. When we finally have our thoughts on the truth, when we dwell in His holy hill, when we lift our eyes to the hills from whence comes our help, when we seek first His Kingdom and His righteous- ness, when we forgive each other and love each other, we are doing the Word! When we do the Word, He will make our paths clear. We will be blessed because we have laid down our agenda and taken up His.

> *Then said Jesus unto His disciples, If any man will come after Me, let him deny himself, and take up his cross, and follow Me* (Matthew 16:24).

> *Follow peace with all men, and holiness, without which no man shall see the Lord* (Hebrews 12:14).

Practical Application

Do you ever feel condemned? Perhaps you need to stop and take a look to see if you have been judging your neighbor. What do you think of your boss? How about the family with the new car next door? Do you want to critique the preach- er's sermon?

As you were reading this chapter, did anyone come to mind that you have not been able to forgive? Perhaps you cannot forgive yourself. Perhaps you believe you have forgiven, but you are still tormented by what they did. Take these individ- uals before the Lord, and confess before God that you need help forgiving. Ask Him to cleanse you from the pain associ- ated with that person. Ask Him to remove all defilement from that person. Ask Him to remove from others defilement that you may have perpetrated.

It may be that you are bringing on your own condemna- tion (see Romans 8:1). Just get right with God. Confess your judgment, forgive yourself, and keep on keeping on.

This is "doing the Word" which will get rid of the torment-ers in your life and enable you to start experiencing more joy, peace, and good things. It doesn't mean everything will be perfect, but when challenging things happen, you won't fall to pieces. You won't fall into a blame game; you will respond from a healthy heart, which will result in peace for yourself and blessing for all those around you.

Have you heard the phrase, "When momma ain't happy, ain't nobody happy"? It is actually a true statement that we can apply to ourselves. When we're not at peace, no one around us has peace, but when we are at peace, people around us are more likely to be at peace, too. That is, of course, if they too have learned that this is through relationship with Jesus Christ of Nazareth, our Lord and Savior.

For more insights on dealing with Guilt and Condemna-tion, pick up Linda's book called "Guilt and Condemnation."[3] It will help you find your freedom!

Endnotes

1. "Nothing But The Truth So Help Me God" by Linda Lange www.truthfrees.org or www.amazon.com.
2. "Forgiving From the Heart" by Linda Lange www.truthfrees.org or www.amazon.com
3. "Guilt and Condemnation" by Linda Lange www.truthfrees.org or www.amazon.com

Chapter Nine

What Was I Imagining?

What we think comes out of our imagination. Every moment we have to choose what we will allow ourselves to imagine. Will we imagine things the way God wants us to so we can do this and greater things shall we do in Jesus' name (see John 14:12), or will we imagine we cannot do that and head down disaster street with the devil's imagination for us?

Our thinking comes largely from our imagination. Because of this, we have to know what is pure imagination (fiction) and what is true (fact). We need to know how to use the imagination for things of God, and not for the enemy. We heard someone once say, "All our problems take place between our ears." Well, it's time to change that so we can get a handle on our life, our heart, and what we are thinking. The Scripture that comes up over and over in this book is Second Corinthians 10:5-6. If you haven't memorized it yet, perhaps now would be a good time.

> Casting down imaginations, and every high thing that exalteth itself against the knowledge of God, and bringing into captivity every thought to the obedience of Christ; and having in a readiness to revenge all disobedience, when your obedience is fulfilled (2 Corinthians 10:5-6).

According to the common view, God is not real and demons are a figment of the imagination. Can anyone see New Age thinking here? Innocent people may fall prey to the idea that the devil is just make believe. This is what the devil wants people to "think." As long as he stays hidden, he has power.

Before we move on, let's see what imagination actually means. In the English language, imagination is defined as the formation of a mental image or concept of what is not real or present. It is also a mental image or idea.[1] The Greek word for imagination, logismos (pronounced log-is-mos), means reasoning, conscience, imagination, or thought.[2] Imagination comes from the root word image.

The Power of Images and Words

Images can come from someone's words, thoughts, or visions. We often speak in word images when trying to get someone to understand us. Jesus used parables to bring people into understanding.

All these things spake Jesus unto the multitude in parables; and without a parable spake He not unto them (Matt. 13:34).

These images all seem to come to us through different brain waves. And as you may now know, that means they can have their origins of influence on us in the natural from things people may say or do to us, or through theta brain waves, which is where we connect spiritually as we hear from God, or from the lying devil and demons.

Words and thoughts are so important because they form images in us that cause us to respond. Whoever said that sticks and stones can break our bones, but names can never hurt us was certainly delusional. Many of the words that you hear strengthen the thoughts or images that you entertain. If a negative or doubt-filled word is what you hear mostly, then it strengthens those negative thoughts, feelings, and emotions. These are the very ingredients for sickness and disease and all manner of problems in your life.

However, as we have been teaching, if you mostly hear positive and faith-filled words, then it strengthens those thoughts, feelings, and emotions, releasing all sorts of good chemicals into your body and producing health and all manner of blessings.

The images that you decided to receive are what caused you to believe, and that is really a part of your faith. Our imaginations are fed by those things we mentally entertain in our thought life. For example, a young pregnant woman will imagine what it will be like when her baby is born.

How vital it is that we learn to be attentive to what we are thinking about! Eventually, we will begin to act out what we have seen in our imaginations. One woman said that she got an abortion because she "imagined" her child being deformed. She actually pictured trying to care for a deformed child. Gripped with fear, she terminated the birth. Where do you think that thought came from? Was that a "God thought"? Of course not. This lady entertained wrong thoughts because she didn't have the true thoughts embedded in her to make good decisions.

How do you know if you are not thinking a God thought? When you make a statement or think a thought, end it with, "in the Name of Jesus Christ." That'll help you learn quickly how much you have been listening to that other kingdom!

There is an old Indian proverb that says: "If your heart is filled with fire, lightning bolts will fly out of your mouth."

Our words are containers for life and death. And we get to choose!

> Proverbs 18:21 *Death and life are in the power of the tongue: and they that love it shall eat the fruit thereof.*

Here's another example: a man who decides to dwell on thoughts of pornography will eventually manifest somewhere, and then he will reap what he sows. It can easily lead him into adultery if he is married causing worse things to come upon him. Jesus told us if you so much as lust after a woman, you have committed spiritual adultery (see Matt. 5:28). The wages of sin is still death, according to Romans 6:23.

Even wondering why the Lord even gave us an imagination is using your imagination. Maybe God gave us an imagination like He has so that we can conceptualize His vision for us.

He used His imagination to create the world and the fullness in it, all the creatures.

> *The earth is the Lord's, and the fulness thereof; the world, and they that dwell therein* (Psalm 24:1).

Before a thing can be manifested or understood, the film screen in your "mind's eye" is where your imagination begins to form ideas and thoughts, derived from life experiences and reading material.

We would be wise to follow and allow the Gospel truth to dictate how we form our perceptions. God gives us the opportunity to speak our mind and put the Word into action, especially when we stay humble and completely submitted to Him. The Lord is then able to give us the vision (a picture in our mind) that He wants us to see, so we can believe it through faith with the Holy Word of God. It has a lot to do with what we believe God will do because nothing is impossible to Him, the "sky" isn't even the limit!

> *Faith cometh by hearing, and hearing by the word of God"* (Romans 10:17).

God uses the imaginations of people to shed light on His Word; the promises the Lord has given us are still for us today if we meet His conditions to receive them. The promises are there so we can have the faith to receive His vision for us.

We do not try to make anything happen, but by simply obeying the Lord things are going to happen. Let's say that you are thinking of going on a journey somewhere. You plan it out, and you start imagining what it would be like once you got there. And while thinking, you hear things like, "Begin praying now for safe passage, for divine appointments with people to share your faith." That person will then be open to more opportunities in the Lord than just a vacation. We have personally seen the Lord heal people and do miraculous things just because of a willingness to share His imagination with others, to share His Word. He sent His word and healed them; He will deliver you, too (see Psalm 107:20).

The Divine Ingredient

The Lord God has a magnificent imagination. No one can come close to His creativity! He had nothing to "copy" from; He had to think all this up on His own. We cannot even understand how He always was and always will be. There is no beginning and no ending.

Stop and take a look around you. Even the house you are living in was created by God because without the trees, you wouldn't have walls. Or, if you happen to be reading this in a mud hut somewhere on this planet, it's a fact that the Lord God also created the dirt used to form the mud hut, the planet, and the ever-expanding universe to hold it in.

No one could create water, only God—some have tried, but it still comes from something God made. He created every beast of the field, every living thing, the universe, everything. It's fascinating to me that all of creation was created from His Word—resonating sound. Perhaps when we realize how powerful words are, we will choose ours more wisely.

I asked my friend, Barry (a brilliant scientist who invented and patented some amazing new ways to recreate sounds) a question on his understanding of sound waves. Thinking of the Genesis account of creation, did he think that sound waves were really the smallest particle, and not the electron, the neutron, or the proton?

Barry shared that he likes to think of all electromagnetic radiation (the electromagnetic spectrum) as the divine ingredients used by God to make everything. There is such a thing as sympathetic resonance as well, wherein one vibration in a range can affect another, and so on. Remember watching an old movie where the singer hits that high note and all the glass in the room breaks? This is what we are talking about—sound that is directed to such a degree that it can change the molecules around it.

We believe, of course, that the Genesis account is true, and therefore God used words or sound waves to create the world and everything in it. Jesus even said that stones could cry out if man didn't (see Luke 19:40).

The Lord cannot lie, so that must mean there are sound waves in every created thing. Sound is the base ingredient in the compositional makeup of all things created, then. As found in Genesis, God formed man out of dust (see Genesis 2:7). The Hebrew word for dust is "aphar" which means smallest particle—it does not mean dirt, as so many people have been taught. Keep in mind the Bible was not written in English, so we may need to go back and study the original language to gather a better understanding. Also, when some theologians start to quote from the Greek, keep in mind there are a number of different versions of Greek. So we need to be good students of the Word. The Lord tells us in Proverbs 25:2 *"It is the glory of God to conceal a thing: but the honour of kings is to search out a matter."*

Since God created everything, then He surely knows how to fix everything, He has the main ingredient, His Word! He created things with His Word, from things that were not. If he can do something with nothing, just think what He could do with something! Even our messes. And know this, you have the same authority, to speak those things that are not as though they are.

Sound is powerful, and it was the sound of God's voice that put things into existence. It's that "divine ingredient" we are trying to explain here. In the Bible, some heard thunder when God spoke from Heaven saying, *"This is My beloved Son, in whom I am well pleased"* (Matthew 3:17; Mark 1:11; Luke 3:22) and others heard His voice.

The main point we're conveying here is that nothing is impossible with God, whatever the issue, be it small or large. Trust the Lord to work out the details, and thank Him and praise Him for what He has done and what He is doing, because even in your praise and thanksgiving it resonates sound that has power.

In bioresonance therapy, some researchers are working with sound waves to see if that can help possibly heal someone by reading his or her voiceprint and taking steps to adjust or help balance out the chemistry of that patient according to their findings. Machines print out your voiceprint, and researchers are hopeful that they may be able to indicate where any deficiencies may be going on in a person. However some of these modalities are still rather questionable like hair analysis. Trying to figure out if certain vitamin or minerals are not adequately helping a person stay in homeostasis.

Dr. Terri[3] found that there were too many inconsistencies with this approach, where others claim it has helped. From our perspective in ministry, most issues start in our thinking and how that dictates all our perceptions of ourselves, others, and God Himself and the world around us. We are certainly not against treatments that help relieve suffering, but often many of these approaches are only an attempt to bypass the penalty of the curse, that comes when we disobey the Word of God.

Deuteronomy 28 tells us we will be blessed and stay healthy if we obey the commandments of the Lord or if we will not obey the Lord, then every sickness and disease has a legal right to come and mess with us. Many say, "I'm being attacked of the devil." Well, then deal with that areas he has access to and he'll have to stop! The enemy can only traffic in darkness, and so whatever is in you that is NOT of the Kingdom of God, he can gain access to your life.

We have referenced several doctors here, and one thing they all agree on is that people are not taking every thought captive to the obedience of Christ, because if they were, they wouldn't be sitting in the waiting room as much.

Most all medicine and alternative medicine has some connection with occultic practices of some sort. Occultism simply means hiding the truth. An example of this would be if you were to look through a microscope and see the most beautiful star. Then you grabbed your friend standing next to you and said, "Look at this awesome star." But between the time you looked and your friend looked, a comet passed in front of the star, and the light of the real star lit up the comet, so the friend said, "Oooh, that's awesome." Occultism is representing itself as truth when it is not, it is a counterfeit. I'll say it this way—we "bypass" the truth to find another way to get the same results.

The apostle Luke was a physician and yet we do not read a single place where he treated anyone other then the most powerful treatment by using the authoritative Word of God. Again we are thankful for all those dedicated physicians who give so tirelessly of themselves to help those who are suffering.

There was a physician who said, "If Christians would practice what they believe I would see less of them in my waiting room."

That doctor, though he was not a Christian, knew this truth. He must have read the Bible along the way and saw what Christians were supposed to believe. We see just as many Christians as non-believers in doctor offices today. This ought not to be so.

But, sometimes we need some help as in the cases of accident, or some measure of time to get sanctified. It's okay to seek out professional help if you have addressed your heart issues with the Lord and He directs you to do so.

Among many counselors there is safety (Proverbs 24:6)

If you would come to us for ministry for this sort of issue, we would probably explain the Gospel to you. We would tell you how much the Lord God loves you and wants you blessed and healed. We would explain to you how your thoughts are working, find out where the point of access was, who broke your heart, and where you allowed in a spirit of envy and jealousy—which we find is often behind things like osteoporosis or where you have auto-immune issues and migraines —which we find is often caused by self-hatred and self-conflict. We would go with you before the Lord, have you turn away from those unclean things in your life, and pray the prayer of faith so that you might be healed in Jesus' name (see 2 Tim. 2:24-26).

As interesting, and potentially valid, as all these advances in medical science are, they usually come down to yet another attempt to bypass the penalty of the curse (see Deut. 28).

There is power in sound, in resonance, in our words. Proverbs 18:21 comes to mind here: *"Death and life are in the power of the tongue: and they that love it shall eat the fruit thereof."* These studies on sound waves and resonance are only another example of science proving what God has known and revealed in His Word all along: that there is power in the tongue.

So yes, we are entering into a time where scientists are starting to discover some significant information about how these things seem to be working. However, no one we know of has been able to give a definitive account yet on how this world and universe came into being except the One who created it all.

God said, let there be light, and instantly there was light (see Gen. 1:3). There was no debate about it, nor did anyone need more confirmation before the existence of light could be agreed upon.

Some time ago, NASA scientists claimed to have discovered sound waves producing musical harmonious notes emanating from black holes in space (which are known as collapsed stars).[4] Why would music be coming from black holes? Psalm 148 tells us that the Lord commands everything to worship Him, and music is a wonderful way to express that worship:

> *Praise ye the Lord. Praise ye the Lord from the heavens: praise Him in the heights. Praise ye Him, all His angels: praise ye Him, all His hosts. Praise ye Him, sun and moon: praise Him, all ye stars of light. Praise Him, ye heavens of heavens, and ye waters that be above the heavens. Let them praise the name of the Lord: for He commanded, and they were created. He hath also stablished them for ever and ever: He hath made a decree which shall not pass. Praise the Lord from the earth, ye dragons, and all deeps: fire, and hail; snow, and vapors; stormy wind fulfilling His word: mountains, and all hills; fruitful trees, and all cedars: beasts, and all cattle; creeping things, and flying fowl: kings of the earth, and all people; princes, and all judges of the earth: both young men, and maidens; old men, and children: Let them praise the name of the Lord: for His name alone is excellent; His glory is above the earth and heaven. He also exalts the horn of His people, the praise of all His saints; even of the children of Israel, a people near unto Him. Praise ye the Lord* (Psalm 148).

It's no wonder He wants us to sing praises to Him with our mouth—making a joyful noise—it could be that we are changing the atmosphere around our lives?

What is God Trying to Write on the Imaginations of His People?

The prophet Daniel wrote that in the end times, "knowledge shall be increased" (Dan. 12:4). And Acts 2:17 says that in the last days, God will pour out His Spirit: sons and daughters will prophesy; young men will see visions, and old men will dream dreams. Sounds like God will be using our imaginations here.

The Word of God says that you shall cast out devils, lay hands on the sick, and they shall recover (see Mark 16:17-18). John 14:12 tells us that we are supposed to do the works Jesus did, and even greater works. (We think many of us would be satisfied just to do the works Jesus did, never mind the greater works!) This includes things like having life more abundantly. Living as a royal priesthood of believers. Knowing we are God's chosen people.

His Word says that *"He shall supply all your need according to His riches in glory"* (see Phil. 4:19). Is anyone richer than our Father in Heaven? Truly, the Lord is never short of cash, nor is He worried about the economy at present. He sees everything, and He has a good plan to bless those who meet His conditions and worship Him in spirit and in truth. Aren't these the images Father God wants to imprint upon your imagination?

The Word of Lord says that *"all things whatsoever you shall ask in prayer believing, you shall receive"* (see Matt. 21:21-22). That's what He wants you to begin to imagine and think on. Trade in your negative, evil thoughts for holy, godly ones. Amen.

The Word says that *"all things are possible with God"* (see Matt. 19:26). So that would suggest in the strongest terms possible you need to believe before you can receive. Papa God's Word says that *by Jesus' stripes you were healed* (1 Pet. 2:24).

That's what He wants you to keep imagining until you receive the complete manifestation of your healing or restoration. Even the alternative medical community has found this to be true as it relates to cancer. They teach that if you imagine your good cells eating the bad cancer cells, the patient can actually improve in health. And as you know, Proverbs 23:7 says that as a man thinks in his heart, so is he. We're not talking about mind over matter; We're talking about getting our thoughts lined up with the Word of God so that the manifestations of our thoughts follow.

That is why Smith Wigglesworth started every meeting with "Only believe!"[5] And signs and wonders and miracles followed him.

Imagining Life Over Death

In Mark 5:35-43, a ruler of the synagogue came to ask Jesus to heal his daughter; yet, while He was on the way to minister to her, the daughter died. But that didn't stop Jesus; He went to her anyway, telling the father that she was asleep, not dead. Those around heard Him and began to laugh, so Jesus told them to leave the room. Jesus touched the child's hand and said, *"Talitha cumi,"* which means, *"Damsel, I say unto thee, arise"* (Mark 5:41). She sat up, and they gave her food to eat. When people hear about death, they will naturally imagine that nothing can be done, that it's all over now. However, here we see the Lord Jesus said to the father, **"Only believe"** (Mark 5:36).

Jesus was obviously trying to get the father of this child to imagine or believe what God could do. Could it be because Jesus knew that if this man believed that death was the permanent ending of his child's life, then that is what he was going to receive?

However, if he would dare to imagine and believe the ability and power of God to resurrect, then that's what he would receive. "Only believe" means to cast out all spirits of doubt, unbelief, and fear. "Only believe" means to believe the Word of God—not to exalt any other thought or image from any other place. It means to cast down *"every high thing that tries to exalt itself against the knowledge of God"* (2 Cor. 10:5).

If you continue in His Word, you will know the truth, and it will make you free.

We are told to capture every thought to the obedience of Christ. If you really do that, you would never be stressed and fearful and murmuring and complaining again. Just imagine that, if you will, no pun intended. Because when you trust the Lord, you will be blessed.

Martha and Mary's Discussion with Jesus

In John 11, there is this amazing story of Jesus knowing that Lazarus is dying and appearing to purposely wait until Lazarus dies before coming to his rescue.

Lazarus' sister Martha is the first to meet Jesus when He arrives:

> *Then said Martha unto Jesus, Lord, if Thou had been here, my brother would not have died. But I know, that even now, whatsoever Thou wilt ask of God, God will give it Thee. Jesus saith unto her, Thy brother shall rise again. Martha saith unto Him, I know that he shall rise again in the resurrection at the last day* (John 11:21-24).

Jesus goes on to give Martha one of the greatest theological lessons taught in the Bible: *"I am the resurrection, and the life: he that believeth in Me, though he were dead, yet shall he live"* (John 11:25).

Now catch this if you can: a few minutes later, the other sister Mary says essentially the same thing to Jesus:

> *Then when Mary was come where Jesus was, and saw Him, she fell down at His feet, saying unto Him, Lord, if Thou hadst been here, my brother would not have died* (John 11:32).

But instead of another theological lesson, this time Jesus weeps, walks over to the tomb where Lazarus rests, dead for four days, and resurrects him. Could it be that Mary had the passion and understanding to move the Lord's hand?

In Luke 10:38-42, we meet Martha and Mary for the first time. They appear to be two single sisters living together with their brother. While John's Gospel gives us the details of Lazarus' resurrection, Luke only mentions the two women:

> *Now it came to pass, as they went, that He entered into a certain village: and a certain woman named Martha received Him into her house. And she had a sister called Mary, which also sat at Jesus' feet, and heard His word. But Martha was cumbered about much serving, and came to Him, and said, Lord, dost thou not care that my sister hath left me to serve alone? Bid her therefore that she help me* (Luke 10:38-40).

Martha is very distracted: Jesus has come into her house, and she is busy serving her guests. Martha asks for someone to help her, and Jesus tells her she is worried and distracted by many things. According to cultural expectations of the day, Martha is doing exactly what she should by entertaining and feeding her guests. It was natural for her to feel that Mary should have been helping her in the kitchen. Wasn't that her proper place—helping to prepare a meal instead of sitting with the men?

But Jesus responds to Martha's complaint in Luke 10:41-42:

> *"Martha, Martha, thou art careful and troubled about many things: But one thing is needful: and Mary hath chosen that good part, which shall not be taken away from her."*

Jesus turns the traditional belief of a woman's place upside down with his assertion that women should also learn the Word of God. By placing the study of the Word of God above the socially and culturally imposed gender roles of homemaker, Jesus makes it rather clear that a woman is greater than what she does. Her worth and dignity are not just from childbearing. Her status is not dependent upon her relationship to a man or her role in society, but upon her relationship to God.

So women, as much as men, need to get their thinking about who they are in God's kingdom straightened out once and for all. Using their imaginations to see them as God sees them.

Heaven is a Real Place

We need to look past this life and see eternity so that we can keep a heavenly perspective. There are a number of Scriptures that describe the New Heavens and the New Earth. We have to use our imagination to try and see those things. It's quite exhilarating when we do since this world is only a type and shadow of things yet to come. We cannot even come close to "imagining" the spectrum of colors that will be there. That alone can keep us in a state of awe, knowing what God has in store for us.

To look past this life into eternal life is not only biblical, but brings hope and peace to our souls:

> *For the Lord Himself shall descend from heaven with a shout, with the voice of the archangel, and with the trump of God: and the dead in Christ shall rise first: then we which are alive and remain shall be caught up together with them in the clouds, to meet the Lord in the air: and so shall we ever be with the Lord. Wherefore comfort one another with these words* (1 Thessalonians 4:16-18).

Many people see Heaven as a distant place and never really wanting to think about it because it involves dying. If Christian's are afraid to die, they need revisit the scriptures. First of all, we will never die, nor taste the sting of death (see 2 Corinthians 15:55). And secondly, that is how we enter into the presence of God for all eternity. We have heard people say, "I'm not afraid to die, but the dying process." There is no difference. If you are afraid of the dying process, then you have lost faith in God to keep you during that time and giving you the strength to endure.

There was a story of two men who were put into prison for their faith. They were going to be burned at the stake the next day. That evening while talking, they had a candle burning. The one fella waved his hand over the candle and said, "I cannot do this, just that little candle flame was too painful to bare." The other fella said, "God isn't giving you faith for that candle, but He will give you faith for the burning at the stake."

Stephen was an example of this. He was being stoned to death yet looked up and saw Jesus standing in the Heavens. He had the strength and ability to endure (see Acts 7:55-60).

We encourage you to begin to imagine what Heaven will be like. It will bring you faith, strength and courage.

Casting Down Evil Imaginations

While we are still here on this planet, we need only one thing: to have an intimate relationship with our Lord. We need our imagination to do that because we cannot usually see the Lord today unless He decides to deal with us in such a direct way, as He did with Saul of Taurus in Acts 9—knocking him off his horse, appearing and speaking audibly to him. However, when we mediate on His Word and spend time with Him, He will begin to speak to us about things and situations going on in our life and around us.

While leaving a mounted police class I did with my horse the Lord stopped me and said, "I want you to go lay hands and pray for that women over there, I am going to baptize her in the Holy Ghost right now." I started to have a discussion with the Lord that I would need several hours to teach her first, but the Lord said firmly and lovingly, "Just do what I am saying."

So I asked this woman—who I hardly knew—if she wanted to be baptized in the Holy Ghost, and she said she had been praying for that a lot lately. So right then and there, she and her husband both received the baptism of the Holy Spirit. Within a few days they started seeing amazing results: people they prayed for were getting healed and getting converted—whereas before even though they were raised in the church—nothing like that seemed to happen.

There had been moments where I was shaking hands with people I just met and the Lord would tell me what to pray and they would be healed right then, even though I did not have time to teach them what the Gospel had to say about healing and miracles. The Lord can instruct us through visions and dreams to go and pray for someone, and when we follow through, we will see miraculous things happen; even people healed from accidents.

But this wouldn't happen so easily if we did not believe the Bible (John 14:12) and did not imagine how the Word of God always works. It is not our reputation at stake here. We are a friend of our Lord Jesus Christ of Nazareth.

> John 15:15 says, *"Henceforth I call you not servants; for the servant knoweth not what his lord doeth: but I have called you friends; for all things that I have heard of my Father I have made known unto you."*

It is He who gets all the glory and honor, because He gave us the knowledge of God through His sacrifice. Just allow His imagination to take over whenever possible. As you imagine good things as we are instructed to do in places like Philippians 4, you, too, will see similar results.

It is time to start imagining things as the Lord would do instead of the disasters the devil would like you to imagine.

So practice paying attention to what you are thinking about, watch carefully what you imagine, and only believe and receive what the Lord has commanded us to believe and receive. Don't meditate on a single image from the enemy. Begin to profess out loud so both invisible kingdoms hear you. Say this out loud as you read: "Papa God, I want only Your thoughts, Your words, Your dreams, and Your visions to be exalted in my life."

The Bible says that the Word is even higher than the name of Jesus!

> *I will worship toward Thy holy temple, and praise Thy name for Thy lovingkindness and for Thy truth: for Thou hast magnified Thy word above all Thy name* (Psalm 138:2).

For example, you can pray all you want and call on the name of Jesus, but if you are not obeying His commandments, if you are not "in" Him every minute of the day, it may not work so well for you.

We have received questions like, "Why did that happen to my good Christian friend?" First of all, Jesus said there is none good but one (see Matthew 10:18). Secondly, it's very clear that we can tell if someone is really rooted and grounded in love is how they deal with hardships. But people sometimes forget the Lord and His goodness, and when they come up against an obstacle they fall to pieces then they run to God. We believe that the Lord "keeps our comings and goings" when we abide in Him every single minute of the day so that when something happens, we have what we need to remain in faith, calm and peace. Keeping God on our mind 24/7 is assurance for our protection. That is what the Bible says. Test it for yourself. It is scriptural to believe God and breath Him in and out every single minute. Otherwise God wouldn't have instructed us to do so.

In Him we live and move and have our being (Acts 17:28).

Psalm 121:5 *The Lord is thy keeper: the Lord is thy shade upon thy right hand.*

Too many wait for disaster to happen to start praying. What if we prayed continually? What does the scriptures say? To pray without ceasing (see 1 Thess. 5:17). That means to continually "know" that God is with you. That you include Him in every area of your life. That you acknowledge Him in all your ways. This will protect you.

Now it's always good to run to God when things happen. Sometimes it takes things to happen to get us to run to Him. But "what if" we were always WITH Him? What if we were always IN Him? What if our mind was always on Him? There would be peace in our mind our spirit. Isn't that what we all want anyway?

You are going to have to cast down and not exalt words and images in your mind's eye that try to be above the Word of God.

When the devil comes and tells you that you are going to get sick and die, you cannot exalt that word; instead, you must speak out loud when possible and declare the Word of God, which says, in Psalm 118:17, *"I shall not die, but live, and declare the works of the Lord."*

This is the time to tell the devil and his demons to shut up and go in Jesus' name. Don't keep exalting those evil spirits' assignments and images for you, by believing and putting its evil power and authority above the Word of God.

Take the devil's words, cast them down, and trample all over them; bring your thoughts into captivity by making the devil's words obedient to Christ.

Begin to speak over your life. Say something like this: *"Devil, you are the father of lies, and I refuse to hear anything you say. Get out of here and take your stinkin' thinkin' with you. Let me remind you where you are spending eternity, devil, and all you evil spirits."*

This way you are declaring and exalting the Word of God and not receiving one image from the enemy. Try it for a day and see how much you get blessed.

Yes, you can speak to the Devil, Jesus did when He was tempted at the end of his 40 day fast. He spoke the Word! But don't have a conversation with him like Eve did, and you know how that turned out. Proclaim the truth. Stand on the word.

When the devil tries to bring a thought or image into your mind, just say, *"I will not receive that,"* and begin instead to declare the Word of God. Remember, we walk by faith, not by how things may look at the moment. So how do you know what is a "devil" thought? In case you don't know this answer, it's anything that causes you to doubt God's love, His Word, and His design for your life. It's anything that promotes fear, anxiety, and stress, or robs you of your peace. That is why it's so important to read the Word for yourself so that it is written on your heart and mind so that you don't sin against Him (see Ps. 119:11). Some people are sinning against God and don't even know it. Their thoughts are not lined up with God's thoughts. we are only trying to help you think like God thinks. When you do that, you will be blessed.

Keep in mind, however, if you have been struggling with that same thought for a long period of time, there may be more going on that just casting down that imagination. It could be you have given that thought a "right" to torment you. How? If there is any unforgiveness or bitterness in your heart concerning that "thought" it leaves the door wide open. So be sure to address any individuals who are connected to that thought, and apply forgiveness. Then when that thought comes up, if it does, you are able to defeat it by replacing it with the Word of God.

There is also a balance here too. Because scriptures say to "agree with your adversary quickly" (see Matthew 5:25). Sometimes when we get a thought or image there is some truth to it. We may need to have a little talk with the Lord about it. The devil cannot tell the truth, but he can twist the truth. Guilt comes when we haven't dealt with some sin in our heart (See Leviticus 5:5). Guilt is the enemy's way to bring you under condemnation.

Mixed with Faith

Whatever image you receive and believe will eventually become mixed with your faith, and that is what you are going to have. That is the simplest way we know how to explain it.

Read your Bible and you will find out what the Word of God says God's vision is for you. Start to declare God's vision out loud. Immediately cast down from your mind any thoughts that are contrary to what God has said, boldly declare the Gospel truth, and speak blessings instead of curses. When you complain about someone you are supposed to love, you are bringing curses into your life. If that person is a born-again believer, you better not be tearing them down. Jesus said that person is His friend.

> *Henceforth I call you not servants; for the servant knoweth not what his lord doeth: but I have called you friends; for all things that I have heard of My Father I have made known unto you* (John 15:15).

Do you really want to speak against someone who Jesus says is His friend?

As you keep spending time with Him, you will begin receiving revelation that will change your life. The revelation may come by way of the Word of God, a dream, vision, or a prophetic word. The imagination or the vision that you receive is the reality that you will get.

There was a pastor who said that after he gave a message, a woman came up and told him she had a word from God that he was going to be in a terrible accident and maybe die. This pastor immediately rebuked the devil in her. He realized divination and occultism were trying to kill him. If he had received that into his spirit, he might have experienced that evil premonition. Praise God, he knew how to fight back with the Word of truth when he heard the devil's lies.

How do we know this wasn't from God? Because the Word says so: Psalm 118:17 says, *we are to live and not die and proclaim the goodness of the Lord.*

If you accept the devil's imagination of the things he is saying to you and accusing you of, then you will receive the devil's results.

Those thoughts of failure are going to begin to manifest in you and around you. These things come from an unloving spirit, and from generational familiar spirits of poverty, self-pity, and shame. It's a form of idolatry and pride, a mind-set that causes you to think that you will never amount to anything, so you are not able to get employment or move in the power of God. You'll be constantly irritable, causing those around you to be affected by spirits of heaviness, fear, control, and unloving spirits. The devil and his entire evil spirit army want you to exalt these images above the Word of God so they can defeat you before you can do any good here. He wants to preoccupy you so you forget about bringing Heaven to earth.

The Lord's prayer says, *"Thy will be done in earth, as it is in heaven,"* but will not happen if you do not get with God's program for your life (Matt. 6:10).

The devil sends his thoughts to us through theta brain waves trying to get you to accept it into your imagination. Truly it is the devil who imagines you sick, defeated, diseased, and impoverished; he tries to get you to accept what he is imagining for you, by your faith.

Remember, whatever you believe, let it be done unto you, whether good or bad. And when you feel fear, it's not you; it's a devil trying to manifest his character through you to try and destroy your faith. You are a vessel—the Bible says you are the Temple of the Lord, if you have received Him by faith—and whatever you agree with in thought, will fill your vessel. The only thing the devil can use to gain access to your vessel is fear. And if he can get you to agree with him in your thinking, then you are snared (see 2 Timothy 2:23).

Faith works both ways. The atheist has to have much more faith to believe the lie than the born-again believer does to believe the truth. Why should a born-again believer put any faith in the devil's lies?

The devil would like you to believe he has the clear edge, but the battle was finished at the cross, and Jesus took the keys to this world back from the devil at His resurrection. We still have to appropriate what was done by believing and receiving, and obeying the Lord's commandments.

Since the devil lost at the cross, his purpose now is to get you to doubt what took place. He used the same tactic on Adam and Eve by gaining access to their imagination. That way he can play out his evil purposes and get you to receive images of spirits of doubt, fear, and unbelief, which will cause you to reject Papa God's Word.

When the serpent spoke to Eve in the Garden of Eden, he was trying to get her to receive his imagination for her. His purpose in the Garden was to get the same vision of disobedience and destruction that got him kicked out of Heaven to come into the lives of Adam and Eve. Once they put their faith in the devil through the serpent, which was his image, all hell broke loose, so to speak.

Immediately Adam and Eve received the results. Their spiritual eyes were opened, and they began experiencing things like shame and fear, which they did not even know existed before they sinned (see Gen. 3:1-10).

Had Adam and Eve continued in God's vision and image for them, things would have turned out quite differently; they would have received the Word's result as it was intended. Instead, they got kicked out of paradise, just like the devil who got kicked out of Heaven, because of the image that was imprinted on their thoughts.

Believing any image or vision the devil gives you jeopardizes your position (remember occultism wants you to believe a counterfeit) and you will lose your God-given power—that means your own thoughts and words will work against you instead of for you. You will not be in homeostasis in your body or circumstances; you will lose your peace.

One third of the angels were fooled by believing Satan's image or vision for them, a vision of overthrowing Papa God. How the Holy Spirit must have grieved to see them fall from their positions of power and authority. As evil spirits, they cannot fulfill their need to express themselves unless they are allowed to manifest through you because they have no bodies of their own. Thus, evil spirits try to steal your power by getting you to receive their evil vision of defeat and failure.

The devil's ultimate goal is to get a person to accept his spirit of fear and to doubt the Word of God.

He is called the great deceiver for a reason—because he is great at deceiving people.

In Genesis 3:4-5, Satan deceived Eve into accepting an image that is contrary to God's Word. She accepted a spirit of doubt, which caused her to become insecure. Somehow, the serpent insinuated that God was holding out on her:

And the serpent said unto the woman, Ye shall not surely die: For God doth know that in the day ye eat thereof, then your eyes shall be opened, and ye shall be as gods, knowing good and evil (Genesis 3:4-5).

Unfortunately, all of us have had to live with the consequences of that wrong decision. Praise the Lord for sending Jesus to provide us with a way out of this mess. We cannot afford to let the devil have any access to our imagination. We are going to have to cast out every lie and replace it with the Gospel truth. Test all the spirits; test all your thoughts against the knowledge of God's Word. Maintain a heavenly perception; lift up those arms and hands and give a victory shout of holy joy! After all, when you study the whole Bible, you see that we win in the end. Hallelujah!

Miracles

It is natural to think of death as a permanent end of life, but God's Word says that we should raise the dead (see Matt. 10:7-8). I experienced such a miracle. While visiting Pleasant Valley Church in Thomaston Georgia, my heart stopped. My good friend, Pastor Henry Wright cast out the spirit of death and I was revived. Not only that, but I was healthier than before that happened. Other ailments I had disappeared. (You can read about it in "Nothing is Impossible" —it's my personal story of being raised from the dead.)

> *And as ye go, preach, saying, the kingdom of heaven is at hand. Heal the sick, cleanse the lepers, raise the dead, cast out devils: freely ye have received, freely give* (Matthew 10:7-8).

Pastor Henry had a vision that he was able to cast out a spirit of death and raise the dead and because of that belief, he was able to. Just think if he didn't this book would not have been written and the many truths and freedom you are already realizing may never have come to pass.

But, it all depends on which vision we believe. When we choose to trust the Lord, we will see miracles—even when they did not have faith for it.

Our faith trumps anyone's unbelief. Remember the story of the men who let their sick friend down through the roof? (See Mark 2.) It was their faith—not the sick person's faith—that made him whole!

Then we read in Matthew 13:57-58 *"And they were offended in him. But Jesus said unto them, A prophet is not without honour, save in his own country, and in his own house. And he did not many mighty works there because of their unbelief."*

What is this saying? It is saying they didn't believe who Jesus was. He was "that local carpenter man" so their attitude of who Jesus was meant they simply did not bring their sick out to him. So only a few sick people were healed there. There was not one case of someone not being healed because they simply did not have enough faith to be healed, as is so often taught in many churches. The fact is, everyone He prayed for was healed, even in the garden where he was betrayed when one of Jesus' followers cut off the ear of the servant of the high priest. Jesus put that man's ear back on his head and healed him before he was taken to a mock trail and crucified.

Jesus healed everyone who came to Him, and He is the same today. If you are willing to meet the conditions according to the Bible you will be healed, you will be restored, because nothing is impossible with God. Your job is to keep the commandments, by loving the Lord God with all your heart, soul, mind, and strength, and love others as you love yourself.

Twenty-three times in the Bible it states that Jesus "healed them all," or that he "healed everyone." It was not because their unbelief hindered or limited His powers in any way possible—that just did not happen. It was simply that He did not bring those who were sick to Him because they didn't believe who He was.

We encourage you to study this for yourself. Don't take our word for it, take "the" Word for it. We have conveniently listed Scriptures that support this truth. Please take the time to read them for yourself

Matthew 4:23; 8:14; 9:35; 11:5; 12:15; 14:14; 35:36; 15:30; 19:2; 21:14; Mark 1:32; 3:10; 6:5; Luke 4:40; 5:15-17; 17; 6:17; 7:21-23; 9:11; 7:17; Acts 10:38

When we study the lives of God's people in the Bible and in recent times, we see that those who manifest God's power have always disciplined themselves to cast down imaginations that exalt themselves against the Word of God. The Word of God is the final authority all the time. Papa God and we are in charge here, not the devil.

The devil continually tries to get his ungodly images to be exalted above the Word of God. The moment you bite into his bait, he starts to reel you in. Then your imagination gets empowered by your faith in the wrong things, which can then become a reality. The word exalt means to magnify, to make something bigger than it is. Too many Christians magnify the devil's thoughts of defeat, rather than exalting the Word of God. Come on, it's true, isn't it?

The first place it all starts is in your mind. Every day there is a battle being fought for your imagination, and some people seem to overlook that fact. Each moment you get to decide if you will think like the Lord or think like the devil. You have to choose; no one can choose for you.

Beloved, believe not every spirit, but try the spirits whether they are of God: because many false prophets are gone out into the world. Hereby know ye the Spirit of God: every spirit that confesseth that Jesus Christ is come in the flesh is of God: and every spirit that confesseth not that Jesus Christ is come in the flesh is not of God: and this is that spirit of antichrist, whereof ye have heard that it should come; and even now already is it in the world (1 John 4:1-3).

Casting down imaginations involves refusing to accept the devil's thoughts for you. It's really up to you; only you can be victorious over the enemy. Jesus is not going to make you into a robot to ensure that you make the right choices.

Practical Application

Each of us knows there are certain thoughts that we must no longer receive or entertain in our minds. We have already seen the devastation from them. So why hold on to them any longer? Entertaining those stinking, evil thoughts is like opening the front door of your holy temple and saying, "Come on in and wreak havoc in me. Here are my life savings: you want them? Here are my dreams and visions: you want to destroy them?"

Watch for words and phrases such as:

- You always
- I can't
- It's impossible
- I hope not
- I can
- It won't
- I am not able
- I don't think so
- I do not know
- Nothing ever works out right for me
- Maybe if

- Why can't I ever
- It will never work out in the end

These thoughts and feelings and words will not help you do what Jesus did, or aspire to do greater things in His name, will they?

Stop yourself from even using these words that are thoughts from the enemy for your failure. Today is the day the devil did not make. It is time you cast those old programs out. Delete them. When in doubt, cast it out.

Don't accept it, and stop entertaining it! It is a thing of the past; do not go back to it like a dog who revisits his vomit (see Prov. 26:11; 1 Pet. 2:22).

Instead, put on the sacrifice of praise. Think about what the Word of God says about you and your circumstances.

> *Rejoice in the Lord always: and again I say, Rejoice. Let your moderation be known unto all men. The Lord is at hand. Be careful for nothing; but in every thing by prayer and supplication with thanksgiving let your requests be made known unto God. And the peace of God, which passeth all understanding, shall keep your hearts and minds through Christ Jesus. Finally, brethren, whatsoever things are true, whatsoever things are honest, whatsoever things are just, whatsoever things are pure, whatsoever things are lovely, whatsoever things are of good report; if there be any virtue, and if there be any praise, think on these things* (Philippians 4:4-8).

Painting by Caspar McCloud

This picture depicts things that may be going on in our thoughts and imaginations. Decide today what you will think on.

Endnotes

1. Dakes Bible, footnotes Matthew 9:30.

2. www.bibleapps.com

3. Dr. Teresa Allen, DO, Internal Medicine Physician: 7047 Halcyon Park Dr., The Fit Centre, Montgomery, Alabama, 36117.

4. "Black Hole Sound Waves," NASA Science News, http://science.nasa.gov/science-news/science-at-nasa/2003/09sep_blackholesounds/.

5. Smith Wigglesworth, Greater Works: Experiencing God's Power (New Kensington, PA: Whitaker House, 2000).

Chapter Ten

HOW A BROKEN HEART CAN CAUSE DISEASE

Everyone has had hurt feelings from time to time in this world. No matter who you are, young or old, rich or poor, it is pretty hard to avoid as we maneuver through this life.

Linda was talking to someone who obviously had a broken heart from the things he was sharing with her. However, when she suggested he might have a broken heart, he said quickly, "No, I don't have a broken heart; I'm not like a woman." Then she began to explain what a broken heart really was, "It's when you have been hurt by someone and it still hurts deep inside when you think about it. It's a result from a broken relationship where someone has abandoned you or seemingly stopped loving you. All these factors contribute to produce a broken heart." He paused for a moment and then said, "Perhaps I do have a broken heart after all."

Recognizing something is the first step toward dealing with it. You will then be in a position to resolve it because, as Jesus Himself said, if we ask, knock, and seek, we shall find the answer:

For every one that asketh receiveth; and he that seeketh findeth; and to him that knocketh it shall be opened (Luke 11:10).

When we discover this for ourselves and we allow the Lord Jesus to come heal our broken heart, we are actually preventing and eradicating disease. However, if the broken heart and spirit of unforgiveness remain for a long period of time, they can cause complications in your health today or years from now, if left unattended.

We are going to talk about our spirit, soul, mind, and body and how a broken heart contributes to biological diseases and manifestations. Also, how the reverse of that is true when we apply the Word of God to our broken heart. We're going to teach you how to appropriate John 14:12 into your lives and ministries. The works He did and even greater works shall we do because He went to the Father for us.

Allergies

We have discovered that the Lord did not design us to have allergies. Take, for example, the case of a small child who is watching a trainer work his horses. They gallop past the child who is standing next to the fence in a corral, throwing dust and dirt into the air and into the child's eyes. The child begins to cry out, suddenly unable to see properly.

He grows up, and whenever he is near a horse, he begins to have an allergic reaction. Allergies are simply a hypersensitive reaction to any substance. A traumatic event suffered as a child triggered great fear; it is a spirit of fear that is behind all allergies. That spirit of fear programmed the memory of events now long forgotten, warning that horses will cause an allergy attack if you get too near them.

Another example would be a young child whose family broke up and who was forced to live with a foster family who had a rose garden. As an adult, whenever she is near the smell of roses, she begins to get a runny nose and watery eyes. Those old programs would be activated, and even though many years have passed, the mind recalls and associates the smell of roses with the trauma that was never properly dealt with. The end result is an allergy attack.

All allergies deal with a substance that induces some state of sensitivity when the substance comes into contact with the body's tissues or memories of it. It is an acquired, abnormal response, and that means the immune system has been tampered with. God did not design you to have allergies. Allergies are something that an invisible, intelligent kingdom has brought to mankind. Once these adults have been properly ministered to, the allergies just vanish; the immune system functions as it was designed to do. Please keep in mind that there are also generational issues that need to be addressed. Allergies can be passed on like any other disease or condition. The sins of the father are being passed on to the third and fourth generations of those who do not love and obey the Lord and His commandments.

For those with allergies, these hypersensitive reactions which do not affect most people can be triggered by a wrong thought or by some environmental factors. There are people who are very affected by such things as certain foods, pollens, molds, dust, and microorganisms. Their bodies, which have a compromised immune system, will produce a substance called cortisol to help suppress the inflammatory response to a known allergy attack. Cortisol is a steroid hormone secreted by the adrenal cortex. When that happens over the long term, your body's natural defenses begin to break down.

The white corpuscles, macrophages, and killer cells are bringing death to cells your body needs to stay healthy. When you stop participating with the spirit of fear that is often behind the allergies, you will most likely be healed.

There was a woman who had allergic reactions every time she mowed her lawn. After ministry, she went out to mow her lawn again and realized she wasn't having allergic symptoms. What happened? Did the grass suddenly get nonallergenic, or did she apply the Word to her life?

> *Then said Jesus to those Jews which believed on Him, If ye continue in My word, then are ye My disciples indeed; and ye shall know the truth, and the truth shall make you free* (John 8:31-32).

Here are some questions to ponder. Is there anything in your life that you are avoiding because of some discomfort? Was there a trauma in your life around the time you started having allergies? Are there blacked-out times in your life where you simply cannot bring up memories? Do you have a hard time with certain people because they remind you of your mother or father? Do you have a hard time with confrontations? Do you have fear?

These questions will help you see what you need to deal with. Ask God to heal your broken heart in each and every situation. However, there is a main factor to realize, and that is we need to forgive everyone in these circumstances. A broken heart can only come from another individual. So that individual needs to be forgiven so God then is able to heal your heart. If you don't, the enemy can come and mess with you. There has to be a reason he has access, as Proverbs 26:2 says—the curse cannot come without a cause.

The enemy messed with the lady with grass allergies because she had fear and unforgiveness in her heart. When we deal with those things, applying what God has said, we will come out of that fiery trial without any residue. Look at those Hebrew children who were thrown in the fiery furnace, yet they weren't burnt at all. They didn't even smell like smoke! All residue of that traumatic event was gone. We believe that if they hadn't believed God, things would have come out differently. Perhaps they would have gotten out of the fiery furnace—but would have a fear of fireplaces. Whatever you are allergic to, or running from, you need to deal with the trauma because you will then find your freedom.

Now the Bible tells us it's the honor of kings to search out a matter.

> *It is the glory of God to conceal a thing: but the honour of kings is to search out a matter* (Proverbs 25:2).

> *If any of you lack wisdom, let him ask of God, that giveth to all men liberally, and upbraideth not; and it shall be given him* (James 1:5).

He gives you what you ask for. How do we know? Because that is what He said He would do. If you ask for discernment, He will give discernment. If you ask for wisdom, He will give wisdom. If you ask for healing, He will give you healing.

> *Ask, and it shall be given you; seek, and ye shall find; knock, and it shall be opened unto you: for every one that asketh receiveth; and he that seeketh find-*

eth; and to him that knocketh it shall be opened. Or what man is there of you, whom if his son ask bread, will he give him a stone? Or if he ask a fish, will he give him a serpent? If ye then, being evil, know how to give good gifts unto your children, how much more shall your Father which is in heaven give good things to them that ask Him? (Matthew 7:7-11)

Many people are perishing from lack of knowledge. From reading this book so far, you now understand that there is a real, invisible, evil kingdom that is out to steal, kill, and destroy. But that evil kingdom cannot touch you unless you give it permission by disobeying the commandments of the Lord. We could not see germs until Louis Pasteur put them under a microscope in the late 1800s, yet the Bible describes germs and how to protect ourselves from them in the Old Testament. What you cannot see can hurt you. But God sees it all, and when we trust and obey the Word, those germs have no leg to stand on!

There are so many flu viruses, we can't keep up, that is causing so much fear in people's hearts that there are now more people with mental illness coming into the emergency rooms than those with injuries! Just follow the money trail. Do you see how many people are waiting in lines to get the flu shot? They run there in droves because of fear. Fear is making the industry rich. Perhaps in some cases it helps, but if you want to boost your immune system, get a shot of truth, and get your broken heart healed.

The medical community is actually linking flu shots from ten years ago with health issues today; some fillers used in flu shots are better used for motorcar engines[1] for example. In addition to mercury, flu vaccines also contain other toxic or hazardous ingredients like Aluminum—a neurotoxin that has been linked to Alzheimer's disease, Triton X-100—a detergent, Phenol (carbolic acid), Ethylene glycol (antifreeze), Betapropiolactone—a disinfectant, Nonoxynol—used to kill or stop growth of STDs, Octoxinol 9—a vaginal spermicide, and Sodium phosphate. We have to ask, "What were they thinking?"

Why would you want to inject that into your body? Perhaps you never knew this? Perhaps no one disclosed the side effects? We need "all" the truth when making decisions for ourselves and our families. We just can't go around trusting people who don't have our best interests in mind. But we can trust God because He does have our good in mind. The enemy is a real foe and will use anything to cause you to faint in your mind and lose your faith in God.

Abide in Him

But what does God say about all this? Psalm 91:10 says, *"There shall no evil befall thee, neither shall any plague come nigh thy dwelling."*

What is the condition for that? It's found at the beginning of that verse:

> *He that dwelleth in the secret place of the most High shall abide under the shadow of the Almighty. I will say of the Lord, He is my refuge and my fortress: my God; in Him will I trust* (Psalm 91:1-2).

You must trust and believe with your whole heart. How do we do that? By dwelling in Him continually. We dwell "in" Him by trusting Him. We dwell "in" Him by talking to Him, by acknowledging Him in every step we take. We dwell "in" Him by including Him in every are of your life; having a daily intimate relationship with Him. We need to know Him through and through; and speak faith out of our mouth.

Have you ever wondered why Christians have hardships? The truth is, things happen, it's just how a person handles it will be the outcome. Will they continue in faith or fall to pieces. That will determine how much you have been dwelling "in" Him. When we "stay" in that place and a hard thing comes our way, we will stand and not be moved.

Did you know that you can have a broken heart towards God? When you have prayed about something and it hasn't come to pass, it can cause a broken heart if you don't know the Father's heart about it. It can turn into thinking God doesn't want you well. Or God doesn't love you. Or God is too busy elsewhere. This has to be resolved now. Take a moment, if this is you, and ask the Lord to forgive you for accusing Him of not loving you like you need to be loved. This is where many of you are stuck. By repenting and receiving forgiveness, you will be restored. You will, once again, sense His love and presence. You will be able to believe again. But you have to get rid of all blame and anger with your loving Heavenly Father.

We've received calls from Christian's with a rap sheet of illnesses and issues that they want us to help them unravel. The truth is, if we learned how much God loved us in the first place and received His love, we wouldn't be in the mess we are in today. Scripture says that hearts are going to grow cold in the latter days. Why? Because we are going to be lovers of ourselves more than lovers of God. Well, what do you see today? All sorts of auto-immune diseases and sicknesses. New ones are being seen every day. It's because hearts of people are broken! They don't know how to repair it. They don't know Jesus is the healer of a broken heart. They don't realize forgiveness is key. They are loving themselves selfishly. Scriptures say we are to love ourselves, but not the self-interest kind of love, but love ourselves SO THAT WE CAN LOVE OTHERS. And that love shown to one another demonstrates that we are Children of God, because of our love one for another (see 1 John 4:7).

Can you see how this world is today? If we don't love one another, hate is at the door. Remember what we said earlier, you will do one or the other at all times, either love or have fear, and fear is behind hate. That is why this world is what it is today. Behind every issue is not loving one another; envy and jealousy, anger, hate, bitterness, unforgiveness, retaliation, control, manipulation, coveteousness, strive, vanity, etc., are all resulting in not loving one another.

> *This know also, that in the last days perilous times shall come. For men shall be lovers of their own selves, covetous, boasters, proud, blasphemers, disobedient to parents, unthankful, unholy, Without natural affection, trucebreakers, false accusers, incontinent, fierce, despisers of those that are good, Traitors, heady, highminded, lovers of pleasures more than lovers of God; Having a form of godliness, but denying the power thereof: from such turn away* (2 Timothy 3:1-5).

The Bible teaches us that Satan and his army are the source of all sickness and diseases; they are behind most problems in this world. But the Lord has given us power over all of them:

Behold, I give unto you power to tread on serpents and scorpions, and over all the power of the enemy: and nothing shall by any means hurt you. Notwithstanding in this rejoice not, that the spirits are subject unto you; but rather rejoice, because your names are written in heaven (Luke 10:19-20).

You give permission on some level when you or someone in your generations listen and submit to that other kingdom. We have to believe we have power to overcome, and it is done through our faith. We must believe God and all He has said to defeat the wicked one. When our hearts are clean before the Lord, the enemy has no leg to stand on and he has to go away. We give the devil permission to send his minions into our lives when we harbor unforgiveness, etc., in our lives. We must repent for what is not of God. Because anything that is in us that is not of God gives the enemy permission to be there. There is a quote, "The enemy can traffic in darkness." We have to ask the Lord to show us any darkness in our hearts so we can be restored.

We are then invited by the Lord to ask and receive anything we want, not just what we need. No matter what you have been taught in church, on television, or from the neighbor next door—what does the Bible really say about it?

If ye abide in Me, and My words abide in you, ye shall ask what ye will, and it shall be done unto you (John 15:7).

And in that day ye shall ask Me nothing. Verily, verily, I say unto you, Whatsoever ye shall ask the Father in My name, He will give it you (John 16:23).

And Jesus answering saith unto them, Have faith in God. For verily I say unto you, That whosoever shall say unto this mountain, Be thou removed, and be thou cast into the sea; and shall not doubt in his heart, but shall believe that those things which he saith shall come to pass; he shall have whatsoever he saith. Therefore I say unto you, What things soever ye desire, when ye pray, believe that ye receive them, and ye shall have them (Mark 11:22-24).

What more proof do we need? Do we need to see someone raised from the dead before we believe the Lord?

In other words, when we obey the Lord, we can ask anything we can believe for and receive the blessing—for our physical and health needs, and for our financial, business, and spiritual needs. They are all covered when we obey and ask in Jesus Christ of Nazareth's name.

The old Hymn says it right, "Trust and obey, for there's no other way to be happy in Jesus, but to trust and obey."

When David went up against the giant Goliath with a slingshot and a few stones, he went in faith. He went believing that God was going to deliver the Philistine into his hand (see 1 Sam. 17:44-49). He spoke with authority about how he was going to do it too. He knew it wasn't the slingshot and stones that were going to kill the Philistine because David gave all credit to God by: "This day will the Lord deliver you into mine hand" (1 Sam. 17:46). He had spent so much time knowing God's thoughts and heart he didn't have to stop and wonder if God would help him. He knew it. He had no doubt and acted accordingly. He obeyed the Word of God. And believing is being obedient.

Then said they unto him, What shall we do, that we might work the works of God? Jesus answered and said unto them, This is the work of God, that ye believe on him whom he hath sent (John 6:28-29)

In Daniel chapter 3, Shadrach, Meshach, and Abednego had that kind of faith. King Nebuchadnezzar commanded them to bow down to his idol, but they refused! All three of these gentlemen told the king that they believed that their Lord the living God would deliver them out of certain death from the fiery furnace. They then added that even if He did not, they still wouldn't bow down to any silly idols, but only trust in the true living God.

The fire was so hot that the men who threw them in the furnace died on the spot. But the Lord honored their faith that day, and they walked out of a fiery furnace without so much as a hair on their head singed or even the smell of smoke on them.

Maybe it is time to ask yourselves what idols you have been bowing down to. God will not share you with the devil and his demonic army.

God's promises are unlimited, so don't put limits on what the Lord can and cannot do. He is God almighty, and He loves you and wants the best for you all the time because He is a good Father to all His children.

Ask Rightly

Our faith is often challenged when we ask and do not receive. Why does that happen? Scripture gives at least three possible reasons: because of sin, because we asked for something that is out of God's plan, and to bring glory to God.

Perhaps you say, "I do ask, but He doesn't seem to answer me." Then let's pose another question. Have you met the conditions for "receiving" what you ask for?

Both Isaiah 59:1-2 and Jeremiah 5:25 indicate that we prevent good things from happening to us.

> *Behold, the Lord's hand is not shortened, that it cannot save; neither His ear heavy, that it cannot hear: but your iniquities have separated between you and your God, and your sins have hid His face from you, that He will not hear* (Isaiah 59:1-2).

> *Your iniquities have turned away these things, and your sins have withholden good things from you* (Jeremiah 5:25).

Turn away from those things that are hindering you from receiving blessings. The Bible says we are to seek first the Kingdom of God and His righteousness (see Matt. 6:33). Many aren't seeking God as Father, but are seeking Him to get stuff. This isn't to bring you under guilt or condemnation, but to get you to see where your heart is. The Lord wants to give you good things, but He is a holy God. How can He bless you when you are participating with unholiness? 2 Peter says it so clearly:

> *Grace and peace be multiplied unto you through the knowledge of God, and of Jesus our Lord, according as His divine power hath given unto us all things that pertain unto life and godliness, through the knowledge of Him that hath called us to glory and virtue: whereby are given unto us exceeding great and precious promises: that by these ye might be partakers of the divine nature, having escaped the corruption that is in the world through lust. And beside this, giving all diligence, add to your faith virtue; and to virtue knowledge; and to knowledge temperance; and to temperance patience; and to patience godliness; and to godliness brotherly kindness; and to brotherly kindness charity. For if these things be in you, and abound, they make you that ye shall neither be barren nor unfruitful in the knowledge of our Lord Jesus Christ* (2 Peter 1:2-8).

The second reason is that we ask outside of God's better plan for us—we are asking "amiss." Sometimes we simply aren't asking according to His will. Perhaps we are asking for selfish gain and pleasures according to our lustful desires. See, when we "abide" in Christ and know His heart and mind, we will ask according to what is best for us. We all need to keep a check and balance on our motives; let us pray we always approach the throne of God with the right motives from a right heart. First John 5:14 says, *"And this is the confidence that we have in Him, that, if we ask any thing according to His will, He heareth us."* However, James 4:3 says, *"Ye ask, and receive not, because ye ask amiss, that ye may consume it upon your lusts."* If you are asking in faith and not receiving, perhaps you are not praying according to God's plan.

That leads us to a third reason: To bring glory to God. Did you know that it's not necessarily a mistake when we go through hard times? God allows things to come into our lives to help us grow up in our faith. If He led Jesus by the Spirit into the wilderness (see Mark 1:12-13), why wouldn't He lead us into hardships, too? We read that angels ministered to Him when He was led by the Spirit into the wilderness to be tempted by the devil. That gives us hope that we aren't alone in these hard times, that we have ministering angels!

> *And immediately the spirit driveth Him into the wilderness. And He was there in the wilderness forty days, tempted of Satan; and was with the wild beasts; and the angels ministered unto Him* (Mark 1:12-13).

Jesus was victorious. He didn't fall into temptation. He proved His love for His Father in Heaven. He trusted His Father God with His life.

Let's take at look at the Israelites. They were tested in the wilderness, too. But their outcome was quite different. Why? Because they didn't obey the commandments. They complained, murmured, and didn't trust God to deliver. Their hearts were far from Him.

> *And thou shalt remember all the way which the Lord thy God led thee these forty years in the wilderness, to humble thee, and to prove thee, to know what was in thine heart, whether thou wouldest keep His commandments, or no* (Deuteronomy 8:2).

If we really knew God, we would gladly do what He said without question! Because we would know that God loves us and only wants what is best for us.

A person who can trust God in the hardest times—without fear, worry, frustration, complaining, and murmuring—is a person who truly knows Him personally. A person who knows God can trust Him and every Word He has said.

Deuteronomy 8 goes on to say that He allowed them to be hungry so they would understand it's not about "food" or "clothing" but His faithfulness toward them; to take care of them in every way needed.

> *And He humbled thee, and suffered thee to hunger, and fed thee with manna, which thou knewest not, neither did thy fathers know; that He might make thee know that man doth not live by bread only, but by every word that proceedeth out of the mouth of the Lord doth man live. Thy raiment waxed not old upon thee, neither did thy foot swell, these forty years* (Deuteronomy 8:3-4).

If there are conditions to His forgiving us, why wouldn't there be conditions about "receiving" from Him?

> *But if ye forgive not men their trespasses, neither will your Father forgive your trespasses* (Matthew 6:15).

We encourage you to stop for a moment and take an inventory of your own heart and thoughts about this. Are you seeking God with your whole heart? Do you find yourself lacking in faith? Do you still struggle with doubt and unbelief? What is your motives when you pray? Then talk to the Lord right now. Tell Him all that is in your heart. Remember the man who cried out to Jesus of Nazareth, "Lord, help me in my unbelief."

> *And straightway the father of the child cried out, and said with tears, Lord, I believe; help Thou mine unbelief* (Mark 9:24).

Ask Him to help you learn to seek Him every single day for who He is, not what He can give. Ask Him to help you learn to pray according to His heart. It is so important to get our thinking right! That is what this book is all about. When we get our thoughts lined up with God's thoughts, we will ask for the right things, and we will begin seeing amazing things happen in our lives!

Effects of a Broken Heart

The Holy Spirit will teach us that when we allow ourselves to entertain ungodly thoughts we compromise our immune system.

Someone with a broken heart has been injured emotionally and spiritually by someone who was supposed to love them and did not. When some people become victimized, you will find a spirit of fear has joined them, which didn't come from God (see 2 Tim. 1:7).

The Bible shows us that it's a broken heart that compromises your immune system. The Lord has healed a number of broken hearts in this ministry, including ours. Why not you? If the Lord is no respecter of persons, He wants to heal your broken heart, too. Maybe He can't right now because you are being destroyed from lack of knowledge. The Lord is not going to violate who He is, let you keep your sin issues, and then bless you in them. He is a Holy God and changes not.

We want to explore why things are not working out as the Bible says they should: why your prayers are not being answered; why you have been going to church year after year and confessing the promises of God, and it's not working for you; why you keep giving more seed faith and it's not growing for you; why you can't get out of debt; why you are still taking medicine and having panic attacks; why you can't get healed.

You may have read many books and gone to all those seminars, and you are none the better for it. Why? Perhaps it is because you are dealing with a broken heart. There is an invisible enemy going about as a roaring lion, seeking whom to devour (see 1 Peter 5:8).

Your problem is not with the Lord who loves you. Your problems are with the devil and his evil kingdom because you do not yet understand your battleground.

Many will quote Hebrews 4:12, but seldom do they quote verse 13:

> *For the word of God is quick, and powerful, and sharper than any twoedged sword, piercing even to the dividing asunder of soul and spirit, and of the joints and marrow, and is a discerner of the thoughts and intents of the heart. Neither is there any creature that is not manifest in His sight: but all things are naked and opened unto the eyes of Him with whom we have to do* (Hebrews 4:12-13).

What is the connection between the spirit and the bones? Scriptures say that envy and jealousy dries up the bones (see Proverbs 14:30). Maybe your bones are losing calcium? Maybe the blood in the bones are drying up? Where is the marrow found? In the bones. A broken spirit dries up the marrow. There must be more to walking in faith than just John 3:16. The Bible has a lot of stuff about our enemy... your life...your business...your immune system...

It goes on to say that those thoughts and intents are creatures that you cannot see. Yes, creatures that you can't see!

> *Neither is there any creature that is not manifest in his sight: but all things are naked and opened unto the eyes of him with whom we have to do* (Hebrews 4:13).

Causes of a Broken Heart

In ministry, we have discovered that there are several things that can open the door that can lead to a broken heart.

Emotional abuse: Beginning in childhood, emotional abuse can come from someone who taunted you, ignored you, or played head trips on you. This is where all the other abuses stem from, the mind games. The individuals who victimized people this way were well on their way to becoming verbal, physical, and even sexual abusers themselves.

Verbal abuse: Teachers and parents and those in authority have often said hurtful things that have become a part of our memory.

Physical abuse: Again, that can start in early childhood development: the school bully who has others hold your arms and hits you repeatedly, or a parent who uses you as a punching bag.

Sexual abuse: This is rampant everywhere, even within the church! It's time we deal with this and stop sweeping it under the carpet. You don't realize how many people, who are sitting right next to you in the pew, were victims of sexual abuse.

Growing up in a legalistic and performance-oriented environment: How well did you meet the expectations of a parent all the way from grades to chores? Those are the sorts of families that whatever you do it is just not quite good enough. If you make straight A's your earthly father might say, "Well you could have done better and gotten all A pluses, you slacker."

All these abuses are perpetrated by people who did not receive the love they needed in their own lives. As the saying goes, hurting people hurt people. As another saying goes, you cannot give away what you don't have. Many individuals giving abuse needed to be loved.

Anger is a result of these things too. It's proven that men who have anger issues have had a broken relationship with their mother. Anger comes from fear, period. So if you struggle with anger, pinpoint who didn't love you, and forgive them.

Who is still afraid of their parents? You may even be a parent yourself with kids of your own. However, if you're loved by people, you won't be afraid of them. Fear has torment. Fear is an evil spirit. We believe that 95 percent of all psychiatric issues and diseases are rooted in fear.

We are really talking about relationship issues here, as well as our sense of personal identity and belonging. Who am I? Why am I here? Who really cares?

We'll never tire of sharing this passage of Scripture because it's the greatest commandment of all:

> *Jesus said unto him, Thou shalt love the Lord thy God with all thy heart, and with all thy soul, and with all thy mind. This is the first and great commandment. And the second is like unto it, Thou shalt love thy neighbor as thyself. On these two commandments hang all the law and the prophets* (Matthew 22:37-40).

If you are not able to love your neighbor, you are in sin. If you are not able to love yourself, you are in sin. How, then, would you be able to say you love the Lord? This is all about relationships. It's about separation from Papa God, from Jesus, and from yourself.

We find that many people in churches don't like themselves, the same with those outside the church. Ministers are people just like anybody else and we have to deal with these things just like you do. The Bible says that Paul even struggled with his sinful nature; the things he wanted to do, he did not always do, and the things he didn't want to do, he found himself tempted to do:

> *For we know that the law is spiritual: but I am carnal, sold under sin. For that which I do I allow not: for what I would, that do I not; but what I hate, that do I.*

If then I do that which I would not, I consent unto the law that it is good. Now then it is no more I that do it, but sin that dwelleth in me (Romans 7:14-17).

God designed us to love and be loved. It's His nature, and it's supposed to be ours as well. Are our ways His ways? We need to be getting into the Word each day, from moment to moment. We need to think more every day the way God thinks, so we are being changed and molded into His image. We need to be able to see outside of God's Kingdom so we also know what we are not supposed to be like. Before we open our mouths to speak out of anger, count to 20. If that does not work, count to 50! The Bible says that a man slow to speak is slow to wrath! This takes self-control and discipline, which are fruit of the Spirit! So we can "help it" because God has given us the power to do so.

Wherefore, my beloved brethren, let every man be swift to hear, slow to speak, slow to wrath: For the wrath of man worketh not the righteousness of God (James 1:19-20).

Satan wants your blood and wants to control your immune system. Fear, anxiety, and stress release too much cortisol— the "fight or flight" response.[2] The spirits of bitterness, anger, resentment are trying to make fear part of your personality, keeping you in a perpetual state of panic. Your body will start conforming to an image of death. Fear attempts to overthrow faith and hope. What is destroying the immune system has little to do with nutrition. It's not so much what you eat; it's what is eating you!

Doctors can give you a regime of herbs and vitamins and supplements. But if you don't go after the spiritual root issues, you are wasting your precious time. Most of these supplements aren't even getting to cell membranes. They're going down the toilet. Most doctors are not going to tell you the truth: that you really have a broken heart because you don't feel loved, you don't feel accepted, or you don't feel valuable.

You are a candidate for disease if you don't deal with this openly. God designed your body to serve you. Behind all allergies is a spirit of fear. You've been programmed and tricked into believing your body cannot handle what God created, such as dairy or sugar. We have a very good and wise pastor friend who likes to say, "The Lord wants to give you back your milk and honey." If He gave the children of Israel a land flowing with milk and honey, why would he not give it to us, too? Mind you, we're not recommending that you consume mass amounts of milk and sugar. But we aren't to be afraid of them either.

> *If the Lord delight in us, then He will bring us into this land, and give it us; a land which floweth with milk and honey* (Numbers 14:8).

The enemy wants you to believe that what God created is evil. You've been had with a lie from that evil kingdom.

When the Lord heals people's immune systems, they can eat whatever they want. (Keep in mind that eating whatever you want may not be such a good idea—and consuming sugar before you are healed from diabetes is not walking in faith but walking in danger.) However, eating things the Lord has provided for us in their original, organic state always seems the best idea.

The bottom line is that if you want to be free from allergies, you need to get back in touch with love and forgive everyone so that your immune system will be restored. Then whatever foods you do decide to eat will be processed properly in your body. Your body is able to remove toxins when your body is fully functional. And don't forget to be thankful. In everything you do—or eat—be thankful.

Allergies are a love issue. Lactose intolerance is based in insecurity.[3] Your enemy is very intelligent; just because you can't see him does not mean he is not speaking to you. The Bible teaches us this, so you better know what voice you are following all the time.

Our battle is not with flesh and blood, but against an invisible kingdom that is trying to steal, kill, and destroy.

> *For we wrestle not against flesh and blood, but against principalities, against powers, against the rulers of the darkness of this world, against spiritual wickedness in high places. Wherefore take unto you the whole armor of God, that ye may be able to with-*

stand in the evil day, and having done all, to stand (Ephesians 6:12-13).

Spirits of Guilt and Shame

But the Lord can see all those that come from that invisible kingdom trying to kill you off, like fear. Fear is a spirit. As children of God, we should be able to discern an invisible being. Fear is behind many diseases. And there appear to be thousands of different kinds of fears: there are magazines and Websites listing thousands of them.

The enemy has been sending you thoughts and has spent years training you in ways that are not God's ways.

> *There is nothing from without a man, that entering into him can defile him: but the things which come out of him, those are they that defile the man....For from within, out of the heart of men, proceed evil thoughts, adulteries, fornications, murders, thefts, covetousness, wickedness, deceit, lasciviousness, an evil eye, blasphemy, pride, foolishness: all these evil things come from within, and defile the man (Mark 7:15;21-23).*

Guilt and Shame come from fear. We have to discover the "sin" in that guilt and shame, and take it to the Lord. It may not even be yours! It could come from a generation before you. That is why we have to go to the Lord in these issues, because He knows the answer.

Scriptures for Your Heart

We have identified some Scriptures to help you find healing in your immune system for problems that stem from a broken heart. We hope these encourage you and give you hope.

> *My son, attend to my words; incline thine ear unto my sayings. Let them not depart from thine eyes; keep them in the midst of thine heart. For they are life unto those that find them, and health to all their flesh. Keep thy heart with all diligence; for out of it are the issues of life (Proverbs 4:20-23).*

Heaviness in the heart of man maketh it stoop: but a good word maketh it glad (Proverbs 12:25).

Hope deferred maketh the heart sick: but when the desire cometh, it is a tree of life (Proverbs 13:12).

Practical Application

We believe that whenever you are hurting, wherever there is a broken relationship, whenever you feel you weren't loved properly you have suffered a broken heart.

So think about this for a minute and ask yourself if you fall into one of these categories. The only true way to get healed from a broken heart is to forgive, so we need to identify those things in our lives. Write down your painful memories—yes, they can be painful at the moment you write them down, but that is good. It means that they are coming to the surface so God can remove them. Don't be afraid of the feelings or of facing things that are hard; they have to come to the surface so that you can be free of them. At times, God is like a refiner, sitting by the pot of gold, turning up the fire just enough to bring the impurities to the top (see Malachi 3:2-3). Your life may be heated up at times, but know that it's a good thing because He is getting you ready to remove the impurities.

A Prayer For You to Pray

The following prayer will help to mend your broken heart.

Papa God, I recognize that I have a broken heart. It was from a broken relationship and You said to forgive all those who have sinned against us. I take responsibility now and choose to forgive each person who broke my heart. I choose to also forgive myself. I ask for Your love to heal me now, and repair all the damage that was done in my heart. Forgive me if I blamed You for my condition, Lord. Please forgive me and restore me to Your heart. I want a whole heart, transparent and clean. I commit my heart to You, completely, and trust You with it. Thank You for healing me, restoring me, and mending every relationship in my life. In Jesus Christ of Nazareth's name. Amen.

Our Prayer For You

Papa God, we come today and give You all our praise and worship. We come now into your gates with thanksgiving in our hearts. We come before Your throne of grace asking You to remove the curses from our lives as we line up with Your Word each day. We thank You for the precious shed blood of our Lord Jesus of Nazareth that covers us now.

We thank You for the Holy Spirit and for Your Word, for the Gospel of Your Kingdom, and for Your desire to see Your child healthy and well, not sick, beaten up, and broken. We thank You that Your heart is that they would prosper even as their soul prospers. So, Papa God, we believe that You are the healer of the broken heart, and we bring our broken hearts to You now. We are so grateful that it is by Your grace through faith, a gift of complete healing and deliverance. Thank You for ministering to these dear ones, Lord, and holding them close to You. Let them know You have not abandoned them or left them, ever, and that Your Word is true. You will never leave them nor forsake them. Their hearts and lives are in Your hands eternally. Help them believe this, Lord.

Let them know that You want to have an intimate and personal relationship with them and that they can have an encounter with the You who was and is and is to come. You are holy and righteous; help them now to come and relate to You in knowledge and responsibility, to be in covenant with You and seek first Your Kingdom and Your righteousness, and to trust that You will take care of all the rest of the details of their lives. Jesus said that it is Your pleasure to give us the Kingdom (see Luke 12:32). Come have your way with them, Lord. We pray this in Jesus of Nazareth's name. Amen."

Endnotes

1. Dr. Teresa Allen, DO, Internal Medicine Physician: 7047 Halcyon Park Dr., The Fit Centre, Montgomery, Alabama, 36117, and Dr. Joseph Mercola, 3200 W. Higgins Rd. Hoffman Estates, IL 60169. http://swineflu.mercola.com.

2. Mayo Clinic, "Stress Management: Win Control Over the Stress in Your Life," http://www.mayoclinic.com/health/stress/SR00001.

3. Pastor Henry Wright, A More Excellent Way (new Kingston, PA: Whitaker House, 2009); www.beinhealth.com

Chapter Eleven

BELIEVE IN HEALING

We can know lots of things the Bible teaches, but these truths need to penetrate our heart and mind so that the fruit we bear pleases God. Our health is a by-product of our relationship with the most High God: Papa, Jesus Christ of Nazareth, and Holy Spirit. Our thoughts on what we believe about healing will determine our healing as well.

We need to truly know that God is full of mercy and love. We need to ask the Lord to help us put on the mind-set of Christ and do those greater works (see John 14:12). We need to watch and pray always that we may be accounted worthy to escape all the things that shall come to pass on this earth, and, having done all, to stand. As we go through this chapter, we invite the Holy Spirit to come and teach us so that His blessings overtake us.

> *Verily, verily, I say unto you, He that believeth on Me, the works that I do shall he do also; and greater*

works than these shall he do; because I go unto My Father (John 14:12).

Watch and pray, that ye enter not into temptation: the spirit indeed is willing, but the flesh is weak (Matthew 26:41).

Wherefore take unto you the whole armour of God, that ye may be able to withstand in the evil day, and having done all, to stand (Ephesians 6:13).

Let's start by seeing what Jesus said in Matthew 20:16: *"So the last shall be first, and the first last: for many be called, but few chosen."* This is a narrow path we walk called holiness; you must choose to answer the call. For now, you get to decide what voice you will follow.

Because strait is the gate, and narrow is the way, which leadeth unto life, and few there be that find it (Matthew 7:14).

Not every one that saith unto Me, Lord, Lord, shall enter into the kingdom of heaven; but he that doeth the will of My Father which is in heaven. Many will say to Me in that day, Lord, Lord, have we not prophesied in Thy name? and in Thy name have cast out devils? and in Thy name done many wonderful works? And then will I profess unto them, I never knew you: depart from Me, ye that work iniquity (Matthew 7:21-23).

This passage has tripped so many people up. We have received calls asking if they were going to lose their salvation because God will say He never knew them. Let me set your mind at ease. If you love the Lord with all your heart, soul, mind and strength, and desire to serve Him and do His will, then "He knows you." Just stay in faith and walk this present life out being a doer of the Word. It is not always easy—stuff happens—but we need to keep our eyes on the Lord and His promises just as Peter did, who walked on the water as long as he kept his eyes on the Lord and not the situation.

For which cause we faint not; but though our outward man perish, yet the inward man is renewed day by

*day. For our light affliction, which is but for a mo-
ment, worketh for us a far more exceeding and eternal weight of glory; while we look not at the things
which are seen, but at the things which are not seen:
for the things which are seen are temporal; but the
things which are not seen are eternal* (2 Corinthians
4:16-18).

Always remember, we have an advocate when we do
goof up—Jesus Christ.

*My little children, these things write I unto you, that
ye sin not. And if any man sin, we have an advocate
with the Father, Jesus Christ the righteous:* (1 John
2:1)

So there are no excuses to remain clean and holy before the Lord. Remember, in our weakness, He is strong
(see Hebrews 11:34).

Wrong Beliefs About Healing

Often when sharing the Gospel as it relates to healing, this
is the response we get: "Please, Pastor, just pray for me; just
pray for my healing." Most of the time, they have already
exhausted all of their pastors and elders with anointing of
oil and prayers of faith. All of their friends have prayed for
them as well. They have even prayed for themselves, yet for
some reason (which is what this book is about), it just does
not seem to be working in this dimension. Or any dimension
for that matter.

And at the end of the day they are still none the better and
are now looking anywhere else to get prayed for. They are
looking for a "miracle" or "divine healing." How many people who claim to be healed at a healing crusade are actually
healed—and if they are, how many are able to keep their
healing if they do not understand what got them into trouble
in the first place? We know several people who were healed
at a healing line, and stay healed. We believe it is because
they continued doing those things we are explaining in this
book. They became not just a hearer of the Word but a doer
of the Word.

Now, we do pray for individuals because God does show mercy on whom He will show mercy, and will work miracles. But in our experience, these are far and few between because God would rather get to their heart condition and heal them in body, soul, and spirit so when He does reach out from Heaven and heal, the person stays healed.

The Lord does not give us gifts and then take them back again. Neither will He heal you and then take back the healing. Therefore, we want to suggest to you that if the devil can put sickness and diseases on someone, he can certainly take them off them if somehow it will take that person further away from the Lord and His truth.

Some then say that they do not believe that all diseases, including things like cancer, are the result of someone dealing with individual sin. After all, they are believers and have been going to church a long time. Or their friend who has a deadly disease is such a godly person they cannot imagine how some personal sin could be the real cause of it. So we ask you, "Is there any evidence of cancer or heart diseases in Heaven? Is there any evidence of any sort of sickness or illness in Heaven?"

Obviously not, and we are supposed to be bringing Heaven to earth. As in the Lord's prayer says, "in earth, as is it in heaven" (Matt. 6:10).

Do you know what God calls these things that cause sickness and disease? He calls them evil spirits. It's just that medicine has come along and put a name on them. People often find comfort once they have a name put to their condition, and easily buy into the lie that is giving the sickness or diseases a "right" to stay.

Some believers understand original sin, but not individual, personal sin because they have been taught that Jesus paid it all. He did; the question is, are you appropriating what He did for you?

They will often even try to argue some scriptural basis for this point of view, which will always include the suffering of Job and the apostle Paul with his "thorn" in the flesh. Some will even say that God has a plan for each of us, and while we may not fully understand the big picture, we need to accept

His will, saying, "Your will be done, Lord." They conclude that if they are sick, it's because it's the Lord's will. We sometimes hear people say that God gave them their diseases. If God has "blessed" you with a disease, why would you then seek medical help for that condition and interfere with the plan of God for your life?

Their faith is to just take anything that comes as a part of the obedient Christian life. They want to pray, "Oh, Lord, if it's Your will, then heal me or my friend," without dealing with the rest of the conditions set forth by our Lord. (For example, if you do not forgive others, then God will not forgive you.)

When a family member or friend dies from some dreadful disease at 40 years of age, these believers will often make up excuses: that they were so godly they just finished their assignment early on earth, or that God loved them so much He took them early. The Bible says that a man's days on this earth are between 70 and 80. Dying any earlier than that is premature death (see Ps. 90:10). They've been had with a lie and apparently just do not know the Word of God very well. That is a common problem because many churches have simply not been teaching the whole Bible message. Teaching partial truth is like putting together a piece of equipment without proper directions; there are lots of parts left over, and you are not sure where they are supposed to fit exactly.

We aren't saying that every person's sickness is a direct result of some personal sin, for that simply is not true, either.

Jesus Heals the Blind Man

John 9 presents us with an intriguing case that addresses the connection between sin and infirmity. And this is one case that also causes confusion in the church today.

And as Jesus passed by, He saw a man which was blind from his birth. And His disciples asked Him, saying, Master, who did sin, this man, or his parents, that he was born blind? Jesus answered, Neither hath this man sinned, nor his parents: but that the works of God should be made manifest in him (John

197

9:1-3).

Jesus then healed the blind man of his blindness. So what was for the glory of God? The blindness or the healing? The healing, of course.

In these times, the Jews believed that a pious soul was re-incarnated as a reward and that souls who were wicked were put into eternal prisons to be punished forever, according to the Jewish historian Flavius Josephus.[1]

Some Jews and some in Asiatic nations believed souls came back into bodies as a penalty for sins committed in pre-existent states. There was a controversy going on here when the Lord Jesus addressed this issue. The question being asked by the disciples—who also had similar beliefs—was really whether some physical infirmity was the result of one's sins before birth, in the womb, or by the parents.

Hindus identify the sins of the reincarnated previous life with afflictions of the present. If someone has epilepsy, it is because that person had poisoned someone in a previous life, rather than understanding the possibility that it really is the work of a deaf and dumb spirit, as according to the Bible in places like Matthew chapter 12:22-28, where it records Jesus informing us what was behind the diseases and sickness.

Theories of reincarnation connect previous sins to current sickness and diseases, which are quite paganistic and totally unscriptural.

The truth of the matter is simply that these things are caused by the fall and sin of man. Always remember the devil wants to steal, kill, and destroy any way he can, and if he can get you to think like him, he's got you. Here are a few Scriptures that refer to the connection between the oppression of the enemy and physical infirmity:

> How God anointed Jesus of Nazareth with the Holy Ghost and with power: who went about doing good, and healing all that were oppressed of the devil; for God was with Him (Acts 10:38).

> And you hath He quickened, who were dead in trespasses and sins; wherein in time past ye walked ac-

cording to the course of this world, according to the prince of the power of the air, the spirit that now worketh in the children of disobedience: among whom also we all had our conversation in times past in the lusts of our flesh, fulfilling the desires of the flesh and of the mind; and were by nature the children of wrath, even as others. But God, who is rich in mercy, for His great love wherewith He loved us, even when we were dead in sins, hath quickened us together with Christ, (by grace ye are saved;) (Ephesians 2:1-5).

And ought not this woman, being a daughter of Abraham, whom Satan hath bound, lo, these eighteen years, be loosed from this bond on the sabbath day? (Luke 13:16)

In this passage in John 9:2-7, we might suggest that because of continued generational sins, there were imperfect and undeveloped cells in this man's body; perhaps overwork, spirits of worry and fear, accidents, and some violation of natural laws also contributed to the cause of the man's blindness. This is not to say this was the cause of his blindness, only that God's blessings and healing power manifested whatever the cause for the blindness.

Jesus did not state the cause of the blindness to answer the disciples, but He made it very clear that God was certainly not the cause of it. God is the healer, and Satan is behind all sickness and disease. If Satan can mess up someone's DNA, God can restore it to its original design. He can do this simply because He is God, because He created all things, and because He loves you. We do not know the cause of this man's blindness, but we do know for certain God was not the cause of it. So Jesus answered their question as to whether the man or his parents sinned.

Jesus went on and healed the blind man. If the blindness was from God, then Jesus was interfering with His Father's plan and would be in rebellion; yet, we know Jesus told us that He and the Father are one (see John 10:30).

So much for God putting diseases on you!

Did God Cause Job's Suffering?

Those who claim that there is scriptural evidence that God puts diseases upon His people always point toward Job's suffering and Paul's thorn in the flesh. In our view, however, Job had a spirit of fear that is opposite of faith, and that is a sin:

> *For the thing which I greatly feared is come upon me, and that which I was afraid of is come unto me* (Job 3:25).

> *...for whatsoever is not of faith is sin* (Romans 14:23).

Job said the thing he feared the worst came upon him: that is opposite of faith. And without faith it is impossible to please the Lord (see Heb. 11:6). But Job got right with the Lord, and he was restored. He was healed so that is not a good argument to debate with me. In fact, the Bible has much to say on why Job suffered. You are going to reap what you sow. If you plant corn, you are not going to harvest tomatoes.

Let's take a closer look at Job's life, starting in Job Ch. 4:

> *But now it is come upon thee, and thou faintest; it toucheth thee, and thou art troubled. Is not this thy fear, thy confidence, thy hope, and the uprightness of thy ways? Remember, I pray thee, who ever perished, being innocent? Or where were the righteous cut off? Even as I have seen, they that plow iniquity, and sow wickedness, reap the same* (Job 4:5-8).

Does this mean that God is punishing Job? No! Papa God is orchestrating things to help Job get to the place where the Lord can bless him again, and he is doing the same with us. Remember, God never changes!

> *Behold, happy is the man whom God correcteth: therefore despise not thou the chastening of the Almighty* (Job 5:17).

If we truly understood God and trusted Him completely, we would be protected from what people said about us; we wouldn't fear destruction or famine or even the beast of the land.

Thou shalt be hid from the scourge of the tongue: neither shalt thou be afraid of destruction when it cometh. At destruction and famine thou shalt laugh: neither shalt thou be afraid of the beasts of the earth (Job 5:21-22).

We would be more like Shadrach, Meshach, and Abednego in Daniel 3. We would trust in the Lord even when facing a certain death sentence into a fiery furnace.

The devil comes but to kill, steal, and destroy when you allow him to. How?

When you allow his evil thoughts to become one with you, you start thinking like he does instead of like God.

If thou wert pure and upright; surely now He would awake for thee, and make the habitation of thy righteousness prosperous. Though thy beginning was small, yet thy latter end should greatly increase (Job 8:6-7).

Could this be saying that his heart was not pure and upright? If Job was known as a "righteous man" and this was said about him, what is being said about us? Could this be the reason we may not be getting the results from our prayer life? So, perhaps we need to do a few things; perhaps we need to really forgive more; perhaps we really need to repent more; perhaps we really need to believe God more. Only you and the Lord can decide those things, but whatever it is, take the time to ask Him to help you. We know for a fact He will answer that prayer!

For thy mouth uttereth thine iniquity, and thou choosest the tongue of the crafty. Thine own mouth condemneth thee, and not I: yea, thine own lips testify against thee (Job 15:5-6).

We need to watch what comes out of our mouth because there is life or death in our words (see Prov. 18:21).

Art thou the first man that was born? or wast thou made before the hills? Hast thou heard the secret of God? And dost thou restrain wisdom to thyself? (Job 15:7-8)

In this passage, it was Job's friend Eliphaz who asked him, *"Should a wise man utter vain knowledge, and fill his belly with the east wind? Should he reason with unprofitable talk? or with speeches wherewith he can do no good? Yea, thou castest off fear, and restrainest prayer before God."*

Earlier we spoke of people who can help discern our yucky stuff, and here is a great biblical example. It appears Eliphaz saw pride in Job and that's why He asked these questions. Sometimes we can be so hard-headed that God uses others to help us see the truth within ourselves.

Job 15 goes on to tell us a list of sins that Job got himself into before he finally got right with the Lord. Job had to get rid of that spirit of pride.

Job 33:14-28 tells us that God tried to deal with Job's pride, but he would not listen; therefore, these things came upon him. How many times has God tried getting your attention, but you wouldn't listen? How many times have you said, "I wish I would have listened to that small voice inside of me; then I wouldn't have had to go through this."

We just need to talk to the Lord every morning and ask Him to help us hear Him better so that we can avoid some of these things we get ourselves into.

We can go even deeper with all this, but you get the picture. No ones who studies the Book of Job could possibly ever make this argument work that God puts sickness and diseases on His children.

Paul's Thorn

The next thing people use to justify sickness and disease is about the apostle Paul. It's our strong position and conviction that the thorn everyone says is a sickness or disease is not.

This thorn in the flesh that Paul mentioned has been used and misused by Christians to justify submitting to nearly any problem that comes along. It's one of the best excuses people seem to come up with to help them justify that it's really OK to be sick and full of diseases and that your suffering from a disease while serving the Lord is your way of suffering for the cause of Christ. Some even go as far as calling it "their cross to bear." Actually, the cross that we are to bear is living a self-less life unto the Lord, not some disease or sickness.

Let's examine Second Corinthians 12:7-10 and see what we can glean from it so we can put this to rest.

We may not be able to tell exactly what that thorn was, but we can tell you what it was not.

> *And lest I should be exalted above measure through the abundance of the revelations, there was given to me a thorn in the flesh, the messenger of Satan to buffet me, lest I should be exalted above measure. For this thing I besought the Lord thrice, that it might depart from me. And He said unto me, My grace is sufficient for thee: for my strength is made perfect in weakness. Most gladly therefore will I rather glory in my infirmities, that the power of Christ may rest upon me. Therefore I take pleasure in infirmities, in reproaches, in necessities, in persecutions, in distresses for Christ's sake: for when I am weak, then am I strong* (2 Corinthians 12:7-10).

Look at verse 7: *And lest I should be exalted above measure through the abundance of the revelations...* (2 Corinthians 12:7).

This says the thorn came lest Paul should be exalted above measure. Many believe and teach that this statement means that the thorn in the flesh was to keep Paul humble so he could be the great man that he was. Then they make God out to be evil saying He would need to use a disease to humble Paul. We have already clearly taught that God does not give a disease for any reason. The Bible tells us that God is good (see Matthew 19:17; James 1:17; 1 John 1:5). But this helps those justify their sickness and disease, falling back into that "permissive will" stuff. So please hear us out; it may save your life.

We need to stop here and address the word "humble." First Peter 5:6 says, *"Humble yourselves therefore under the mighty hand of God, that He may exalt you in due time."* It's our choice to be prideful or be humble, and it will depend on who we submit to or listen to. We don't believe this is about pride. When you submit to God, you are humbling yourself before Him, and you will be exalted by God when He decides. And Humble, simply put, means to believe God.

Now Let's Tackle This Thorn Theory

The "thorn in the flesh" came to Paul after he had an abundance of revelations. He was "armed and dangerous with the Word of God" and was a threat to the kingdom of darkness.

We can see in other passages where the word "thorn" is used, and it has nothing to do with sickness or disease.

> *But if ye will not drive out the inhabitants of the land from before you; then it shall come to pass, that those which ye let remain of them shall be pricks in your eyes, and thorns in your sides, and shall vex you in the land wherein ye dwell* (Numbers 33:55).

> *Know for a certainty that the Lord your God will no more drive out any of these nations from before you; but they shall be snares and traps unto you, and scourges in your sides, and thorns in your eyes, until ye perish from off this good land which the Lord your God hath given you* (Joshua 23:13).

Here we find people who were enemies of God were spoken of as being "thorns in your sides" and "thorns in your eyes." Frankly, we cannot tell you what that thorn was, but we can tell you what it wasn't, and it wasn't a disease or sickness. That's the point we are making here.

Moving on with verse 7: *"...the messenger of Satan..."* (2 Cor. 12:7).

The word messenger here in Greek is "aggelos," meaning an angel or messenger.[2] Aggelos is translated "angel" 179 times and "messenger" seven times. It is never translated as a disease or physical infirmity.

So "the" messenger, not just any messenger, was sent to Saint Paul. It appears that Satan sent his top-ranking messenger because he knew the impact Paul's life was going to play on the world. So this tells me he sent his strongest force to kill Paul off with stonings, persecutions, and just plain sinfulness in the world. So, what does a messenger do? He brings a message. Since it was a message from Satan, it was designed to bring defeat of some kind, to try to steal, kill, and destroy him—this is the thorn we are talking about.

Moving on with verse 7: *"...to buffet me..."*

Let's take a look at the word buffet. According to the Strong's concordance, buffet means: to wrap (hit) with a fist (a blow specifically with the hand).[3] Saint Paul was persecuted, beaten and left for dead, he was thrown into jail several times, and even stoned. He endured many forms of abuse for the cause of Christ. Again, these have nothing to do with sickness or disease.

When we look at what we've studied so far, this is what we see: A messenger from Satan who spoke lies and hypocrisies into the minds of individuals weak with their own lusts and sins, and used them to come against Paul so they would go and try to take him out. The enemy cannot just come and do something. He has to use a vessel, but it starts in a person's thinking, and once he gets you to agree in thought, then he has you doing his will. And that is what we are talking about in this book—who are we listening to? In Paul's day, who were "they" listening to?

And now the last part of verse 7: *"...lest I should be exalted above measure."*

Paul is the first to admit that his life was not his own, and that what he did for Christ was not to be exalted, but only Jesus was to be exalted. He chose to humble himself, and applied what John 3:30 says, "I must decrease so God could increase." This is not about pride, but about human nature, sinful nature that is in every single person.

Now on to verse 8: *"For this thing I besought the Lord thrice, that it might depart from me"* (2 Cor. 12:8).

Wouldn't you ask God to make those persecutions stop? How many of you have asked the Lord to stop a certain situation because it hurts too much and causes you grief. Remember, Paul was a man, too. So we have to conclude that "this thing" wasn't a disease or sickness, but rather persecutions—as it goes on to say.

And He said unto me, My grace is sufficient for thee: for my strength is made perfect in weakness. Most gladly therefore will I rather glory in my infirmities, that the power of Christ may rest upon me (2 Corinthians 12:9).

We need to stop here and take a look at the word weakness. It's a major key here! The Greek word is "astheneia," and means want of strength, weakness, or infirmity. Infirmity here suggests a moral or mental flaw, not a disease. It's clearly that he was in a "weakened state of mind or body." So then, in order to continue the work of the Lord God, He needed the power of the Holy Spirit through Christ to give him what he needed to patiently endure.

It says: *"...the power of Christ may rest upon him."* Now, this is where we can talk about "taking up your cross to follow Him." Laying down our own comforts, desires, cares and sins, and taking up a life to follow Jesus. And of course, Paul goes on to say that he took pleasure in this because He knew He was being what God wanted him to be. Him being weakened was due to all these beatings and physical and mental abuse, not from some sickness.

And verse 10 says: *Therefore I take pleasure in infirmities, in reproaches, in necessities, in persecutions, in distresses for Christ's sake: for when I am weak, then am I strong* (2 Corinthians 12:10).

So then Paul resolves to say, OK, I will be content with this, and will trust you Father to complete the work that you have called me to do. Several times in Scripture it talks about "being thankful in everything" (see 1 Thess. 5:18), "Rejoice always" (see 1 Thess. 5:16) and better yet, "I have learned to be content in all things" (see Phil. 4:11). He learned through trials and persecutions to be content. He knew because he experienced it himself. And besides, Paul lived to complete the work he was sent to do. If he had a disease or sickness, how could he have endured prison life?

If you know anything about prisons in those days, they weren't like they are today that is for sure. It was a stinky, unsafe, and an unsanitary place. They didn't treat the prisoners well, either. So again, Paul did not have a sickness or disease, it would have taken him out years ago before he could finish his writings, and where would we be? As a matter of fact, what he endured was before he was sent to prison are the very things that made him "strong" so he could endure those conditions and finish the work.

We have to stop and ask ourselves the same thing. Is what we are going through today preparing us for the days ahead? We would have to say yes. We are living in precarious times, as you may know, and all our trials and persecutions are to prepare us for what lies ahead, just as with Paul.

As a matter of fact, what the devil meant for evil, God turned it to good, because it made Paul even stronger!

But thou hast fully known my doctrine, manner of life, purpose, faith, longsuffering, charity, patience, persecutions, afflictions, which came unto me at Antioch, at Iconium, at Lystra; what persecutions I endured: but out of them all the Lord delivered me. Yea, and all that will live godly in Christ Jesus shall suffer persecution (2 Timothy 3:10-12).

As you can see, no health issues were listed here, it's all about character, nature, or relationship issues. That brings us to another point, his relationship with Barnabas. As you read in Acts 15 they ministered together for some time with great success. But they had a disagreement and parted ways, and it wasn't a pleasant split. Could it be that his broken relationship with Barnabas caused his pain? How many of us have painful relationship issues? It can actually wear you down if not dealt with. Have you ever said, "They are a pain in my neck?" That is why forgiveness is so important.

Even Jesus told his captors they had no power over what was going on accept the Father permitted it. It was for the good of the whole world.

Jesus answered, Thou couldest have no power at all against me, except it were given thee from above: therefore he that delivered me unto thee hath the greater sin (John 19:11).

We may not always see what is going on, that is what faith is for. Trusting God who does, and we are promised that everything is going to work out for good!

What about Joseph? The things that happened to him were not very pleasant, but because of it, he saved a nation from starvation.

But as for you, ye thought evil against me; but God meant it unto good, to bring to pass, as it is this day, to save much people alive (Genesis 50:20).

Later we learn that Barnabas and Paul reunited. Could it be that's when Paul was "delivered" from his pain? Because we just read that Paul was delivered "out of them all."

And the contention was so sharp between them, that they departed asunder one from the other: and so Barnabas took Mark, and sailed unto Cyprus (Acts 15:39).

We know in ministry that when people are reconciled to others, or even just forgive them from their heart, they begin to heal, emotionally, physically (relationally) and spiritually.

Fight the good fight of faith, lay hold on eternal life, whereunto thou art also called, and hast professed a good profession before many witnesses (1 Timothy 6:12).

I have fought a good fight, I have finished my course, I have kept the faith (2 Timothy 4:7).

And we know that all things work together for good to them that love God, to them who are the called according to his purpose (Romans 8:28).

We need to study this for ourselves, and allow the Holy Spirit to teach the truth that makes us free. Because the bottom line is that the Lord will provide for us and take care of us, and His grace is sufficient for us. He will take care of every detail of our lives. Whenever we are attacked by an angel of Satan's army, our hope is in God, we look for the grace promised by God. Only then can we be strong in His power.

When we live godly in Christ Jesus, we are going to suffer persecution for it. Nobody likes it, but that is the way it is. Those who persecute us, we need to forgive and even bless (see Matt. 5:44). We have to be Christ-like and forgive them, and ask the Lord not to lay these charges against them because they know not what they do.

> *Blessed are ye, when men shall revile you, and persecute you, and shall say all manner of evil against you falsely, for my sake. Rejoice, and be exceeding glad: for great is your reward in heaven: for so persecuted they the prophets which were before you* (Matthew 5:11-12)

Satan has used this and other traditional teachings from the Church about Paul's thorn to bring many Christians to a place of submitting to the devil (in our thinking) from our own life situations instead of submitting to the Lord's. But praise God; you shall know (in your thoughts) the truth, and the truth shall make you free.

Did Paul Have Eye Problems?

There are a few other passages of Scripture that people have tried to argue and insist that Paul's thorn in the flesh was eye problems. Let's look at Galatians 4:13-16:

> *Ye know how through infirmity of the flesh I preached the gospel unto you at the first, and my temptation which was in my flesh ye despised not, nor rejected; but received me as an angel of God, even as Christ Jesus. Where is then the blessedness ye spake of? For I bear you record, that, if it had been possible, ye would have plucked out your own eyes, and have given them to me. Am I therefore become your enemy, because I tell you the truth?*

Saint Paul here is saying that he preached the Gospel to these Galatians folks through an infirmity of the flesh. In verse 15 he makes reference to these people actually being willing to pluck out their own eyes and give them to him but this is referring to Paul being willing to lay down his life for these people; it does not mean in any way Paul has some sort of eye disease. He was concerned that false teachers were trying to win the people's love and take them away into false religions.

Some people have said that Paul's thorn was some sort

of eye disease that was characterized by runny and puffy eyes. Where did they get this information? It is not found anywhere in the Holy Bible. Again, we need to read the Bible for ourselves and be as the Berean (see Acts 17:11-13) were, who did not just take someone's word for it but went to study for themselves and that surely pleased the Lord.

We need to take a look at who Saint Paul was speaking to when he said this. He was writing to the people who lived in the region known as Galatia, which had as its major cities Derbe, Lystra, and Iconium.

Paul was stoned and left for dead (see Acts 14:2) in Lystra, a city of Galatia. No doubt that his friends and fellow believers prayed for him to be healed and resurrected. The Greek word "anistemi" is used here meaning to raise up back up 111 times in the Bible, and 40 times it means resurrected.[4]

Paul was brought back or resurrected, and the next day Paul walked to Derbe, another city of Galatia, and began preaching to them. If you had been stoned as he was and left for dead and were brought back to talk about it the next day, you might possibly have some puffy eyes, along with multiple cuts and bruises. Again, all this was not the result of some disease.

He also says in verse 13 that his infirmity was "at the first," which gives us the impression it was a temporary thing that he soon recovered from. The other Scripture people often use to say Paul's thorn was bad eyes is found in Galatians 6:11: "Ye see how large a letter I have written unto you with mine own hand."

There are those who want to teach people that Paul's eyes were so bad that he had to write in large letters, to again give the excuse if God did not heal Paul why would the Lord heal you today.

That is nonsense! Be Berean here. It appears he is simply referring to the long letter he had written to the Galatians in his own hand.

And finally we read in Second Timothy 3:11, *"Persecutions, afflictions, which came unto me at Antioch, at Iconium, at Lystra; what persecutions I endured: but out of them all the Lord delivered me."* And that just about says it all.

Satan has used misunderstanding like this and other traditional teachings from the Church about Paul's thorn to
bring many Christians to a place of submitting to the devil
(in our thinking) instead of the Lord. But praise God; you
shall know (in your thoughts) the truth, and the truth shall
make you free.

When Jesus Christ of Nazareth had a church service, He
preached the Gospel, healed people, and cast out evil spirits.
That is what the early church practiced. That is what we are
supposed to practice.

Positioning for Healing

Acts 10:38 tells us the devil is behind sickness and disease:

> *How God anointed Jesus of Nazareth with the Holy
> Ghost and with power: who went about doing good,
> and healing all that were oppressed of the devil; for
> God was with him* (Acts 10:38).

We do not agree that if God wants to heal someone He will
heal them no matter what they happen to do as long as they
just keep praying and whatever happens is OK. This is that
permissive will stuff again. The Bible says that God will have
mercy and compassion on whom He will, so if you don't get
your miracle, what are you going to do? We are going to cooperate with God and come in line with His Word in that area
of our life. Because if prayer isn't working then we need to get
to work and find out where the enemy thinks he has some
legal right to us!

In 1 John 5:16-17, it tells us not to even pray when we see
someone sin a sin which is unto death because there is more
going on than just needing a miracle here.

Lets face it, not that many people who go up in a healing line are healed. It is wonderful for those who are, but
what about the ones who went up believing to be healed and
weren't? Then someone suggests maybe they did not have
enough faith. That can't be the correct answer. God gives every one a measure of faith and it only takes a mustard seed
amount to get a job done.

Is any sick among you? let him call for the elders of the church; and let them pray over him, anointing him with oil in the name of the Lord: And the prayer of faith shall save the sick, and the Lord shall raise him up; and if he have committed sins, they shall be forgiven him. Confess your faults one to another, and pray one for another, that ye may be healed. The effectual fervent prayer of a righteous man availeth much (James 5:14-16).

Healing and forgiveness goes together like peanut butter and jelly. They go hand in hand together. How is someone going to be forgiven of sins without going before the living Lord Jesus Christ of Nazareth and dealing with issues?

The Lord is telling us here that as we confess our faults, our sin issues before each other it will bring us to a place where we can receive healing. Why is it because as we talk about those deep dark sins we committed that the enemy of your souls is holding over you accusing you of, by confessing them the enemy loses his grip on you. All of a sudden you realize no matter what you have done, no matter how bad it was God still loves you and His love covers a multiple amount of sins. Because a spirit of fear has torment and God's perfect love casts out all fear.

If any man sees his brother sin a sin which is not unto death, he shall ask, and he shall give him life for them that sin not unto death. There is a sin unto death: I do not say that he shall pray for it. All unrighteousness is sin: and there is a sin not unto death (1 John 5:16-17).

What is a disease unto death? Is it possibly a disease that is brought on through bitterness and unforgiveness? For example, research shows that cancer is a disease that can cause death.[5] We don't believe God is going to heal someone and also leave all that yucky stuff that got them into such a place of bitterness that allowed such a horrible disease to manifest in them in the first place. He wants the person to deal with the sin issues that produced the incurable disease; otherwise, if someone received a "miracle," what would stop the disease from returning? Many people want to argue that

Jesus just healed people without any conditions attached.

Jesus told the woman caught in adultery in John 8:11 she was not condemned to go and sin no more and the man in John 5:14 who suffered with an infirmity 38 years after he healed him to go and sin no more, lest a worse thing happen to you.

We really do not see any promise in the Bible that does not have a condition attached. There is always an if-then with the promises of the Lord. He still loves you, but like a young child at the dinner table there is no desserts if you do not finish the meal. We are to remain in His love and finish the race.

We have tried to show you that there are invisible creatures that are affecting your thoughts and running programs in your body that cause malfunctions and breakdowns to occur.

The Bible warns us that to simply cast out these things, these spirits, but also warns us that it is very dangerous if we do not deal with the issues that allowed them to enter in the first place.

Matthew 12:45 says that seven more wicked spirits can enter in if the person does not stay right before the Lord.

How many people have prayed for individuals with these types of illnesses who didn't get healed? How many elders anointed them with oil, praying the prayer of faith to no avail?

We are to minister to them instead. Find out what is bothering them, who hurt them, and broke their heart. Help to get them to repent and forgive. It might take awhile to get someone to a place of understanding where the Lord can come and heal them. How can our Holy God heal someone in their sins? He would have to change who He is then, to get them to repent and forgive. It might take awhile to get someone to a place of understanding where the Lord can come and heal them. The Bible says Jesus went about preaching the Gospel, healing the sick and casting out demons.

That means he must have taught the people first before He healed them. Which negates the idea of all those people who think Jesus healed all sorts of people and left them stranded in their sin issues so the enemy could quickly reenter them with legal right.

However, we know He wants to heal them; that is what His Word says.

Who forgiveth all thine iniquities; who healeth all thy diseases (Psalm 103:3).

All we know is I was dying of heart diseases before I went to Pleasant Valley Church in 2001. Almost a decade later I wrote this: "Praise God; I am still going strong without any medicine and without heart issues, living in the Word of our Lord. I am being a doer of the Word the best I am able. I have ministered what I have learned to countless people and have seen the Lord heal many of them and perform some miracles. I cannot take credit for any of it. My job as a believer is the same as yours: to share the Gospel, which includes healing as a part of the salvation package."

If someone we call a friend sinned against us, we hope they would come to us, make things right, and ask for forgiveness—just as we would want to do if we sinned against a friend.

Jesus calls us friends. How much more should we go back and repent of our sins after we have been saved and forgiven? This is what the Bible teaches. The Bible says, "What? Should we sin some more so grace abounds? God forbid!" (See Romans 6:1-3.) However, when we entertain an evil spirit like bitterness against someone or ourselves, the evidence speaks for itself. God says He cannot forgive us if we do not forgive others. How can He heal us if we do not repent of these things?

There is much to understanding this, and the more we learn about it, the more we realize we do not know very much. But we do know one thing the Lord promised for those who believe: He would confirm His Word with signs, wonders, and miracles (see Mark 16:20). We are seeing that. The question is, are other believers seeing that as well?

In your church, no matter how wonderful and kind the people are, if you are not experiencing that reality, we would really begin to question, why not? Because that is part of the

Gospel, and there is no denying that the Lord is the same yesterday, today, and tomorrow (see Heb. 13:8). When did the gifts of healing pass away? Divine healing for the body is perfectly scriptural. We have seen people who were hospice patients recover when they got their hearts right before the Lord and met His conditions.

But the Lord gives us the choice. You get to decide who to follow moment by moment. We as disciples are commanded as the early church was to observe all the commandments Christ gave the disciples (see Matt. 28:20).

We must also consider the sins of our fathers that have been passed on from generation to generation. They show up in genetically inherited diseases and undesirable character traits that are passed along from generation to generation.

Drug and alcohol addictions are said to "run in families." The curses for sin can be passed on generation after generation until someone finally stands before the Lord, repents, and turns from the iniquity of it. The Holy Bible gives us many examples in the Old Testament of people standing before God and repenting for the sins of their forefathers. This breaks the curse off of our lives and off of our children's lives. The Old Testament is still for our instruction in righteousness. Nehemiah 9:2 says, *"Israel...stood and confessed their sins, and the iniquities of their fathers."*

Jesus explained in Mark 7:14-15 that defilement comes from within, out of the heart of men. It does not come from without. This is the basis for freedom from diseases and broken relationships—even to the healing of a nation. It is the path to freedom from generational curses.

In order to get rid of the defilement, Jesus told us to "repent: for the kingdom of heaven is at hand" (Matt. 4:17).

Practical Application

This teaching may have been hard to hear, but necessary. If you have thought incorrectly about where disease comes from, simply repent. Take a moment now to pray to Papa God about your thoughts, and ask Him to help you line your thinking up with His.

Take a moment to examine your thought life. Do you believe He wants you well? Do you believe Jesus still heals? Do you believe He is our deliverer from all our trials? When? When we are doers of the Word. This isn't a time to fall into fear; it's a time to stand up and be counted among the many Christians who suffered for the cause of Christ. He wants us to walk fearlessly, bold, courageous, and free, filled with love, forgiveness, compassion, and truth. Matthew 10:16 says, *"Behold, I send you forth as sheep in the midst of wolves: be ye therefore wise as serpents, and harmless as doves."*

We are only on this planet momentarily; eternity is the real place! Choose today whom you will serve.

Endnotes

1. The Works of Josephus, Complete and Unabridged New Updated Edition. Translated by William Whiston, A.M., (Peabody, MA: Hendrickson Publishers, Inc., 1987).

2. James Strong, Strong's Exhaustive Concordance of the Bible (Peabody, MA: Hendrickson Publishers, n.d.), s.v. "aggelos" (Greek #32).

3. Strong, s.v. "kolaphizo" (Greek #2852).

4. Strong, s.v. "anistemi" (Greek #450).

5. American Cancer Society, "Heredity and Cancer," http://www.cancer.org/docroot/CRI/content/CRI_2_6x_Heredity_and_Cancer.asp?sitearea=.

Chapter Twelve

PREPARING TO OVERCOME

Military commanders understand their enemy's strategies so they can defeat them. Armies that are victorious in battles must prepare and train before they go into battle. They learn their enemy's weakness; they see what weapons they are using. We must also prepare ourselves by staying in the Word and casting down every thought and imagination the enemy's kingdom tries to give us. We must wield the sword of the Spirit, which is the Word of God, and use all the resources and weaponry with which God has equipped us. What is the fight we fight? To maintain God's vision for us. If whatever you are thinking or imagining does not line up with the Word of God, cast it out (see 2 Cor. 10:5). Only accept the thoughts and imaginations that line up with the Word of God.

James 4:7 says that by submitting to God, you will be able to resist the devil every time, and he will flee.

In other words, people struggle to resist the devil because they are not submitting themselves to the Lord. Some of us think that we can do it ourselves without the Lord. Maybe we believe more of what the devil is saying than what God is saying. Whatever the case, it's time to get that right with God.

Discipline is part of becoming a disciple of the Lord so you can move in His power and might, mixing your faith with His truth.

Has anyone struggled with feeling "out of control?" For example, you just can't refrain from eating that last piece of chocolate cake. Or where there is a spread, you eat more than you usually do. There needs to be self-control in every area of our lives, including what we eat. Not having self-control is like a city with it's walls down and anyone can come in and out and pilferage it.

> *He that hath no rule over his own spirit is like a city that is broken down, and without walls* (Proverbs 25:28).

In the book of Romans, it talks about food. And if you eat it in fear, you are in sin.

> *And he that doubteth is damned if he eat, because he eateth not of faith: for whatsoever is not of faith is sin* (Romans 14:23).

We have the power and ability to change our thinking and habits. Remember, where your mind goes your body follows. So as you start to do something you would rather not do, stop and think what you were thinking? Perhaps you need to forgive someone? Perhaps you need to have a little talk with the Lord? See, if we decide to keep our mind on Him 24/7, we may walk in self-control more often. But we have to believe we can. Again, what are you thinking? Will you agree with the devil and believe you can't change or will you believe the Word of God that says the complete opposite?

The devil tries to keep your mind full of other things so your mind is too busy to think about what the Bible says. He wants to distract you, trip you up, and get you snagged along the way. Maybe he gets you to watch too much television so that you have a worldly perspective that makes you weak in your spirit. Maybe you're still thinking about the movie or show that you just saw, or meditating on some problems at home or at work. Those problems would not even be there if you kept your mind stayed on the Lord:

> *Thou wilt keep him in perfect peace whose mind is stayed on Thee because he trusteth in Thee* (Isa. 26:3).

Someone who prays without ceasing will be in tune with spiritual things. Prayer always works: If it does not change the circumstances, it will at least change your perception of them so eventually the circumstances do change. If prayer does not work, it's time to get to work and find out why.

When we stay in a place of prayer and worship as we study the Bible, we receive a greater confidence in the things of God, causing us to have the ability to cast out all of the devil's images of sickness and defeat. How can you ever cast out all those evil imaginations if you don't have Papa God's Word constantly in your thoughts?

The devil will try to overwhelm you with his thoughts. Being overwhelmed is not from Papa God. He never gives you more than you can handle. These things come straight from the kingdom of darkness. He is the one who causes problems, and he is the one who orchestrates crises in your life. Maybe it's time to fast and pray so that you can get the victory. Maybe if we read about the wonderful things offered in the Bible instead of filling our mind's libraries with the worldly imaginations that lead to destruction, we might see some good things come our way. It is the Word of God that strengthens us, and when it's spoken from our heart, it always defeats the enemy.

Receiving Answers to Prayer

I sent the following lyrics of a song I wrote to a friend:

Freedom comes in Jesus' name if you're a doer of His Word. Then surely all your prayers will be answered.

He asked, "How can I be promised that all my prayers will be answered?" The way I answered was with this Scripture:

> *Verily, verily, I say unto you, he that believeth on Me, the works that I do shall he do also; and greater works than these shall he do; because I go unto My Father. And whatsoever ye shall ask in My name, that will I do, that the Father may be glorified in the Son. If ye shall ask any thing in My name, I will do it. If ye love Me, keep My commandments* (John 14:12-15).

If people are not getting prayers answered, the issue may be disobedience. Perhaps they are not as obedient as they think they are. Maybe they are fellowshipping with devils and not really seeing it. That is what is called being "self-deceived." But Papa God sees it all, and He is not deceived.

Often people do not understand that they could be blocking their own prayers because of sin (see Isaiah 59:1-2; Jeremiah 5:25). That is why we need to fellowship with other believers, so we can see the truth that will make us free. In order to see if we have issues in the area of fear of man, we have to be around people of authority. In order to see if we have issues with impatience, we need to drive in traffic. If someone irritates you, that is actually a good sign. It means that you have some heart issues to deal with. We need others to help us see what is in ourselves so we can get free! It's the truth (about what we see in us) that helps free us.

If you were asked if you are entertaining a spirit of fear and you say, "No, I have no fear." And then in the course of the conversation begin asking you if you are afraid of getting a disease, or afraid of dying or afraid of making a mistake. Usually people would respond with, "Actually I do have some of those thoughts." Now they've discerned that they are in fact entertaining a spirit of fear that God did not give them. Could this be what is hindering their relationship with God? Could this be what is hindering their prayer life? So we need each other to help us see clearly so we can recover ourselves from the snare of the devil. We need to make a proclamation about what we just discovered. Share this revelation truth with someone. It's the blood of the lamb and the word of our testimony that overcomes the enemy (see Rev. 11:13).

Jesus even said, *"Father, I know that you always hear Me, but I pray out loud now so these nearby can hear Me and believe."* Then He raised Lazarus from the grave.

> *Then they took away the stone from the place where the dead was laid. And Jesus lifted up His eyes, and said, Father, I thank Thee that Thou hast heard Me. And I knew that Thou hearest Me always: but because of the people which stand by I said it, that they may believe that Thou hast sent Me* (John 11:41-42).

Okay, you may say, that was Jesus, and He is the Son of God. He was given all power in Heaven and on earth; we are not Him and never will be. But then we must go back to John 14: *"He that believeth on Me, the works that I do shall he do also; and greater works than these shall he do; because I go unto My Father"* (John 14:12).

We just miss it because we do not stay in the Word all the time; we lose that heavenly perspective and take on an earthly perspective. Papa God wants us to move in His signs, wonders, and miracles; the devil wants to get us to think like he does and entertain defeat and sickness.

Our position is that it is possible to have all your prayers answered according to the Bible when we cast down every high thing that tries to exalt itself against the knowledge of God (see 2 Cor. 10:5).

Derek Prince[1] once said that all his prayers were answered because he always prayed according to the will of God. But this can only happen when you know God's thoughts and His will. Some say that it is not God's will to heal. Who told them that? It wasn't the Word of God because the Bible is filled with Scriptures that tell us otherwise. Who are you going to believe? Because, as you have believed, let it be done. If you don't believe in healing, then don't expect to be healed. If you don't believe God loves you, then you will have a hard time loving yourself and others.

The Lord gives us freedom of choice to think like Him, or to think like the world and the devil.

What's Our Point?

You have to be a doer of the Word for blessings to manifest this side of Heaven. Often, people make up theological reasons to explain why prayer did not work. We hope that from reading this book, you have what you need to defeat the enemy and see good results for your life. Scripture says, "Thy will be done in earth, as it is in heaven" (see Matt. 6:10). We should be encouraging each other to bring Heaven to earth by walking in love and peace continually as best we can.

When Jesus cursed the fig tree, it took a day or so for it to die. Just because we do not see something happen immediately, it is no reason to give up. If Papa God said it, we just believe it; we trust in Him and lean not on our own understanding. People will know we are Christians by our love for one another. We need to exalt the Word of God above the words of the devil and his imaginations. We need to stay in faith and cast down every stinking thought that goes contrary to God's Word—so we expect the manifestation of His Word in our lives.

If you don't see an immediate manifestation of God's Word, then the devil will try to make you feel like a failure as a believer. He wants to cast doubt on what God said just as he did in the Garden of Eden: "Has God really said?" (see Gen. 3:1). Once you have declared the Word of God above the imaginations of the enemy, then the battle will be victorious. As you continue to exalt the Word of God and cast down every imagination, wait patiently on the Lord until the full manifestation of the victory that we have in Jesus' name occurs. Having done all, stand (see Eph. 6:13). That means, now wait on God. Don't grow weary in well doing for in due season you will reap if you don't faint or give up (see Gal. 6:9).

There was a man who lived in a village in another country they called "The rain maker." During an interview he was asked why they called him that. He said it was because when they needed rain, the people would ask him to pray. He would draw a circle on the ground, sit in it and pray until it rained, even if it took days. Now that is someone who doesn't give up.

We need to do all we know to do, and then stand and wait on God.

> *Wherefore take unto you the whole armour of God, that ye may be able to withstand in the evil day, and having done all, to stand* (Eph. 6:13).

Sometimes we aren't doing anything but waiting on God to do it. That is error. When Jesus said, "It is finished" that is what He meant. He's done all He is going to do. He left us His peace. He left us the keys to the Kingdom. He left us in charge of this planet. He left us the power of the Holy Ghost to lead, guide and direct us. He left us to teach nations, make disciples, do what He did and more. So why are we sitting around waiting? What do waiters do when you go to a restaurant. They serve. They don't sit around and tell you to go get your own order. This is the same with waiting on God. Do all you know to do, then wait… in faith. We believe during the waiting time. We don't doubt, we don't fall into fear. We wait believing.

Let's do all we can do, and then see what God does. This also pertains to our thoughts. Have you ever regretted saying something but didn't know how to fix it? Well, the enemy wants to put guilt on you and oppression from it. So here is how you apply this scripture. You repent to God for your part, and pray that the Lord restores that person. Sometimes we don't even have to talk to that person, but sometimes God tells us to. Each situation is different, but suffice to say, we have to stop falling into guilt. Take responsibility for your part, and let God take care of the part you can't do. Let's repeat that. Do what you know to do, and what you can't do, that's what you trust God for.

Asking God for something in prayer is just that. Are we asking God for something we can do? If we are, we may not get that prayer answered. But if we are asking God for something we cannot do, that's a prayer we'll see answered. We believe that God has given us everything we need to live this life. Our bodies were made to heal itself as it lines up with the Word of God. Relationships are restored when we apply forgiveness.

Did you know the father of the prodigal son didn't go looking for him but when He saw his son coming in the distance, he ran to him and kissed him on his neck? Sometimes we have to take the first step toward the Lord so He takes His steps toward us.

> *Come now, and let us reason together, saith the Lord: though your sins be as scarlet, they shall be as white as snow; though they be red like crimson, they shall be as wool* (Isaiah 1:18).

The Bible says that the Lord sent a "helper" to help us, not do it for us. Let's begin changing our thinking about this and imagine ourselves representing the Father on this earth.

Now this takes some imagination. But if you think about it, it's actually quite fascinating. The Bible says that there is healing in His wings (see Mal. 4:2). we like that. Because people sometimes find themselves between a rock and a hard place, and they feel trapped. But nothing is impossible with God. No matter what you are facing, He is able to deliver you. Trust Him and stop trying to figure it all out. That's what it means to stand.

Rejecting Stinkin' Thinkin'

Many Christians are defeated before they even get started by the imaginations that they are receiving. They are defeated with spirits of sickness, poverty, and unfulfilled dreams.

As soon as they begin to feel uncomfortable symptoms, they begin to receive the devil's imaginations that he sends with the symptoms. If you sneeze, the first think you think is, "Oh no I'm getting a cold." And it's further from the truth, it was probably that dusty room you cleaned that day and the sneeze is just cleaning it out. But if you open the door to that thinking, the thing you fear may come upon you.

Perfect peace comes to those whose minds are stayed on the Lord. And perfect peace causes our immune system to work properly to fight off any viruses that may come.

What if the bank and bill collectors decide to collect what you owe them today? What will you do? The moment that you begin to think on and accept negative imaginations, you sow a seed for these things.

Some seeds seem to have a quick result, just as some plants grow more quickly than others. Again, you cannot put your faith in the devil's imaginations and expect to be victorious in God.

When you grab hold of this concept that you have the ability in your own thoughts to choose what pathway you are going to take, fear based or faith based—it must make the devil and his demons mad because his job is to get you to be miserable all the time. Misery loves company, so stop fellowshipping with him and his misery. Choose today; only you can do it. He has imagined you very sick and defeated, and the devil wants to transfer that imagination to you so it will manifest in you. This is when you must really work your faith and believe the report of the Lord that you shall not die but live and proclaim the Word of the Lord. You speak the truth out loud.

How many times have you found you are about to pray for a sick person or cast out a devil out of someone, and immediately the enemy comes to you, saying, "What if they don't get healed or delivered?" Listen, it's not your reputation at stake here. When this happens, you have to speak out loud what is going to happen in Jesus' name before the devil can try and steal anything from you or the person you are ministering to.

Immediately cast down and declare what is going to happen according to the Holy Word. The battle for the healing or deliverance is most likely won before we even lay physical hands on someone to pray for them. The battle is won by whose imaginations you have received—God or the devil's. Matthew 21:22 says, *"And all things, whatsoever ye shall ask in prayer, believing, ye shall receive."*

The believing comes before the receiving. If you believe Papa God's imagination, take in His Holy Words, His visions and thoughts for you, what do you think you shall receive?

If you who are evil know how to give good gifts to your children, how much more will God bless those who do this? (see Luke 11:13).

When you go to lay hands on the sick, you must already believe that they will be healed; otherwise, you might as well not even go there. If you have asked God for some provisions, you must already believe that He is going to give it to you, before you actually receive it. That is why "abiding" in Him all day long is so important. You are already being equipped and prepared for what is coming down the pike. You don't have to say, "hey devil wait a minute while I fast and pray and seek God." You are already in that mode.

> *And the spirit cried, and rent him sore, and came out of him: and he was as one dead; insomuch that many said, He is dead. But Jesus took him by the hand, and lifted him up; and he arose. And when he was come into the house, his disciples asked him private-*

*ly, Why could not we cast him out? And he said unto them, This kind can come forth by nothing, but by prayer and fasting (*Matthew 9:26-29).

Did Jesus go and pray and fast before he cast out that spirit from that man? No. He was in a constant state of prayer and fasting.

There is a passage that talks about the disciples unable to cast a devil out of a man who was being tormented severely. The disciples asked Jesus why they couldn't cast it out. Jesus said, "This cannot come out only by prayer and fasting." It's not that a person says, "I'll be back later to cast that out after I have fasted and prayed." What this means is that if we live in a state of prayer (pray without ceasing) and fasting as Isaiah 58:6-9 talks about (to minister one to another), then we can cast out that demon.

Stop letting the stinking enemy steal your faith in God's imagination for you, especially if there is a waiting period before the full manifestation. We are to walk by faith, not by how things look in the natural. The devil will try to introduce fear by getting you to focus on how things look. We serve a supernatural God who can cause you to walk on water; anything is possible with the Lord when you keep your eyes on the Lord Jesus and imagine things the way He does. That is why the scripture says to walk by faith not by sight (see 2 Corinthians 5:7).

Whose imagination or report are we going to believe and receive? If we choose to cast down the imaginations of the enemy, then we are going to have to actively and continually guard our mind, and speak the Word of God, moment by moment if that is what it takes.

> But the word of the Lord was unto them precept upon precept, precept upon precept; line upon line, line upon line; here a little, and there a little; that they might go, and fall backward, and be broken, and snared, and taken (Isaiah 28:13).

Are you going to entertain those thoughts of failure from the devil? Hey, it's your mind and your battle; don't let the devil write his imaginations on it!

All the devil wants is to deceive us and erode our faith in the Word of God. Discipline yourself to immediately cast down ungodly imaginations. We cannot do that for you. The biblical way to cast down imaginations is through speaking the Word of God immediately when the enemy sends his imaginations.

Jesus is the perfect model for our warfare. For example, in Luke 4:1-15, when the devil uses the Bible to tempt Him, Jesus responds with Scripture: *"Get thee behind me, Satan: for it is written..."*

Sometimes the devil can send his imaginations for you through friends or family members. Mark 8:31-33 says,

> *And He began to teach them, that the Son of man must suffer many things, and be rejected of the elders, and of the chief priests, and scribes, and be killed, and after three days rise again. And He spake that saying openly. And Peter took Him, and began to rebuke Him. But when He had turned about and looked on His disciples, He rebuked Peter, saying, Get thee behind Me, Satan: for thou savourest not the things that be of God, but the things that be of men* (Mark 8:31-33).

Jesus saw how Peter was being influenced through theta brain waves and how the devil was speaking through this disciple.

Numbers 13:1-33 talks of 12 men who were sent to spy out the land where God was sending them. Joshua and Caleb came back and reported, "We can take the land," while the other ten brought back a disheartening report. Their thoughts and imaginations got the better of them; they listened to the enemy of defeat, and that's what they believed.

Joshua and Caleb believed God. They wanted to run in and take the land immediately. They believed that with God all things were possible. Because of the faith of Joshua and Caleb, they were the only two in that generation who entered the Promised Land; all the others died in the wilderness. Joshua and Caleb exalted the Word of God and therefore received the promises of the Word.

People often exalt or accept the imaginations and thoughts of the enemy due to peer pressure because they just want to fit in and run with the "in" crowd. They don't want to be rejected, so they will do what others want them to do—just to be accepted. These individuals are listening to the enemy; they aren't hearing God at all, and what they believe they will get.

Remember, whatever you believe—be it good or bad—you may get it. We say, "may" because sometimes the Lord gives us time to retract that request. That is why our prayers seem not to be answered. It's because God knows what that request is going to do and is giving you time to be sure it's really what you want. Have you ever said, "Boy I'm glad that prayer wasn't answered." So is God!

More Than Conquerors

We are "more than conquerors." Why would we need to be "more than a conqueror?" Isn't being a conqueror enough in itself? And what does this have to do with our thoughts? Because we are what we believe.

> *Nay, in all these things we are more than conquerors through Him that loved us* (Romans 8:37).

> *As he thinketh in his heart, so is he* (Proverbs 23:7).

Joshua and Caleb were "more than conquerors." They believed correctly. If you want to live in victory like them, then you'll want to "believe" that you are "more than a conqueror" right now. If you have accepted Jesus Christ and His love for you, then you have the power to be more than a conqueror. It's His love alone that helps us acquire this. However, it's what you believe that makes it real or not, because the truth is, it's already there for us. That is why I've spent so much time discussing our thoughts and getting them lined up with what God says so that we can live victoriously.

Have you ever asked someone how he was doing and he said, "I'm just fine; I'm hanging in there." But you discern that he is not just fine. And his statement "I'm hanging in there" is indication he's having some problems. So it's either the truth or a lie—someone who is dealing with a spirit of fear won't tell you the truth.

We aren't to just "hang in there"; we are to be the head and not the tail, above and not beneath. We tread on serpents and scorpions, not the other way around. We have to get a grip and understand who we are in Christ! We are God's kids. We are heirs of salvation. We are "more than a conqueror." What will you believe? Do you believe He loves you? Do you believe you can do all things through Christ who strengthens you? Do you believe you are more than a conqueror? What are you *really* thinking? That is why we titled this book, "What Was I Thinking" because we need to *really* look at what we are thinking. "Why did you do that?" as opposed to "Why did you really do that?" This question goes deeper into the soul of man. And if we can answer the question at that level, we are half way to our freedom. This is where the rubber meets the road: it is the deciding factor for whether you are a conqueror or not.

Christians travel two roads: a high road and a low road. They both get to the final destination, but one is done with peace (believing God in every area of life), and one is done kicking and screaming (doubt, unbelief, and fear). What road will you choose? That is what being "more than a conqueror" is. Scriptures say that we'll even do "more" than Jesus did. We can't be content with the way things are; we are to aspire to grow more and more in His likeness and grace.

Here are a few examples of the low road: some may struggle with doubt and unbelief. Some may struggle with fear. And some may even struggle with personal and sexual sins like pornography.

What happens is that this person knows these are wrong thoughts so he or she tries to muster up the strength not to entertain them or "do" them. (Remember, where your thoughts go, your body follows.) The person has a "desire" to do what is right because the Holy Spirit indwells, shining the light. A person may even take thoughts captive and not allow the mind to wander extensively during those times, thinking, "I have conquered that moment," only to experience that temptation again. No wonder people fall into guilt and condemnation. Those evil spirits of accusation and guilt can come in like a flood and try to tempt the person again and lie to them saying that they aren't really free and never will be. So often if you take that in and go down under lustful thoughts, actions, and perversions, you will feel you are even more tripped up than before. We need to address these areas in our life that cause us to be tempted; otherwise, we are going to battle them every day. We have to get on a "new" road in our thinking and stop falling into that rut.

So how do we live on that high road? It seems so many people search the Scriptures, not really searching for answers, but searching for another rule to abide by, to add to the list of "do's or don'ts" and only choosing those that they want to do. We can get legalistic, making it all black and white. But the Lord gave us a rainbow of colors and told us that where sin abounds, His mercy and grace abound more (see Romans 5:20). That means no matter how much you think you have goofed up, His love and mercy is greater. Stop looking for another answer; simply admit your wrong doings and thoughts, confess them to the Lord, accept His forgiveness, His love and mercy, forgive yourself and others (if applicable), and press on. That is the Gospel in a nutshell—that is the high road.

"We are more than conquerors," Romans 8 says, "through Him who loved us." So stop being so hard on yourself. Jesus loves you, has all you need to be all you can be, and will always be there for you, no matter what.

We have to have this mind-set so that we walk as "more than a conqueror" and defeat the enemy to gain the victory.

You are not likely to resurrect the dead or heal a sick person in the all-powerful name of Jesus Christ of Nazareth if you have received the devil's evil, defeated imaginations for you. Jesus said in John 14:12-14:

> *Verily, verily, I say unto you, he that believeth on Me, the works that I do shall he do also; and greater works than these shall he do; because I go unto My Father. And whatsoever ye shall ask in My name, that will I do, that the Father may be glorified in the Son. If ye shall ask any thing in My name, I will do it.*

Some people accuse us of teaching out of context. But Matthew 10:7-8 tells us to go and raise the dead, heal the sick, and cast out devils. (See Mark 16:17-18, as well.) What you get is a result of what you believe. Those people who get mad about it just do not want to take any responsibility for what happens in their lives. The Bible says the curse cannot come without a cause (see Prov. 26:2).

John 8:32 tells us the truth will make you free—but first it might make you miserable.

None of us has it all figured out yet; just keep pressing in and seeking the Lord, His Kingdom, and His righteousness, and all the things you hope, ask, or dream of will be added to you. Matthew 6:33 says, *"But seek ye first the kingdom of God, and His righteousness; and all these things shall be added unto you."*

God's Dreams and Visions for You

Sometimes God will speak to us through dreams or visions or a prophet; however, He will always speak to us through His written Word. Many Christians do not know their Bible very well, so they simply do not understand what He has imagined for us.

God wrote His imaginations in your spirit, soul, and mind. This would be a good time to start exalting the Lord, and His dreams and visions for you. Start imaging what it is Papa God has given you, by confessing it out loud, declaring what the Word of God says about it, and casting down every imagination and high thing that the enemy tries to give you that is opposite of what He has told us. Remember, you have to first believe to receive. We like what the Bible says that the father of the boy with the deaf and dumb spirit said to Jesus, *"I believe; help my unbelief."* He knew he needed to believe more to receive the healing of his child (see Mark 9:24).

We have shared with you in every way possible how important it is to line up our imagination (thoughts) with God's. When we do this, the blessings and healing we so desire will come. This is a promise! That is why we need to exercise our faith, waiting patiently for the Lord to deliver.

We need to pray for each other and build each other up, not tear each other down. When we do that, and stay in an attitude of praise and worship, we will receive blessings.

Then shall thy light break forth as the morning, and thine health shall spring forth speedily: and thy righteousness shall go before thee; the glory of the Lord shall be thy reward. Then shalt thou call, and the Lord shall answer; thou shalt cry, and he shall say, Here I am. If thou take away from the midst of thee the yoke, the putting forth of the finger, and speaking vanity; And if thou draw out thy soul to the hungry, and satisfy the afflicted soul; then shall thy light rise in obscurity, and thy darkness be as the noon day: And the Lord shall guide thee continually, and satisfy thy soul in drought, and make fat thy bones: and thou shalt be like a watered garden, and like a spring of water, whose waters fail not (Isaiah 58:8-11).

And all these blessings shall come on thee, and overtake thee, if thou shalt hearken unto the voice of the Lord thy God (Deuteronomy 28:2).

In that day shall this song be sung in the land of Judah; we have a strong city; salvation will God appoint for walls and bulwarks. Open ye the gates, that the righteous nation which keepeth the truth may enter in. Thou wilt keep him in perfect peace, whose mind is stayed on Thee: because he trusteth in Thee. Trust ye in the Lord for ever: for in the Lord Jehovah is everlasting strength (Isaiah 26:1-4).

If what we've shared in this chapter rings true in your heart, then pray this prayer.

Our Father in Heaven, Papa God, forgive me for listening to the lies of the enemy and making his thoughts greater than Yours. I repent and ask for Your forgiveness. I only want Your thoughts in my heart and mind; I desire more of Your truth and Your vision for my life. Help me see as You see, Lord. Let my mind be filled with all that You say, not what the devil has said. I thank You, Papa God, for Your forgiveness, and I choose to receive it. I choose to walk in freedom this day. I renounce in my generations all the way back to Adam, and I repent and renounce in my life for fellowshipping with any unclean spirits. I renounce and repent in my life for all condemnation and gossip and murmuring; for all accusation toward God, self, and others; for bitterness and all its underlings; and for all the wrong things I have imagined. In Jesus of Nazareth's name. Amen.

Our Prayer For You

In the name of Jesus Christ of Nazareth, we take authority over all the works of the enemy, and we bind and break its powers. We cancel the assignment of every stinking spirit that has ever messed with your imagination.

We bind all judgment and criticism, all condemnation, all gossip and murmuring. We bind and break the powers of all accusation and criticism that would come against you through the mouths of other people.

It is written, "No weapon formed against you shall prosper and every tongue that rises against you in judgment you shall condemn for this is the heritage of the servants of the Lord! Their righteousness is of me saith the Lord."

We take authority over self-accusation where you have accused yourself, feeling you've not done enough, or not done it well enough.

We command every stinking evil spirit that has used your imaginations for evil, for guilt, shame, condemnation, false burden bearing, false responsibility, people pleasing, and drivenness, to go right now into the abyss, in the name of our Lord Jesus Christ of Nazareth.

The Word of God is clear that the Children of God have been given the fruit of the Spirit which is love, joy, and peace in the Holy Ghost. Be released to enjoy your life and serve the Lord whole heartedly without fear. In Jesus Christ of Nazareth's Name. Amen.

Practical Application

It's important to take a moment and imagine what you think you look like to Papa God right now. Is it good? Or is it frightful? Do you feel His love, or do you feel abandoned? When you sit at the supper table with the Lord, where do you find yourself sitting? Are you even at the table or sitting under it eating crumbs. Did you know that we can sit with Jesus in Heavenly places? Something to imagine.

Don't forget, the Lord has no fear at all, so He doesn't see things like we do from our earthly perspective. We too often look at things through fear instead of through faith, but He looks at us through faith and love. So, let me ask again, what do you see when you look at yourself through His eyes?

For some of us this would take a "stretch" of the imagination. But that is good; we need to get out of the old ruts in our thinking and explore new possibilities. The Bible says that no one has ever imagined the depths and greatness of His love, so we think we all have some room here to grow in.

> *But as it is written, eye hath not seen, nor ear heard, neither have entered into the heart [imaginations] of man, the things which God hath prepared for them that love Him* (1 Corinthians 2:9).

Just don't imagine any pink zebras with yellow stripes. No, don't imagine that! You see how powerful words are—even written words—so if you spend more time getting to know what Papa God actually says about you in His Holy Bible, those images of who you are will transform your life right into His image! And you will never doubt again how much He really loves you.

Bottom Line

Rule #1: Imagine good things.

Rule #2: See Rule #1.

If this didn't make you smile, find something that does. Put your mind on what brings *you* peace and joy.

Endnotes

1. Derek Prince, They Shall Expel Demons (Grand Rapids, MI: Chosen, 1998); Blessing or Curse (Grand Rapids, MI: Chosen, 1990, 2006); On Experiencing God's Power (New Kensington, PA: Whitaker House, 1998).

Chapter Thirteen

SALVATION MESSAGE

You have learned so many things about how thoughts work, what the Bible says about them, and what we found that science says about them. You learned that some of your thoughts may not even be your own. But there is only one way to be certain you are hearing correctly, and that is to be assured of your salvation. The Bible says that *"His sheep hear His voice."* Well in order to hear His voice and apply all that we have spoken or rather written to you, you need to have the Holy Spirit. This comes by truly believing that Jesus Christ of Nazareth is who He says He is and accepting Him as your Lord and your Savior.

Some of you have already accepted Jesus Christ as your Lord and Savior; others reading this book are still unsure about Him. Whatever the case, this chapter is an excellent source for you to help others or make a decision for yourself. In order for the things I've talked about works in your life, you need the Holy Spirit of Jesus Christ of Nazareth dwelling within you. He is the only way, truth, and life to our Father in Heaven who has all these blessings to give. So you may ask, "What must I do to be saved?"

This is a question that is often asked, and the Bible gives us the answer.

In Acts 16, the apostle Paul and his esteemed colleague, Silas, were incarcerated by men who sought to persecute them for sharing the Gospel message. After being beaten and chained in this dark, smelly, damp prison, Paul and Silas begin to worship the Lord Jesus Christ of Nazareth about midnight.

Can you imagine singing praises to the Lord after being abused and beaten severely just for doing a good and noble thing? Talk about putting on the sacrifice of praise as the Bible says to do (see Heb. 13:15). This means praising the Lord even when you do not particularly feel like it. Because of their faithful devotion, the Lord sent a sign and wonder, and an earthquake came. Immediately everyone's prison chains fell off, and all the prison doors were flung open.

Paul was someone who listened to the Lord without much thought to his own self-preservation. The jailer in charge of the prison was awakened out of his sleep and, seeing what had happened, was about to take his own life. He must have thought that was a better alternative than being tortured and killed by the Romans for losing a prisoner. In this case, he thought he had lost all the prisoners.

But the apostle Paul cried out to him with a loud voice, as he must have known what was about to take place: *"Do thyself no harm: for we are all here"* (Acts 16:28).

What an amazing moment that must have been for this man who was about to end his life in disgrace! Instead of doing himself in, he called for a light, ran in, fell down before Paul and Silas trembling, and asked this question so many of us need to ask:

> *Sirs, what must I do to be saved? And they said, Believe on the Lord Jesus Christ, and thou shalt be saved, and thy house* (Acts 16:30-31).

Confess and Repent

The Bible tells us that if we confess that Jesus Christ is Lord and believe He is the Son of God, that He died on the cross for our sins, and that He was raised from the dead, then we shall be saved.

That if thou shalt confess with thy mouth the Lord Jesus, and shalt believe in thine heart that God hath raised Him from the dead, thou shalt be saved (Romans 10:9).

For all have sinned, and fallen short of the glory of God (Romans 3:23).

Sin has separated us from God who loves us. The first thing we need to do after we believe is ask the Lord to forgive us of all our sins. In Romans 6:23, we read that payment of sin is death, but the gift of God is eternal life through Jesus Christ of Nazareth. There is no other way but through the Lord Jesus Christ of Nazareth. He is the one who paid an untold price for all your sins and took your place on your cross.

We learn in Ephesians 2:1 that the Lord has shown us the truth, so we do not have to keep living in sin and listening to evil thoughts that are not even ours.

Jesus Himself tells us in John 14:6 that He is the only way to God; there is no other way to reach God. Jesus is the living bridge that you must cross over to reach God the Father: *"Jesus saith unto him, I am the way, the truth, and the life: no man cometh unto the Father, but by Me."*

Jesus began His earthly ministry by calling people to repentance (see Matt. 4:17). To repent means to turn away from the sinful things in our lives and start to think more like God thinks. How can we know what God thinks? By studying His Word, the Holy Bible. We have the ability to begin to think and do good instead of evil.

Some people have expressed the idea that all you have to do is believe; however, it is just as important to walk away from sin in your life and walk toward the Lord and those things that are good. There is a Scripture that says, *"I fear lest you complicate the Gospel of Jesus Christ"* (see 2 Cor. 11:3). His message is simple, so don't complicate it; just agree with it and do it.

In Luke 13, again Jesus tells us we need to repent to be saved: *"I tell you, Nay: but, except ye repent, ye shall all likewise perish."*

Again Jesus said that if you love Him, you would keep His commandments (see John 14:15). It's that simple. Loving God will cause you to want to do what He has taught. So instead of making yourself obey, it will become a pleasure just to do it. We can live this life kicking and screaming or just get on board and believe and trust God. By loving Him, believing Him and trusting Him will cause you to be obedient. It's so much easier than trying to "make" yourself obey. Seek first the Kingdom of God and His righteousness, and all these things will be added to you (see Matthew 6:33). Instead of trying to be a good Christian. Instead of trying to do everything right. Seek the righteousness of God in Jesus Christ, and you will have what you need to live like you believe!

Really Knowing Christ

There are some who claim to be Christians, yet at the end of their life when they meet Jesus face to face, He may say to them, *"I never knew you: depart from Me, ye workers of iniquity"* (Matt. 7:21-23).

That will be an awful thing, to find out at the end you weren't even His! What does that really mean? It means that they weren't truly saved. They did all the "churchy" things, but didn't come into relationship with Him. Now don't fall into fear here. Here are some signs to help you decide for yourself if you are really His. Do you have a desire to please Him? Do you have a desire to know Him? Do you want to be changed more in His image every day? Then you are His because you wouldn't be convicted of these things if you didn't have the Holy Spirit teaching you these things.

Then just get on with the program; stop fearing you're not saved and stop listening to the spirit of doubt and unbelief. However, if these aren't in your thoughts, then stop and take the time to make that right. Having intimacy with God means knowing His incredible nature and character and living like we believe. It's not about religion; it's about relationship.

We need to get to know Him, and we do that through Bible reading, fellowship, and prayer. It's really that simple!

The Bible teaches you how to be like Jesus with clear instruction. One area He taught on that is critical to every believer is forgiveness. We are told to forgive everyone that sinned (or sins) against you, and that includes forgiving your-self! As soon as you begin to forgive, you enter into a place of holiness. It doesn't mean you are perfect. It means that when you sin, you take it to the Lord and confess your sins, for He is faithful to forgive and cleanse you (see 1 John 1:9).

Jesus Christ hung on a cross and said to His Father in Heaven, *"Forgive them; for they know not what they do"* (Luke 23:34). Then He led the thief who was crucified next to Him into salvation.

> *And he said unto Jesus, Lord, remember me when Thou comest into Thy kingdom. And Jesus said unto him, Verily I say unto thee, today shalt thou be with Me in paradise* (Luke 23:42-43).

We also read in Proverbs that *"He that covereth his sins shall not prosper: but whoso confesseth and forsaketh them shall have mercy"* (Prov. 28:13). Luke 15:10 says, *"Likewise, I say unto you, there is joy in the presence of the angels of God over one sinner that repenteth."*

If there is no repentance, no walking away from those sin-ful things in your life, then there is no joy either because there is no salvation.

Benefits of Salvation

John 10:28 says the Holy Spirit seals us unto salvation, *"And I give unto them eternal life; and they shall never perish, neither shall any man pluck them out of My hand."*

What a promise and benefit of salvation! Not only that, He's got us imprinted in the palm of His hand so we are ever be-fore His face!

> *Can a woman forget her sucking child, that she should not have compassion on the son of her womb? Yea, they may forget, yet will I not forget thee. Behold, I have graven thee upon the palms of My hands; thy walls are continually before Me* (Isaiah 49:15-16).

This is true for those who have truly committed their lives to the Lord, trusting Him for their life. When we stumble and fall along the way, we can quickly repent and accept the Lord's forgiveness, forgiving others and ourselves. We can keep on keeping on, fighting the good fight until we finish this race (see 2 Tim. 4:7).

Another benefit of salvation is understanding that Jesus provided healing for your body.

> *Is any sick among you? let him call for the elders of the church; and let them pray over him, anointing him with oil in the name of the Lord: And the prayer of faith shall save the sick, and the Lord shall raise him up; and if he have committed sins, they shall be for-given him. Confess your faults one to another, and pray one for another, that ye may be healed. The effectual fervent prayer of a righteous man availeth much* (James 5:14-16).

Another benefit we find is that nothing can separate us from His love.

> *For I am persuaded, that neither death, nor life, nor angels, nor principalities, nor powers, nor things pres-ent, nor things to come, nor height, nor depth, nor any other creature, shall be able to separate us from the love of God, which is in Christ Jesus our Lord* (Ro-mans 8:38-39).

The Lord does not want any of us to perish; He has foreor-dained, determined, and predestined that all should come to salvation. However, not everyone who is called accepts His invitation. This is where "free will" comes in. He isn't forcing you to trust Him or accept Him; however, He's made it very easy to do so.

We need to believe that Papa God is for us and will freely give us all things, that He is the one who sent Jesus and the Holy Spirit to help us out, and that nothing can separate us from the love of Christ.

A very important benefit is the gift of the Holy Ghost. Once we have been born again, something inside us (which is the Holy Spirit) gives us the desire to please the Lord and to do what is right in His sight. That is one of the "signs" you are truly saved. It doesn't mean we will do it perfectly all the time; it means we have a "desire" to please Him. As we grow in the Lord, we will do more right things than wrong—this is what is called sanctification.

Another benefit is asking for and receiving the desires of your heart! Do you have any desires? Do you have any prayers that need to be answered? Mark 11:24 says, *"What things soever ye desire, when ye pray, believe that ye receive them, and ye shall have them."* That includes pretty much anything you can desire for.

Jesus makes this promise in John 15:7: *"If ye abide in Me, and My words abide in you, ye shall ask what ye will, and it shall be done unto you."* So the abiding Christian receives a major benefit from Jesus here, namely, receiving answered prayer.   Notice this happens through Jesus with another conditional sentence. He says here: *"If you abide in Me, and you may or may not, and My words abide in you, and they may or may not, then you shall ask whatever you desire, and it shall be done for you."* we encourage you to do a study of the word abiding—it means to obey.

We believe that it is a true benefit to be able to go to Papa God at any time, confess our faults and sins, and have the power of the Holy Ghost help us refrain from ever doing them again. The Bible says that sin is actually pleasurable, but only for a moment, because the results of it can cause you much pain and suffering and even bring sickness and disease.

> *Choosing rather to suffer affliction with the people of God, than to enjoy the pleasures of sin for a season* (Hebrews 11:25).

Proverbs 26:2 tells us that the curse—which is all manner of evil, broken relationships, sickness, and diseases—cannot come without a reason: *"As the bird by wandering, as the swallow by flying, so the curse causeless shall not come."* You give it the reason when you disobey the Lord and His commandments.

Jesus tells us Himself, *"If you love Me, do what I command"* (see John 14:15). Salvation gives you the power to overcome the world and the devil. Luke 10 says that the Lord will give you power over the enemy when you are adopted into His family through Jesus Christ:

Behold, I give unto you power to tread on serpents and scorpions, and over all the power of the enemy: and nothing shall by any means hurt you. Notwithstanding in this rejoice not, that the spirits are subject unto you; but rather rejoice, because your names are written in heaven (Luke 10:19-20).

After you have been saved by faith and have received Jesus Christ, His Holy Spirit comes and lives in our hearts.

For this cause I bow my knees unto the Father of our Lord Jesus Christ, of whom the whole family in heaven and earth is named, that He would grant you, according to the riches of His glory, to be strengthened with might by His Spirit in the inner man; that Christ may dwell in your hearts by faith; that ye, being rooted and grounded in love, may be able to comprehend with all saints what is the breadth, and length, and depth, and height; and to know the love of Christ, which passeth knowledge, that ye might be filled with all the fulness of God. Now unto Him that is able to do exceeding abundantly above all that we ask or think, according to the power that worketh in us, unto Him be glory in the church by Christ Jesus throughout all ages, world without end. Amen (Ephesians 3:14-21).

If we confess Christ before all men, Jesus Christ will confess us before our Heavenly Father:

Whosoever therefore shall confess Me before men, him will I confess also before My Father which is in heaven. But whosoever shall deny Me before men, him will I also deny before My Father which is in heaven (Matthew 10:32-33).

This is simple obedience to the Word. Are you going to do it or ignore it? James 1:22-25 says not to be a forgetful hearer but to do what the Word says, and then you will be blessed in your deed. How much simpler can we put it?

Make a Choice

So we have a choice to make here, either be blessed or be cursed. Some people have said, "Well, I just don't believe in Heaven or hell." That is like someone saying that they just don't believe in those invisible germs and bacteria that invade this present world.

Just because you cannot see them with your natural eyes does not mean they do not exist.

Under a microscope they are clearly seen. Through using the Holy Bible, we can clearly see there are other kingdoms that are real, although invisible to us at this moment.

The story in Luke 16 about two men who died is not really a parable. It is a true account of something that really happened, or the Lord Jesus would not have given the man's name.

Let's read of this account:

> There was a certain rich man, which was clothed in purple and fine linen, and fared sumptuously every day: and there was a certain beggar named Lazarus, which was laid at his gate, full of sores, and desiring to be fed with the crumbs, which fell from the rich man's table: moreover the dogs came and licked his sores. And it came to pass, that the beggar died, and was carried by the angels into Abraham's bosom: the rich man also died, and was buried; and in hell he lift up his eyes, being in torments, and seeth Abraham afar off, and Lazarus in his bosom. And he cried and said, Father Abraham, have mercy on me, and send Lazarus, that he may dip the tip of his finger in water, and cool my tongue; for I am tormented in this flame. But Abraham said, Son, remember that thou in thy lifetime received thy good things, and likewise Lazarus evil things: but now he is comforted, and thou art tormented. And beside all this, between us and you there is a great gulf fixed: so that they which would pass from hence to you cannot; neither can they pass to us, that would come from thence. Then he said, I pray thee therefore, father, that thou wouldest send him to my father's house: for I have

244

five brethren; that he may testify unto them, lest they also come into this place of torment. Abraham saith unto him, they have Moses and the prophets; let them hear them. And he said, Nay, father Abraham: but if one went unto them from the dead, they will repent. And he said unto him, If they hear not Moses and the prophets, neither will they be persuaded, though one rose from the dead (Luke 16:19-31).

This was a real event that happened, and it is in the Bible to help people understand that we must decide about eternity here. We have a choice to make before it is forever too late.

Hebrews 9:27 says it is appointed unto men to live once and then the judgment. You only have this life to live; there is no such thing as being reincarnated as some people may think. This life is it, so make sure you choose wisely here.

Trusting God's Word

"But wait a minute," you may say. "Didn't men write the Bible? Why should I accept all of this if mere men wrote this?" Simply put, God Almighty had certain people He chose to write down every word as He decided.

All scripture is given by inspiration of God, and is profitable for doctrine, for reproof, for correction, for instruction in righteousness (2 Timothy 3:16).

The whole Bible contains 66 books: 39 in the Old Testament and 27 in the New Testament. It all will harmonize. This fact is amazing in itself, as the Lord used about 40 different people at different times and ages to write the Bible. It took approximately 1,600 years to complete all the books of the Bible, which all go together as one complete work (just as it might take many years to build a magnificent castle or proper palace).

When you think about it, trying to get 40 different people of different ages and backgrounds to agree on anything would be a difficult task. Think about a company like IBM trying to get 20 people to agree to one idea, like where to go for dinner. At least some of them would most likely not want to eat where the majority decided. The Bible is an amazing work and gift the Lord has given us. If we really want to understand who God is, how He thinks, what He likes, and what He does not like, we would do well to spend time reading His instructions to us.

Many people in this world have countless ideas about all sorts of things from medicine and science to inventions of all kinds. If you go back and read the writings of some brilliant people of the past, you will find that often they were wrong about many things. Archaeologists and other scientists continually discover ancient artifacts, lost cultures, and scientific evidence, just as the Bible indicated all along.

> *I have made the earth, and created man upon it: I, even My hands, have stretched out the heavens, and all their host have I commanded* (Isaiah 45:12).

> *It is he that sitteth upon the circle of the earth, and the inhabitants thereof are as grasshoppers; that stretcheth out the heavens as a curtain, and spreadeth them out as a tent to dwell in* (Isaiah 40:22).

How tragic it is that so often people come up with their own conclusions instead of trusting in the Word of God.

Adam and Eve

To get a clear picture of the ancestry of a believer, we need to start at Genesis, beginning with the man and woman who were placed in a garden and told by God that they could eat anything they wanted, except for fruit from the tree of good and evil. The tree may have looked appealing to Eve because she wanted to be wise, so the enemy used that desire to cause her to sin.

Why would God have allowed evil to be in the world in the Garden of Eden? Perhaps because He needed to test Adam and Eve to see if they would rebel against Him as lucifer once did, taking one third of the angels with him when he was kicked out of Heaven:

> *How art thou fallen from heaven, O Lucifer, son of the morning! How art thou cut down to the ground, which*

didst weaken the nations! For thou hast said in thine heart, I will ascend into heaven, I will exalt my throne above the stars of God: I will sit also upon the mount of the congregation, in the sides of the north: I will ascend above the heights of the clouds; I will be like the most High. Yet thou shalt be brought down to hell, to the sides of the pit. They that see thee shall narrowly look upon thee, and consider thee, saying, Is this the man that made the earth to tremble, that did shake kingdoms...? (Isaiah 14:12-16)

Eve forms a hypothesis based on information given to her by the serpent. If she eats this forbidden fruit, she will be wise, and nothing bad can happen to her. Surely she will not die. She must have thought that Papa God was lying to her somehow, not wanting to share the truth with her, even though He would come and talk and walk with them in the cool of the evening.

Eve decides to do an experiment and observe what happens. She eats the forbidden fruit, and when she does not suffer any immediate results, she decides like any good scientist would, to repeat the experiment on her husband Adam. Once again, the results are the same. Eve has some data to work with. Only now their eyes are opened to see and feel things that they could not have observed before. There was nothing wrong with their eyesight before this experiment. Adam was able to see and name the animals. He was able to see Eve's beauty. They could both see perfectly, but now their spiritual eyes were open, and their knowledge had increased with understanding of good and evil.

You may not believe in gravity, but if you decide to test it and step off of a mountaintop, you will find that indeed there is a law of gravity. There are individuals who say they aren't worried about going to hell because they don't believe there is one. We just hope that these individuals take the time to seek the truth because we wouldn't want them to wake up one day on the other side with flames and darkness looming around them.

Everything in the Bible that God has said is true. He cannot lie; it is not in His nature to do so. So if He says there is a hell, then there is a hell. If Jesus says that He has gone to prepare a place for us and will come back for us, then we need to believe that He has gone to prepare a place and will return to get us (see John 14:3).

Entering the Kingdom of Heaven

We are actually eternal beings, but Satan wants you to think this is all there is, that there is no real place such as Heaven or hell, that you can live any way you choose and still go to Heaven as long as you say you are a good person or prayed the sinner's prayer asking Jesus to be your Savior.

> *He that overcometh, the same shall be clothed in white raiment; and I will not blot out his name out of the book of life, but I will confess his name before My Father, and before His angels* (Revelation 3:5).

Does that mean it's possible for your name to be blotted out of the book of life after it was entered there? What do the Scriptures say?

> *He that overcometh shall inherit all things; and I will be His God, and he shall be My son* (Revelation 21:7).

So you must be an overcomer, which means to believe what the Lord has said and be a doer of the Word of God.

Unbelieving Believers

Scriptures addresses the relationship we have with God. If we don't really believe He exists, then what do we really believe? Unbelief is a major block in our lives and an opening for the enemy. There are many Christians who doubt God is really there for them. When asking people at our conferences if they Love God, every hand goes up. But when we ask them if they have a hard time "receiving" God's love, almost every hand goes up. These are individuals who are unbelieving believers. Oh, they say He is there for others, but have a hard time believing for themselves. It's time to stop and repent right now for not believing He is there for you too.

Next up is the unbelieving. How many church-going people have we heard say, "I don't believe that part of the Bible," or "I do not think that part of the Bible is meant for today?" Please understand that God means what He said, and said what He means. Remember, He is the same yesterday, today, and tomorrow (see Heb. 13:8).

2 Corinthians 1:20 tells us that all of God's promises are for us now, today, personally: *"For all the promises of God in Him are yea, and in Him Amen, unto the glory of God by us."*

Every promise that fits our situation and meets our need is for us now, personally. We believe this verse rebuts any dispensational theories that would try and rob Christians of their kingdom benefits, such as physical healing and having their needs met.

In fact, we see in Mark 16:16 that *"He that believeth and is baptized shall be saved: but he that believeth not shall be damned."*

We are going to have to believe God's Holy Word for something to happen. If you don't believe, you can expect that nothing will happen. Then you will miss out on having a relationship with the Lord, and even miss Heaven, and possibly hear these words, "Depart from Me I never knew you"

> *And then will I profess unto them, I never knew you: depart from me, ye that work iniquity* (Matthew 7:23).

What is the iniquity that God is talking about here? Simply put, not believing, trusting and obeying God. How do we know if we believe God or not, by how we think and act. But it's not time to fall into condemnation, it's time to get right with God in your heart, for He will restore you if you desire it.

We are made up of spirit, soul, and body. Satan's kingdom accesses us and speaks to us at the spirit level, through our thoughts with theta brain waves. Therefore, our thoughts can only really come from one of three places: God, ourselves, or the enemy.

Please keep in mind: the devil is called the "great deceiver" because he really is skillful at deceiving mankind. Hosea 4:6 says that God's people are destroyed for a lack of knowledge.

If we give expression to thoughts from this evil invisible kingdom of darkness, we open doors for this kingdom to become one with us. This is best explained in Romans 7:17, where the apostle Paul refers to the "sin that dwells within." Sin, therefore, is a noun (the body of sin, Satan's kingdom)—or a verb (our sin if we become one with Satan's kingdom and allow it to express itself through our physical body). Sin comes to us by way of thoughts. That is why the Bible urges us to take every thought captive to the obedience of Christ. In fact we have over 60,000 thoughts a day.[1] It's time we start thinking about what we are thinking about. For every thought we have, thousands of electrical and chemical reactions take place. Those negative, unholy thoughts can do great harm to our bodies over an extended period of time.

Don't forget this scripture:

> *Let the words of my mouth, and the meditation of my heart, be acceptable in thy sight, O Lord, my strength, and my redeemer* (Psalm 19:14).

Choosing to Obey or Disobey

Deuteronomy 27 and 28 graphically illustrate the contrast between obedience and disobedience to the Lord our God. Here we find listed every manner of disease and broken relationships known to mankind.

Over in Romans 6:6 tells us that *"our old man is crucified with Him, that the body of sin might be destroyed, that henceforth we should not serve sin."* This passage does not say that the body of sin is destroyed; it says that we are crucified with Christ that it might be; it is now possible not to give in to sin. Paul explains that this is our place positionally, and that we are free from sin through the redemptive work of Christ if we have trusted in Him for our salvation.

We may be secure in Christ, but appropriation of this freedom in this life is our choice. Every day we must choose the blessings of God or the curses of the enemy. We can be led by the Holy Spirit and operate as the hands, feet, and mouth of our loving God, or we can become mediums of expression for evil and let the enemy rein in our bodies as one would rein in a horse to control its direction. As believers in Christ, moment by moment, throughout every day, we must make this choice. If we are children of God, then let us act like it.

Remember, we are containers, jars of clay, you might say. What are we full of? Are we full of God's peace and glory, or are we full of a spirit of pride that caused the downfall of lucifer? What we are really full of will manifest when we have to face certain decisions in our life. How we respond will show us what kingdom we are dwelling in. What do you savor? Jesus rebuked Peter by saying, *"Get thee behind me, Satan, for thou savourest not the things that be of God, but those that be of men"* (Matt. 16:23).

In other words, Peter spoke from that other kingdom! He had selfish reasons; he didn't want to see Jesus taken away because what would happen to him? Was this Peter or a spirit manifesting through him? The fact remains, who are you going to serve? What are you going to allow to fill your vessel? God is looking for a clean vessel to be used by Him.

> *If a man therefore purge himself from these, he shall be a vessel unto honour, sanctified, and meet for the master's use, and prepared unto every good work* (2 Timothy 2:21).

By knowing what we are full of, we can cooperate with God to find freedom from these things.

> *Come now, and let us reason together, saith the Lord: though your sins be as scarlet, they shall be as white as snow; though they be red like crimson, they shall be as wool* (Isaiah 1:18).

Why not start with right now by an act of forgiveness toward someone or even yourself? The very first key to freedom is to forgive—whether you feel like it or not. It is not so much about feelings as it is about obeying the Word of the Lord.

Is there anyone you have not yet forgiven? The Lord tells us if we do not forgive others, He will not forgive us!

> *So likewise shall My heavenly Father do also unto you, if ye from your hearts forgive not every one his brother their trespasses* (Matthew 18:35).

There was a story a few years ago where a man in Africa stabbed a Christian man to death as he left a church meeting. When the church found out, instead of accepting the finality of the situation as so many people would do, chose to pray and believe the Lord would raise their friend up from death. The Lord, in fact, did just that. The man who was brought back to life wanted to go to the jail and see the man who had killed him the night before. When they brought the murderer out, the man whom he had killed told him, "I just wanted you to know that I forgive you and that Jesus loves you." Well, that murderer broke down and got saved on the spot.[2]

There have been many documented accounts of people being raised from the dead and countless amazing healing and miracles in our lifetime, just as the Bible said would happen when we believe that all things are possible with God (see Matt. 19:26).

We see two things here: first, the church believed God could raise him from the dead; and second, the resurrected man followed up that miracle by forgiving the one who had killed him. How powerful is that?

Be Born Again

The question is what are you now going to do with this information?

But as many as received Him, to them gave He power to become the sons of God, even to them that believe on His name: which were born, not of blood, nor of the will of the flesh, nor of the will of man, but of God (John 1:12-13).

If you are ready to be born again and overcome the evil in this world, pray this out loud from your heart:

Father God, I come to You now and confess that I have done sinful things in my life. I have told lies, taken things that did not belong to me, and spoken things that hurt others. I am so sorry that I have done wrong, and I ask that You forgive me now, that You supernaturally wash me clean from all my sins by the precious blood of Jesus Christ of Nazareth. I forgive all those who have ever hurt me and sinned against me in my life, and because

I know that You have just forgiven me, I also forgive myself right now. I thank You for coming into my heart and for Your Holy Spirit who comes and fills me up from the crown of my head to the soles of my feet. Thank You that You mend my broken heart and that You have given me a new heart this day. I dedicate myself to You and make You my Lord and Savior. I pray this in the almighty name of Jesus Christ of Nazareth. Amen.

If you prayed this prayer from your heart, we encourage you to get into a gathering of Bible-believing friends and continue studying the Word of God for yourself.

It is also important to be completely immersed in water as the early church practiced; this is referred to as water baptism. You are demonstrating, in front of Papa God and witnesses both visible and invisible, that you are serious about your commitment to Jesus Christ. Water baptism represents dying, being buried to your old ways, and being raised up out of the water into your new life as a believer.

> *Sirs, what must I do to be saved? And they said, Believe on the Lord Jesus Christ, and thou shalt be saved, and thy house. And they spake unto him the word of the Lord, and to all that were in his house. And he took them the same hour of the night, and washed their stripes; and was baptized, he and all his, straightway. And when he had brought them into his house, he set meat before them, and rejoiced, believing in God with all his house* (Acts 16:30-34).

Did you notice that the jailer is now rejoicing in the Lord? That is supposed to happen when you are born again. It is your passport to paradise.

It is also important to ask the Lord your God to baptize you with His Holy Spirit. If you ask Him in faith, He will do it. Being baptized in the Holy Spirit means you have completely surrendered your life to the Lord, who will then equip you with the power to do all that is written in the Word.

> *And it came to pass, that, while Apollos was at Corinth, Paul having passed through the upper coasts came to Ephesus: and finding certain disciples [that means they were born again Christians], he said unto them, Have*

ye received the Holy Ghost since ye believed? And they said unto him, We have not so much as heard whether there be any Holy Ghost. And he said unto them, Unto what then were ye baptized? And they said, Unto John's baptism [that means they had been water baptized]. Then said Paul, John verily baptized with the baptism of repentance, saying unto the people, that they should believe on Him which should come after him, that is, on Christ Jesus. When they heard this, they were baptized in the name of the Lord Jesus. And when Paul had laid his hands upon them, the Holy Ghost came on them; and they spake with tongues, and prophesied (Acts 19:1-6).

Therefore we are buried with Him by baptism into death: that like as Christ was raised up from the dead by the glory of the Father, even so we also should walk in newness of life (Romans 6:4).

Buried with him in baptism, wherein also ye are risen with Him through the faith of the operation of God, who hath raised Him from the dead (Colossians 2:12).

These are two experiences we are to have after we become believers—being buried with Christ in water baptism, and then enjoying the newness of our eternal life and the empowerment of the Holy Spirit.

God loves all His children; He created us in all different sizes and races: red, yellow, black, or white, we are precious in His sight. *"For ye are all the children of God by faith in Christ Jesus"* (Gal. 3:26).

Living by Faith

Being born again gives us the power to become the sons and daughters of God, by faith. *"But as many as received Him, to them gave He power to become the sons of God, even to them that believe on His name"* (John 1:12).

We are "becoming" sons of God once we believe on His name. In that process, we are learning to be like our Daddy in Heaven (see Romans 8:15). That is what faith is for.

The Bible says we are saved by grace through faith, but that is only the beginning. Salvation is appropriated by faith. If we are saved and sanctified the minute we received Jesus, why would we need faith? We are being saved day by day, and our faith is the ticket.

Ephesians 2:8 says, *"For by grace are ye saved through faith; and that not of yourselves: it is the gift of God."*

If you love the Lord, simply obey Him and do what He has commanded. The simplicity of the Gospel is this: when you sin, confess it! You are immediately restored and are "overcoming" the world. So take your peace. We get into trouble when we have the mind-set that we don't need to confess; we begin to doubt our salvation and fear God in the wrong way. When you have taken all your sins and weaknesses to the Lord, you are "becoming" sons and daughters, and you are "being" saved and sanctified every step of the way. As soon as you enter into a place of forgiveness, you have entered into a place of holiness before the Living God who loves you.

Now the just shall live by faith: but if any man draw back, My soul shall have no pleasure in him (Hebrews 10:38).

> *Even so faith, if it hath not works, is dead, being alone* (James 2:17).

Not only are we to believe, but we are to do what we believe! Once we are converted, we receive the power to overcome evil; previously, we were lost in the world's way of thinking. We may have had a consciousness of right and wrong, but without being born again in Christ Jesus, we can't qualify for His protection plan. We don't get a "redemption" ticket—or a "get out of hell free" card when we blow it! We do not have the power to overcome the darkness and evil of this present world without the power of His Holy Spirit to help us, and His love and grace in us to do it.

But when you have entrusted your life to the Lord Jesus Christ, you do receive a "redemption" ticket; you do receive a "get out of hell free" card because when you do blow it (and you will), you simply confess it to your Heavenly Father. Jesus made it possible for you to be pardoned of all your sins.

You do not have to be perfect, just forgiven. There is only One who is perfect, and we are not Him. Even Jesus said, "Why call me good, there is only one who is good, and that is the Father."

> *And he said unto him, Why callest thou me good? there is none good but one, that is, God: but if thou wilt enter into life, keep the commandments* (Matthew 19:17).

Jesus even said to keep His commandments. So what is that saying to us today? Keep His commandments. This was a New Testament command actually, talking to believers not the unsaved. As a matter of fact, the Bible was written for the believer, with provision for the unsaved! The Bible is the "revelation of Jesus Christ" and without the Holy Ghost within us, we won't see it properly. We won't understand. It won't be alive.

Once we put our faith in Jesus, now the sanctification process starts. As we were saying, we are saved by faith. So we need to continue believing we are saved. It hasn't happened yet. At the day we leave this earth, our faith shall be sight (as the old song goes.)

> *Wherefore, my beloved, as ye have always obeyed, not as in my presence only, but now much more in my absence, work out your own salvation with fear and trembling* (Phillippians 2:12).

It's a day by day choice to follow the Lord. We are given free will to do so with the power of the Holy Ghost to keep us.

> *And grieve not the holy Spirit of God, whereby ye are sealed unto the day of redemption* (Ephesians 4:30).

After we are born again, the Holy Spirit begins to sanctify us daily with the washing of the Word.

> *That He might sanctify and cleanse it with the washing of water by the word* (Ephesians 5:26).

He is able to reprogram our thinking so we begin to think, act, and do more as He would have us do.

Howbeit when He, the Spirit of truth, is come, He will guide you into all truth: for He shall not speak of Himself; but whatsoever He shall hear, that shall He speak: and He will shew you things to come. He shall glorify Me: for He shall receive of Mine, and shall shew it unto you (John 16:13-14).

We get to overwrite those old thoughts and programming the devil taught us and our generations. We get to renew our mind and transform our character more every day into the image God had in mind for us before the foundations of the world were even laid.

And be not conformed to this world: but be ye transformed by the renewing of your mind, that ye may prove what is that good, and acceptable, and perfect, will of God (Romans 12:2).

Be not conformed... that means we can be conformed. It's a choice to follow after the world or after the Word that can renew our mind daily in preparation for that day when we are called home.

Power of the Cross

So often people really misunderstand what happened at the cross; the work of the cross was finished by Jesus through His obedience to the Father. The cross represents the shed blood of Jesus, who took away the sins of the world. But we are also told to pick up our crosses and follow after Him.

And being found in fashion as a man, He humbled Himself, and became obedient unto death, even the death of the cross (Philippians 2:8).

Then said Jesus unto His disciples, If any man will come after Me, let him deny himself, and take up his cross, and follow Me (Matthew 16:24).

The work of the cross and picking up our cross in our day-to-day life must be finished through our obedience to Christ as doer of the Word—by following all His commandments.

And having in a readiness to revenge all disobedience, when your obedience is fulfilled (2 Corinthians 10:6).

If we say we love Jesus, then we must obey Him and do as He has commanded us to do (see John 14:15).

What is the first and foremost commandment? To know God is one God, and to love Him, love ourselves, and love others. That is the Gospel in a nutshell. When you love (which includes forgiving), you fulfill all the commandments!

And Jesus answered him, The first of all the commandments is, Hear, O Israel; the Lord our God is one Lord: and thou shalt love the Lord thy God with all thy heart, and with all thy soul, and with all thy mind, and with all thy strength: this is the first commandment. And the second is like, namely this, thou shalt love thy neighbor as thyself. There is none other commandment greater than these (Mark 12:29-31).

Of course there are people who simply don't want to obey the Lord but continue in sin and follow the lies of the devil. Many people live like the world because they are afraid of what someone will say or do. Matthew 10 tells us we are not to be afraid of men, but of God:

And fear not them which kill the body, but are not able to kill the soul: but rather fear Him which is able to destroy both soul and body in hell (Matthew 10:28).

This would be a good time to put into practice what you have learned. Be a doer of the Word, not a hearer only. A good place to start would be to begin reading your Bible. No matter if we are seasoned Christians or new to the faith, we all need to read our Bibles. We need to get to know Jesus, the author and finisher of our faith. We need to know God and His incredible nature, His love, and His forgiveness. And we also need to know the power of the Holy Spirit so we can release Him to work in our lives. So we can "learn" to be His child. Even Paul said, "I have learned." Everything we have said or done we have "learned" it. We aren't born with instincts like animals, we are born to choose. Whatever we know today or do today, we have learned. So we need to re-learn some things don't we?

If you work for a company, wouldn't it make good sense to learn what your boss likes and does not like if you hope to be promoted? Then you can do what is pleasing in his sight. How much more sense does it make to please the living God? Proverbs 16:7 says, *"When a man's ways please the Lord, he maketh even his enemies to be at peace with him."*

But as many as received him, to them gave he power to become the sons of God, even to them that believe on his name: (John 1:12).

As Christians, we are given the power to **become** the sons of God. The word "become" is a process. Daily serving, daily choosing, daily living unto the Lord. But we can only choose wisely if we have the power in us to do it. That is why it was so important to add the salvation message in this book. Without the leading of the Holy Ghost you will not be able to decipher your thoughts and take back your life.

Your Turn

Take a moment to think about your heart condition. Perhaps you are saved, or perhaps you haven't made that decision for Christ yet. Regardless, please respond here.

If you haven't made the decision to follow Jesus, now is a time to consider doing just that. Take that step of faith by acknowledging your sinful ways to God and by accepting Jesus Christ as your Lord and Savior. Ask Him to help you learn of Him and know His thoughts so that they become your thoughts. Ask Him to give you revelation and insights as you read the Word for yourself. Ask Him to help you see the truth, as it is what will make you free. Have a little talk with the Lord every day. Learn to hear His voice by reading the Bible.

For those of you who have already taken this step of faith, we urge you to step it up: become more determined and seek Him even more than you do now. There is so much more than we can ever imagine!

> *But as it is written, eye hath not seen, nor ear heard, neither have entered into the heart of man, the things which God hath prepared for them that love Him* (1 Corinthians 2:9).

We hope that you have made a decision to reaffirm your relationship with Him—or to meet Him for the first time. we want to rejoice with you and pray with you, so please tell us about it. If you would like to share, please do so by emailing us at:

wwit@truthfrees.org

Jesus loves you, and so do we!

Endnotes

1. http://www.goodtofeelgood.com/blog/your-brain-has-over-60000-thoughts-per-day/.
2. Heidi Baker, Always Enough (Grand Rapids, MI: Chosen, 2003).

Prayers for a Renewed Thought Life

We want to end this book by praying for you specifically in the areas we have spoken of. We spent a great deal of time, sometimes in repetition, to help you to see that we need to pay attention to what is in our heart because out of it flows the issues of life. So if you are ready to make a change; if you want to walk in victory; if you want to find peace in the midst of your storms; if you want your mind to be at rest; if you want to be more healthy; if you are ready to get rid of some of that stinkin' thinkin' and start listening to our Lord; if you are ready to get rid of those evil spirits that have been holding you down and disturbing your life for such a long time, then this prayer is for you to pray:

> Papa God, I renounce in my generations all the way back to Adam, and I repent and renounce in my life for fellowshipping with devils and with a spirit of unforgiveness and accusation, either accusing others or feeling accused by others. Because I know now that the devil is the one who accuses us day and night before You, and that is his way of dividing and conquering us and taking us away from Your holy truth. I renounce and repent in my life for all condemnation, gossip, and murmuring. I repent for all the times I listened to a religious spirit instead of listening to You through the Holy Word.
>
> Please forgive me now as I confess that I have sinned against You and You only. Wash me clean from all unrighteousness and forgive my every sin. I forgive all who have sinned against me, including myself. There have been times I mistakenly thought You did not really love me. I know that You do really love me and that the Lord Jesus Christ of Nazareth took my place on my cross and paid the penalty for my sins. Oh, thank You, Lord, for teaching me the truth; Your truth will make me free. I thank You, Papa God, for my forgiveness, and I choose to receive it; I choose to walk in freedom this day.

Thank You for showing me my thought life and help-ing me to continue to take every thought captive, replacing the lies with Your wonderful truth. Help me to continue to seek Your love because it's Your love that will cast out all fear. Thank You for Your presence, Your protection, Your care, and Your love. Thank You for restoring me to Your heart. I pray in Jesus of Nazareth's name. Amen.

Because we care for you, we want to come alongside and break off anything that could be hindering you and your walk with the Lord. We want to pray that the Lord will fill you with His love, His power, and His sound mind.

In the name of Jesus Christ of Nazareth, authority is taken over all the works of the enemy and bound and all power broken. Every stinking evil spirit of un-forgiveness and accusation assigned is canceled. All judgment and criticism, all condemnation, all gossip and murmuring is bound and cast out. Every power of accusation and criticism that would come against you through the mouths of other people is cast out. It is written, "No weapon formed against you shall prosper and every tongue that rises against you in judgment you shall condemn for this is the heritage of the servants of the Lord!" (See Isaiah 54:17.)

Self-accusation, where we accuse ourselves because of the stinkin' thinkin' that has released all sorts of toxic chemicals into our holy temples, go now in Jesus' name.

Broken hearts, that caused hurt because we lis-tened to the devil and his lies and hurt other people as well, go now. Every neurotransmitter, normalize now.

Every stinking, evil spirit of self-hatred, self-rejec-tion, self-bitterness, guilt, shame, condemnation, false burden bearing, false responsibility, people pleasing, and drivenness go right now into the dry place in the all-mighty and all-powerful name of our Lord Jesus Christ of Nazareth.

We have been given authority to tread upon serpents and scorpions and over all the powers of the enemy, and nothing will by any means harm us. The Word of God is clear that as His children, we have been given the fruit of the Spirit, which is love, joy, and peace in the Holy Ghost. And this is what we are willing to walk in from this day forward.

Pappa God, we pray that Your perfect, unconditional love would flood these dear saints to overflowing from this day on as it's Your love that casts out all fear and torment. We ask You to help them receive Your love for themselves, so they have what they need to live every day as an overcomer, a victor, and as "more than a conqueror."

We thank You for Your precious Son, Jesus Christ, who made a way for them to approach Your throne of grace. We thank You for all the love and blessings You have for them as we lift them to You now, in Jesus Christ of Nazareth's name. Amen.

Our Heart to Your Heart

This book was written to help people come into the knowledge and truth of the Word of God so that they are able to exercise their authority over the enemy and walk in the fullness of God in Christ Jesus all the days of their lives.

We are not perfect; we may not teach things perfectly, but we are doing our best with what we have been given. We don't want any lost; We don't want any sick. We want people set free and delivered from whatever is keeping them down. We want to help you be sure you are secure in you salvation so that you spend eternity with the Lord.

We shared what we did because we love you and have your highest in mind. So, "What were we thinking?" We were thinking about you!

> *Lord, thou hast been our dwelling place in all generations. Before the mountains were brought forth, or ever thou hadst formed the earth and the world, even from everlasting to everlasting, thou art God. (Psalm 90:1-3).*

TESTIMONIES

This is the second version of this book, so many have read it and so we wanted to share some of those testimonies with you. We overcome the devil by the blood of the Lamb and the word of our testimony (see Revelation 12:11). When we share our testimony, it is as powerful as the blood of the Lamb! They work hand in hand. Because without our testimony of sharing what God has done for us, how can we defeat the enemy? Let's share the goodness of God (see Romans 2:4).

I have been a Christian for over 50 years and never learned what I read in this book. I didn't pay much attention to what my mind was capable of, but I realized I had been thinking incorrectly about some things. Now my mind is being renewed, and now I know how to do it. It has even caused me to treat my wife better! This book is like reading the Bible, it's full of scriptures and all working together to bring about a single thought. That the Word of God is sharp and powerful and rightly divides the truth. By taking my thoughts captive I've been able to change in areas that I thought would never change. I'm no longer just thinking about me and what I want, but now I'm thinking of others more. Learning how the mind creates homeostasis was what I needed to continue to stay in peace and stay healthy.

Jim, Sutter Creek, California

This is an excellent book for all, yes all, Christians to read. Experiences in life reveal that the subject of thinking as it is covered in the Word of God has not been routinely taught in the church. This is a book driven toward spiritual growth for all.

The authors deal with this important subject in a progressive learning manner for all ages to read and learn, and to place into their lives.

This is not a book on non-Christian physiology, but one written with teaching us of our brain function to thought patterns as a Christian to overcoming whatever is our specific problem or change needed in this area.

Experiences in ministry reveal that many feel and not think. This book sets the biblical standards for the overall thought process.

It is excellent, and is a needed-reading for each of us.

Pastor Bob

I never realized until I read this book that what I'm rehearsing in my mind produces peace or stress, health or sickness in my body. My destiny can be changed by monitoring my thoughts, so the words I speak will bring blessings. Very practical help for my spiritual growth. Thanks so much.

Carol Meadows, Florida

This is a wonderful book. It is changing the way I am ALLOWING myself to think. I have just started going to Pastor Caspar's fellowship. He is a brilliant and serious teacher of God's Word. He is not afraid to teach the truth. The first time I attended, and he began to speak about the new discoveries of science, I wondered if I was in the right place. Then he flashed a Bible verse on the screen which clearly showed that God has already made that information available to us. His teaching is nothing like I have been used to in the past. You don't have to be a science major to understand the connections he makes between the latest scientific discoveries and the Word of God. I highly recommend this book to anyone interested in learning what controlling your thought life can do for your health—both emotional and physical. This book will help you on your journey to become the person both you and God want you to be.

Ms. Cligie, Amazon.com testimonial

I could not put this book down. I have been a Christian for 25 years and it has always been a challenge for me to "take every thought captive to the obedience of Christ". After reading "What Was I Thinking" it became much easier and I began to recognize immediately when my thoughts did not line up with the Word of Truth. Most of my Christian life has been spent trying to "DO" the right thing, and usually failing miserably, but when I began to "THINK" the right thing, the doing came almost automatically. I believe that if the people of God could master this concept that we would truly begin to bring Heaven down to earth and impact our communities and nation in such a way that our churches would not be able to hold all the people who want what we have.

> I thank God for you, Caspar and the insights He has given you.
>
> *Rick DeBoard, Sutter Creek, CA*

We have a group of people that are reading the book and discussing it and expressing there thoughts on it.

> *Larry Lapmarado*

Reading "What Was I Thinking?" Get your thoughts working for you not against you. By Pastor Caspar McCloud is getting very interesting, and really does make me think about my thoughts. I wish everyone could read this book and think about their thoughts. Maybe the abundance of our hearts would be more about loving each other... I know I am being transformed more and more into the image of God because I have changed my mind on stinkin' thinkin!' I am loving this book.

> *Rex Anne*

BIBLIOGRAPHY

Medical and other information gleaned from the following sources:

- The American Medical Association Family Medical Guide, 4th edition (Hoboken, NJ: John Wiley & Sons, Inc., 2004).

- Daniel G. Amem, MD, Change Your Brain, Change Your Life (New York: Three Rivers Press, 1999).

- Dr. Tony Dale, www.house2house.com.

- Grant Jeffrey, The Signature of God, rev. ed. (Colorado Springs: WaterBrook Press, 2010); The Handwriting of God (Colorado Springs: WaterBrook Press, 1997); Jesus: The Great Debate (Colorado Springs, CO: WaterBrook Press, 1999).

- John G. Lake Anthology: The Complete Collection of His Life Teachings, Roberts Liardon, compiler (New Kensington, PA: Whitaker House, 2005).

- Mayo Clinic online database: http://www.mayoclinic.com/.

- The Merck Manual of Medical Information, 2nd edition (New York: Pocket Books, 2003).

- Bob Giffin, www.7flames.com.

- Rex Russell, MD, What the Bible Says About Healthy Living (Grand Rapids, MI: Fleming H. Revell Company, 1999).

- Wikipedia, free online encyclopedia: http://en.wikipedia.org/wiki/Main_Page.

ABOUT THE AUTHORS
CASPAR MCCLOUD AND LINDA LANGE

Caspar McCloud is an outstanding Virtuoso Guitarist, Singer, and Songwriter, an accomplished Portrait Artist, as well as an Equestrian, Ordained Minister, and bestselling Author, Husband and Father.

He signed to Atlantic Records after leaving his home in England for New York City and was touted as the "next Jimi Hendrix" by Ahmet Ertegun, the CEO of Atlantic Records. As an accomplished musician, he has completed several projects over the years since his first UK release " Messin' Round", In Adoration", The Living Word, Soul Saved, In Our Life Time and World Without Borders, Dead Men Like Me Are Just Happy to Be Alive, with his band

Caspar McCloud & Ministry of Three.

There are also several solo projects like "Mercy, Grace and Love' that feature more of his classical/celtic/ worship acoustic style. He has played and/or recorded with many celebrities and friends including: Michael Shrieve, and Michael Carabella of Santana, Matt Bassionett, of Joe Satriani band- G3 and Ringo Starr band, Eddie Zynn of FogHat, Hall and Oats, Phil Keaggy, Peter Furler and

Jody Davis of the Newsboys (to name but a few).

Caspar is also a world-class portrait artist with a Pre-Raphaelite approach, specializing in Equestrian subject matter. Some of his work in the personal collections of the British Royal Family.

Caspar's first book was his incredible autobiography entitled, "Nothing is Impossible", which portrays signs, wonders and miracles. His second book, "What Was I Thinking" deals with the spiritual roots of disease and the science of epigenetics through the lens of the Holy Bible. His book, "The Shroud of Turin Speaks for Itself" with co-author Simon Brown in UK is #1 on Amazon. Along with his book most recent book, Spiritual Encounter With the Shroud: Caspar McCloud Interviews with L.A. Marzulli

Pastor Caspar has an amazing testimony filmed by TBN. He wants to train disciples and live as the Lord Jesus has taught us to do. He also hosts an internet radio show each Thursday entitled, "Spiritual Encounters". that has included such guests as L.A. Marzulli, Gary Stearmen, Richard Shaw, Tom Horn, Cris Putnam, Bill Salus and others.

He also contributes as a staff writer/researcher for Dr. L.A. Marzulli's magazine, "Politics, Prophesy & the Supernatural" and has been on several conferences/research expeditions in our quest to reveal evidence for Dr. Marzulli's books: "On the Trail of the Nephilim" to equip the saints for ministry.

He is currently Senior Pastor at The Upper Room Fellowship in East Cobb, GA. and has done a number of presentations with L A Marzulli at such events as Prophecy In The News and at the Nephilim Agenda.

He pastors a church called The Upper Room in Roswell, Georgia, when he is not out traveling as a musician and a guest speaker. To Contact Caspar McCloud for more information on his book, music, art, and ministry, go to www. pastorcaspar.com or email pastorcaspar@gmail.com

Hear what others have said about him:

"Caspar McCloud is the next Jimi Hendrix"

—Ahmet Ertegun, President, Atlantic Records

"Why, he is a modern-day renaissance man!"

—The 700 Club

"Caspar McCloud floats in the clouds—heavenly music, spiritual inspiration, a gentle spirit in touch with his God."

—Robert Lacey, Best-selling Author
Royal Biographer for Queen Elizabeth II

"Caspar McCloud is a multitalented artist. He not only makes music with a guitar but with a paintbrush as well. His love of horses is evident in his highly rendered and exquisite equestrian paintings that capture every nuance. Caspar inspires people on many levels."

—Bart Lindstrom, Artist Portrait Society of America

"What is there left to say about the musical genius that is Caspar McCloud? Not only is the man a true gentleman, but he is a gifted painter (as in, the Leonardo Di Vinci kind of painter!) and a sensational Musician! Caspar is as versatile as a Swiss army knife, and like a Swiss army knife, each ability is as sharp and practical as you'd expect...Caspar McCloud is truly a man born to inherit the title 'artist'...."

—Steven Nagle,

Editor, Rock of Ages Magazine, London, England

"...in years to come people will mention these names together. Ken Tamplin, Glenn Kaiser, Phil Keaggy, Bob Hartman, and Caspar McCloud. An honor that most modern day guitar players will never even come close to getting."

—Jeff Hauser
Hands in Motion Ministry

"Caspar McCloud is a really great guitarist with more of the legitimate rock and roll edge that I never had. He is also a devoted husband and father, which to me is even more important then the fact that he is such an excellent songwriter, singer, and guitarist and a very gifted painter and I don't mean house painter—I mean a Di Vinci kind of painter."

—Phil Keaggy

To reach Caspar directly:

email: pastorcaspar@gmail.com
www.theupperroomfellowship.org

Linda Lange is an author, teacher, ordained minister, radio and television host, worship leader, wife, mother, and grandmother of five who has a heart to help others find the peace and joy that only comes from knowing the Lord personally. She is founder and president of a nonprofit organization called "Life Application Ministries" since 1996 and has been helping people, "one heart at a time," discover God in a way that releases blessings into their lives.

Her autobiography, A Matter of the Mind, is her account of what God did in her life that set her free. She has written several other books and workbooks, which you can pick up on her website at www.truthfrees.org or amazon.com.

She has created teaching DVDs and CDs and conducted hundreds of seminars and conferences to help teach these principles. She has a TV program called "Restoring Your Life" that airs every Wed. night on www.tspntv.com at 6:00 PM PST. You can actually access it through any computer device and watch any recorded programming if you missed it at: www.restoringyourlife.tv.

She conducts teleconference mentor classes reaching people all over the world in a private session with other students through a workbook she created called: "Discover the truth that makes you free." She speaks at Women's Aglow meetings, conducts weddings, baptisms, films and produces DVD's of special events, founder of "Help for the Holidays" yearly event helping low-income families and homeless through the holidays. As an outreach for our community, she started the project called "Warm Socks for Cold Souls" a homeless outreach, which is headed by one of her board members who happens to be blind; therefore, provides books and materials she has written to the blind in DVD or audio formats. Ministers to people via telephone and e mail internationally.

Conducts monthly meetings for 25+ pastors in India through translation, equipping them to help minister to their congregations. Sponsored an orphanage in India, provided teaching materials, a wheelchair for one child, clothing, and food. Also on the leadership board for "JOY Ministries (Just Older Youth). Meeting the needs of the elderly in our community.

Also runs a digital book company, helping people self-publish their books. She has  completed over 20 of her own, and over 20 for others, helping make their dreams of being an author into a reality without the expense.

Has a blog that addresses every life issue possible, and many have found healing just by reading them. Available through http://linda-lange.wordpress.com.

She has appeared as guests on television and radio, offering her insights and ministry to help you find the answers you are looking for in your life, so you too can be healed, set free, and delivered from whatever ails you. Many have found help and healing just by reading her Web site!

Hear what people have said about her and her ministry:

"I am so very thankful to have been blessed and healed by the power of God through your Web site, Life Application Ministries. I love what you are doing! I am amazed at the revelation and steps to health and joy that I have received from your teachings."

Ms. S. - Missouri

"After reading about *"how to know if you are saved"* all I can say is WOW over and over again. A light went off! I am so thankful to God that I found your Web site, it was just what I needed to remind me of His Word and give it simplicity where I could understand it. I'm so grateful for your teachings that it literally brought tears to my eyes."

Ms. T. - Florida

"I'm going through a period of finding myself and my relationship with God. I tend to listen only to teachers I know I can trust like Billy Graham and Charles Stanley. Some how I connected with your Web site and I had to stop right in the middle of the study I was doing to study your materials. You have a gift! I am finally making progress in getting on the right path to the Lord. Thank you so very much. Several days ago I thought I was doomed to hell. But now I know the truth."

Mr. T. - Kentucky

You shared your journey with us, only it was more than just a testimony. You went far beyond what would normally be shared. You exposed areas which most people wouldn't have the strength to share. You were honest and transparent in a way that I have rarely experienced. That was pretty astounding all by itself. The Lord has been talking to me about the power that is released when we are transparent before Him and others. The Lord honored your vulnerability and I don't think one of us will ever be the same again. That you for you example and your incredible courage.

K. S - CA

I have listened to a number of your teachings and now reading the book called "What Was I Thinking." I have truly been blessed. I must say that the title of one of your teachings "What does love got to do with it" caused me to burst out laughing. I couldn't believe what you were teaching was exactly how I've been thinking over the years. I have a seminary education (though never in the ministry and have often told my wife I would love to preach a sermon with that title. I would introduce it as coming from the renowned American theologian, Tina Turner, "What does Love got to do with it?" Everything!!!' Thanks to God for the gifting He has endowed upon you. Blessings to you and your family.

Comment came from one of my blogs entitled: Not Everyone Will Like Us. "Wow this has helped me so much. Praise God, I can deal with the defilement, put God back on the throne and dust off my feet. A was truly making some mud pies!

Corsen - on-line connection

"I am so very thankful to have been blessed and healed by the power of God through your Website, Life Application Ministries. I love what you are doing! I am amazed at the revelation and steps to health and joy that I have received from your teachings."

Ms. S. Missouri

"After reading about *"how to know if you are saved"* all I can say is WOW over and over again. A light went off! I am so thankful to God that I found your Website, it was just what I needed to remind me of His Word and give it simplicity where I could understand it. I'm so grateful for your teachings that it literally brought tears to my eyes."

Ms. T. Florida

"I'm going through a period of finding myself and my relationship with God. I tend to listen only to teachers I know I can trust like Billy Graham and Charles Stanley. Some how I connected with your website and I had to stop right in the middle of the study I was doing to study your materials. You have a gift! I am finally making progress in getting on the right path to the Lord. Thank you so very much. Several days ago I thought I was doomed to hell. But now I know the truth."

Mr. T. Kentucky

We defeat the enemy by the blood of the Lamb and the word of our testimony! (Revelation 12:11)

To reach Linda personally please go to:

www.truthfrees.org or email: linda@truthfrees.org.

AUTHOR'S BOOKS

Caspar McCloud:
- Nothing is Impossible
- Spirit of Self-Pity
- Spiritual Encounter with the Shroud
- The Shroud Speaks for Itself (co-Author Simon Brown)

Linda Lange:
- Abandonment and Rejection
- Bitterness and Unforgiveness
- Forgiving From Your Heart
- Truth Revealed
- A Matter of the Mind - autobiography
- Buttons of Self-Worth
- Overcoming Guilt and Condemnation
- Aha Moments - Daily Devotional
- Life Lessons for Children - teaching aid
- Grieving Loss without the Bitter Pain
- Fearless Living Workbook
- Loving God - Book and workbook
- Nothing but the Truth so Help Me God
- Prayer Guide
- Understanding Manipulation and Control
- Discover the Truth that Makes You Free - workbook
- Dealing with Trauma's and PTSD
- Roots - defining spiritual roots
- Do You Have an Un-Biblical Cord?
- Exposing Spirits of Envy and Jealousy
- Holes - what causes leakage in our lives
- Linda also offers free downloadable teachings on her Web site at www:truthfrees.org. via: text, audio and video.

TO ORDER BOOKS, YOU CAN CONNECT WITH OURS OR ORDER FROM AMAZON.COM

CONTACT INFORMATION

If you would like to contact us for further ministry, we can provide assistance or refer you to ministries in your area that could be of service to you.

Caspar McCloud Ministries, Inc.
Pastor Caspar McCloud
1901 Batesville Road
Canton, GA 30115-4902
(770) 380-2749
pastorcaspar@gmail.com
www.theupperroomfellowship.org

The Upper Room Fellowship
www.theupperroomfellowship.org

Life Application Ministries, Inc.
Pastor Linda Lange
P.O. Box 165
Mt. Aukum, CA 95656
(530) 620-2712
linda@truthfrees.org

www.truthfrees.org
http://lindalange.wordpress.com (blogs)
www.facebook.com/restoringyourlifewithlindalange
www.restoringyourlife.tv
and
www.LAMP@lifeapplicationministries org
(Self-Publishing services)

Printed in Great Britain
by Amazon